Living in Christ

Jesus Christ

God's Love Made Visible

Second Edition

Carrie J. Schroeder

Saint Mary's Press®

The Subcommittee on the Catechism, United States Conference of Catholic Bishops, has found that this catechetical text, copyright 2015, is in conformity with the *Catechism of the Catholic Church* and that it fulfills the requirements of Course II: "Who Is Jesus Christ?" of the *Doctrinal Elements of a Curriculum Framework for the Development of Catechetical Materials for Young People of High School Age.*

Nihil Obstat: Rev. Timothy J. Hall, STL
             Censor Librorum
             July 11, 2014

Imprimatur: †Most Rev. John M. Quinn, DD
            Bishop of Winona
            August 7, 2014

The content in this student book was acquired, developed, and reviewed by the content engagement team at Saint Mary's Press. Content design and manufacturing were coordinated by the passionate team of creatives at Saint Mary's Press.

The publishing team included Justin Karr, editor; and Joanna Dailey, contributing writer. Content design and manufacturing coordinated by the passionate team of creatives at Saint Mary's Press.

1162 (PO5689)

ISBN 978-1-59982-431-4

Contents

Unit 3: Jesus: The Definitive Revelation of God

Unit 4: Jesus: The Definitive Revelation of God's Plan

Unit 5: Faith and Our Response to Jesus

Introduction

"Mary of Magdala went and announced to the disciples, 'I have seen the Lord'" (John 20:18).

How amazing it must have been for Mary of Magdala to proclaim those powerful words of faithful witness on that first Easter morning: "I have seen the Lord." Sometimes I have wondered, if I had been there at the empty tomb with her, would I have had the challenges to my faith that I have encountered? The people who saw, knew, and talked with Jesus during his earthly ministry witnessed his miracles firsthand and heard his powerful preaching and storytelling with their own ears. Some even saw him alive after he had risen from the dead. Yet we know from Sacred Scripture that some of the disciples, like Peter and Thomas, did experience moments of profound doubt. They had been blessed with the privilege of walking with Jesus, seeing him face-to-face, feeling his touch, and hearing his voice. With that blessing, though, came the task of accepting that the one they had known personally as their teacher, companion, and friend was, in fact, more than all these things: he was the Word Made Flesh (see John 1:14).

I have come to understand that my own life of faith follows a similar pattern of knowing Jesus yet still experiencing moments when my faith is challenged. I have been blessed with the knowledge that Jesus is alive, present, and active in my life, daily offering me strength, grace, wisdom, guidance, and salvation. And yet, to be completely honest, with that blessing comes what is sometimes a hard task, even a struggle: to understand fully what having a relationship with Jesus means. What does it mean for me to say that I, as a member of the Body of Christ, the Church, dwell in a relationship of love, trust, and friendship with Jesus?

One of the ways I have tried, throughout my life, to answer that question has been through study. When I was a student in a Catholic high school, my religious studies classes were among my favorites. In high school I finally began to explore not just *what* Catholics believe but *why*; not just how to *read* the Bible but how to *apply* it to my life; and not just what prayer *is* but how to *really pray*. Studying cultivated my faith, and that faith grew stronger the more that I learned and put it into practice. After high school I continued to follow a path that I found to be both intellectually and spiritually fruitful: I majored in religious studies in college. When I completed my graduate degree in theology, I began teaching religious studies in a Catholic high school, not unlike the one I had attended years before. Through these many years, study of Scripture and Sacred Tradition has truly helped me to grow my faith in Jesus. Study has enabled me to root that faith—including its more affective or emotional aspects—in something solid, something that truly nurtures, challenges, and enlivens my whole self: mind, heart, body, and spirit.

One of the greatest privileges of my life has been to serve as a religious studies teacher and campus minister. In that role I have been delighted by the opportunity to accompany young people, like you, on their journey of faith. I love your exuberant energy, your joy in living, your passion for justice, your challenging spirit, your intellectual curiosity, and your fierce loyalty: these are wonderful gifts you bring to our Church and to our world! If you bring all of these gifts to bear on your study of Jesus this semester, I guarantee that you will not be disappointed. Your efforts will return to you many times over, in the form of greater clarity of belief, deeper trust in God, and a more profound sense of purpose for your life.

This course begins by reflecting on the greatest mystery of our faith, the Trinity: Father, Son, and Holy Spirit. We then look at how God has revealed himself throughout history and most fully in his Son, Jesus Christ. We will see how Jesus reveals to us what it means to be a child of God and how we are to live and act upon our faith.

As you learn about Jesus through this book and in this course, my sincere hope is that your academic work takes deep root in you, opening your mind, touching your heart, and nourishing your soul, so that you may grow and flourish as the person of faith you were created to be. I pray that all your work may draw you more completely into a loving relationship with the One who came so that we might have life, and have it more abundantly (see John 10:10). May you, like Mary of Magdala so long ago, see the Risen Lord alive and active, and may you be forever changed by that life-giving encounter.

Wishing you every grace and blessing,
Carrie J. Schroeder
Editor, First Edition

Unit

1

The Trinity

In this unit, we will examine the mystery of the Trinity and the development of Trinitarian doctrine in the Catholic Church. Furthermore, we will explore what the terms *monotheism* and *Trinitarianism* really mean to the Catholic faith. Throughout the coursework of this unit, we will discover exactly what makes up each Divine Person, and we will also follow the development of the Church's teachings about the Holy Trinity.

At the core of the Catholic faith is the mystery of the Holy Trinity, the truth that there is one God in three Divine Persons: Father, Son, and Holy Spirit. In chapter 1, we will analyze exactly what it means to be both monotheistic and Trinitarian. We will also consider what Sacred Scripture reveals about the Trinity. As we make our way further through chapter 1, we will learn about the distinct origin and work of each Divine Person in the Holy Trinity, as well as how they are united.

The Trinity is a complex reality to understand and explain. The truth of our Trinitarian faith was revealed to the earliest Christians and is present in Sacred Scripture. Chapter 2 takes us into the development of Trinitarian doctrine. We will see how the early Church worked at developing a clear language about the mystery of the Trinity, including the Church's response to early challenges and heresies about the Trinity and Jesus' place in it. Finally, we will see how the Trinity is a model for human relationships.

The enduring understandings and essential questions represent core concepts and questions that are explored throughout this unit. By studying the content of each chapter, you will gain a more complete understanding of the following:

Enduring Understandings

1. The mystery of the Trinity is the central mystery of the Catholic faith.

2. The Church developed the doctrine of the Trinity over centuries through the early Ecumenical Councils and the work of the Church Fathers.

3. The Trinity is a model for living in relationship with others.

Essential Questions

1. Why is the Trinity considered to be a mystery of faith?

2. How has the Church expressed and explained the doctrine of the Trinity throughout the centuries?

3. How should our human relationships reflect what we see in the Trinity?

Chapter 1

God Is One: Father, Son, and Holy Spirit

Introduction

The faith of Catholics is rooted in the truth that there is one God in three Divine Persons: Father, Son, and Holy Spirit. Belief in one God is called monotheism. Belief that God is three Divine Persons in One is called Trinitarianism. Trying to understand how Catholics can hold both beliefs is confusing for many people. How is it possible to be both monotheistic and Trinitarian? If God is a Holy Trinity, who are these three Persons? How are they united, and how is each Divine Person distinct? Throughout this chapter, we will see how God the Father, the First Person of the Trinity, is the source of all life, the creator of all that is known and unknown. Furthermore, we will witness how God wants us to be in a loving relationship with him. We will explore how the Son, Jesus Christ, is fully God and fully man, having assumed the form of a man to assure us our salvation. Finally, we will investigate the Third Person of the Trinity, the Holy Spirit, as he shares the mission of Jesus to bring us into the Church, the Body of Christ, as adopted children of God.

Article 1: God Is One: Catholics Are Monotheistic

The belief in and worship of only one God is called **monotheism**. Throughout much of human history, people of many cultures have practiced polytheism, which is the belief in many gods. You may have studied some polytheistic cultures, like ancient Egypt, Greece, and Rome, in other courses in school. You may know Hindus or Shintoists who worship many gods. When God began a **covenant** relationship with Abraham, he was revealing an essential truth: there is only one God, the Lord of all the earth. Over time Abraham and Sarah's descendants, who would become known as the Jews, understood and embraced this monotheistic faith.

As Jewish people came to fully understand and embrace this monotheistic faith, they incorporated this belief into their prayer and worship. The Shema, the prayer uttered daily by faithful Jews of ancient times and the present day, begins with these words, found in a slightly different form in Deuteronomy 6:4: "Hear, O Israel! The Lord is our God, the Lord alone!" (*Shema Yisrael, Adonai eloheinu, Adonai ehad*). The Bible, in both the Old and New Testaments, consistently reveals that there is only one true God. For instance, in the Gospel of Mark, a scribe asks Jesus which is the first of all the Commandments (see 12:28). Jesus quotes the words of the Shema, replying, "The first is this: 'Hear, O Israel! The Lord our God is Lord alone! You shall love the Lord your God with all your heart, with all your soul, with all your mind, and with all your strength'" (Mark 12:29–30). Jesus himself tells us there is only one God.

One God or Three Gods?

When the early Christians first began to understand, speak, and write about the **doctrine** of the **Trinity**, many people thought they were rejecting monotheism in favor of polytheism. Even today praying "in the name of the Father, and of the Son, and of the Holy Spirit" may lead some people to mistakenly think that Christians have

monotheism
The belief in and worship of only one God.

covenant
A personal, solemn promise of faithful love that involves mutual commitments and creates a sacred relationship.

doctrine
An official, authoritative teaching of the Church based on the Revelation of God.

Trinity
From the Latin *trinus*, meaning "threefold," referring to the central mystery of the Christian faith that God exists as a communion of three distinct and interrelated Divine Persons: Father, Son, and Holy Spirit. The doctrine of the Trinity is a mystery that is inaccessible to human reason alone and is known through Divine Revelation only.

Nicene Creed
The formal statement or profession of Christian belief originally formulated at the Council of Nicaea in 325 and amplified at the Council of Constantinople in 381.

three gods, not one. Those who mistakenly believe that Catholics worship Mary or other saints may even think we have four or more gods. *The Catechism of the Catholic Church (CCC)* firmly states our belief in one God. "To confess that Jesus is Lord is distinctive of Christian faith. This is not contrary to belief in the One God. Nor does believing in the Holy Spirit as 'Lord and giver of life' introduce any division into the One God" (202). Catholics have always affirmed the truth that God is one. Indeed we profess this each week at Sunday liturgy when we pray the **Nicene Creed**: "I believe in one God."

Why do you think belief in a Trinitarian God can be difficult to understand for some people?

Did You Know?

Three Major Monotheistic Religions

© RUI FERREIRA / shutterstock.com

© dbhalbur / shutterstock.com

© Scott Speakes / Corbis

Only Christians have recognized God as Trinity—one God in three Divine Persons. However, we share our belief in one God with Judaism and Islam.

The very heart of Judaism is monotheism, as reflected in the Shema, which faithful Jews pray daily. Followers of Islam also profess belief in one God. They too proclaim their monotheism as part of their regular prayer. Each day faithful Muslims repeat the *Shahadah*. It is translated: "There is no God but God and Muhammad is the Messenger of God."

The Second Vatican Council spoke of the "common spiritual heritage" shared by Jews and Christians (Declaration on the Relation of the Church to Non-Christian Religions [Nostra Aetate, 1965], 4). In this same document, the council said this about Muslims: "They worship God, who is one, living and subsistent, merciful and almighty, the Creator of heaven and earth, who has also spoken to humanity" (3).

To understand what Catholics share with Jews and Muslims does not in any way lessen the truth of our Catholic beliefs. Rather, it helps us to appreciate and marvel at the many people of different times and places who have recognized the reality that there is only one God, Creator of all.

Article 2: God Is Three-In-One: Catholics Are Trinitarian

The mystery of the Holy Trinity—the mystery of one God in three Divine Persons—is a unique defining trait of Christian faith. The Trinity is the Church's most important and fundamental teaching and the central mystery of our faith, which only God can fully reveal to us. Every prayer we pray and every Sacrament we celebrate is done in the name of this Triune, or three-in-one, God—Father, Son, and Holy Spirit.

The Trinity: United, Yet Distinct

The three Divine Persons are inseparable both in what they are and in what they do. They are inseparable in what they *are* because each Divine Person is fully God—complete, whole, and entire. All of God is contained in God the Father. All of God is contained in God the Son. All of God is contained in God the Holy Spirit. They are inseparable in what they *do* because each Divine Person has the same job description, so to speak. Each of the three Persons is engaged in the work of our salvation. Each acts to create us in love, redeem us, and make us holy. As the *Catechism* states, "The whole **divine economy** is the common work of the three divine persons" (258). The work and mission of Father, Son, and Holy Spirit are inseparable. But each Divine Person contributes his own unique qualities to this common work. It was the Son who became **incarnate**, assuming a human nature. It is the Holy Spirit who is sent into each believer's heart and is sent to guide the Church.

Even though they are inseparable, the three Persons of the Holy Trinity are truly distinct from one another. This distinction does not divide the divine unity. The Father, Son, and Spirit are in perfect communion with one another.

divine economy
Also known as the economy of salvation, this refers to God's eternal plan and his actions for the salvation of humanity.

incarnate, Incarnation
From the Latin, meaning "to become flesh," referring to the mystery of Jesus Christ, the Divine Son of God, becoming man. In the Incarnation, Jesus Christ became truly man while remaining truly God.

The three Divine Persons of the Trinity are also distinct in their origins. It is proper to speak of the Father as the generator, even though all three Divine Persons are eternal, existing without beginning or end. We express this mystery of faith by saying that the Son is begotten of the Father and that the Holy Spirit proceeds from both the Father and the Son.

If the Persons of the Trinity are united, how are they distinct? First, each carries out the work of our salvation in the way that is most proper. For example, God the Father draws us to follow Christ; God the Son became incarnate; God the Holy Spirit gives us the gifts of the Spirit. Second, the three Persons are distinct in their relationship to one another. God the Father is *unbegotten*, meaning he has always existed without beginning or end. God the Son is *begotten* of God the Father. In the words of the Nicene Creed, Jesus is "the Only Begotten Son of God, born of the Father before all ages." The Holy Spirit is sent out into the world, *proceeding from* the Father and the Son.

Primary Sources

The Athanasian Creed

Rarely used today, the Athanasian Creed was once commonly recited in the liturgy of Trinity Sunday. This statement of faith dates back to about the fifth century, and although it was probably not written by the great Doctor of the Church Saint Athanasius (297–373), it bears his name. Below is an excerpt from this beautiful meditation on the mystery of the Trinity:

> For there is one Person of the Father, another of the Son, and another of the Holy Ghost. . . . The Father Incomprehensible, the Son Incomprehensible, and the Holy Ghost Incomprehensible. The Father Eternal, the Son Eternal, and the Holy Ghost Eternal and yet they are not Three Eternals but One Eternal. . . . So likewise the Father is Almighty, the Son Almighty, and the Holy Ghost Almighty. And yet they are not Three Almighties but One Almighty.

The Trinity Is Revealed by God in Sacred Scripture

Although the Church did not fully articulate the doctrine of the Trinity until the Ecumenical Councils of the fourth and fifth centuries, the presence of the Trinity is clear in Sacred Scripture, especially in the New Testament. For example, in Luke's Gospel, Jesus "rejoiced [in] the holy Spirit" (10:21), stating that "[n]o one knows who the Son is except the Father, and who the Father is except the Son" (10:22). In the Gospel of John, Jesus says, "Whoever has seen me has seen the Father" (14:9). Later in the Gospel of John, just hours before his death, Jesus prays to God the Father for his disciples, asking "that they may be one just as we are" (17:11). Finally, at the very end of the Gospel of Matthew, Jesus commissions his disciples to baptize "in the name of the Father, and of the Son, and of the holy Spirit" (28:19). These and other passages help us to understand that the God revealed to us in Scripture is a Trinity of Divine Persons. Let's now take a closer look at the distinct qualities of each of the three Persons of the Blessed Trinity.

The mystery of the Trinity is revealed in the Scripture and Tradition. How would you explain this mystery to someone who has never heard of it?

© kwest / shutterstock.com

How do you use Sacred Scripture to help you understand aspects of your faith, such as the Trinity?

Article 3: The First Person of the Trinity: God the Father

As you've already read in this chapter, God the Father is the First Person of the Trinity. He is the Eternal Source of all that exists. As we profess in the Nicene Creed, God the Father is the "maker of heaven and earth, of all things visible and invisible." Many religions, including Judaism,

filial

Having to do with the relationship of a child to his or her parent.

have understood God as Father, reflecting that God is the Creator and Lord of all the earth. When we profess that God is our Father, we acknowledge that he is the source of all life; that all creation exists because of him. Further, we acknowledge that God is all-powerful and desires to be in an intimate, loving relationship with his creation. He loves us, cares for us, provides for us, heals us, forgives us, and is just and faithful. Even if the love of an earthly father—or mother, or friend, or any other person—disappoints us, God's faithful love will never, ever fail us.

Jesus Reveals God the Father

In the Gospels, Jesus calls God *Abba,* which, in his native language of Aramaic, means "Father." This reveals two things about Jesus' relationship with God the Father:

- Jesus' relationship with God is **filial**—that is, a father-son relationship. In prayer Jesus knew his Father's unconditional love, strength, and guidance. But even more important, Jesus reveals a new way of understanding God as Father—as the First Person of the Trinity, the Eternal Father of the Eternal Son.

- Jesus' relationship with God the Father is an intimate one. In Jesus' prayer, we see him speaking to his Father directly and personally, revealing his inner thoughts and feelings (see Matthew 11:25–26 and Mark 14:36). One way Jesus teaches us about God the Father is through his parables. For example, in the parable commonly known as the Parable of the Prodigal Son (see Luke 15:11–32), Jesus tells the story of a father who loves both of his sons with patience, compassion, and joy. In this parable, Jesus gives us a clear depiction of the gentle, transforming love of God the Father.

We Are God's Adopted Children

Jesus does more than teach about his loving Father. He actually invites us to call God "Father" ourselves. In doing so, Jesus invites us into the close relationship he has with his Divine Father—into the communion of the Holy Trinity. Through Baptism we become God the Father's adopted daughters and sons. Saint Paul writes:

> For you did not receive a spirit of slavery to fall back into fear, but you received a spirit of adoption, through which we cry, '*Abba*, Father!' The Spirit itself bears witness with our spirit that we are children of God, and if children, then heirs, heirs of God and joint heirs with Christ, if only we suffer with him so that we may also be glorified with him. (Romans 8:15–17)

This does not mean that God cares for us only if we are baptized. On the one hand, the Church does not recognize any means other than Baptism to reach true **beatitude**. On the other hand, we believe that God's infinite love and tender mercy extend to all people, even in ways we cannot fully understand.

beatitude
The state of eternal happiness with God in Heaven.

Is God Male?

The answer to that question is a most definite no. To say that God is our Father is to talk about the first Person of the Trinity, the Father of the Eternal Son, who has

Live It!
God Is a Loving Parent

When we call God "Father," we are reminded that we are his children. This means we are blessed with a heavenly Father who loves and cares for us and whom we can always turn to. God is a great parent who wants to listen and provide support. He is always there no matter our mood or situation. We can tell him about triumphs, defeats, hopes, and fears. We can ask for help, advice, or forgiveness.

Have you ever talked with God as if you were talking with a loving parent? For the next three days, write down three or four things each day that happen to you or that you need support or guidance on. It could be as simple as "I got an A on a test," "Volleyball practice was hard today," or "I was really lonely at lunch." At the end of each day, spend time going through the list and talking with God about each item. Tell him what is going on in your life, ask for his help and protection, and thank him for being with you.

adopted us as sons and daughters. It does not mean God is a human being. It also does not mean God is literally male. Both Judaism and Christianity have always maintained that God has no gender. In other words, God is neither male nor female. Jesus affirms this in his conversation with a Samaritan woman when he asserts that "God is Spirit" (John 4:24). The *Catechism* reminds us that God has characteristics we associate with both fathers and mothers when it states: "God's parental tenderness can also be expressed by the image of motherhood,[1] which emphasizes God's immanence, the intimacy between Creator and creature. . . . We ought therefore to recall that God transcends the human distinction between the sexes" (239).

Both the Old and New Testaments use a great variety of symbolic images when speaking about God. Some of these are masculine images, like "the Lord, your God, carried you, as one carries his own child, all along your journey" (Deuteronomy 1:31). Other images are feminine. Jesus tells a parable about a woman searching for a lost coin (see Luke 15:8–10). The woman represents God, who patiently searches for us when we are "lost" in sin. Others are neither masculine nor feminine, like Psalm 19, which describes God as "my rock" (verse 15). Praying with many scriptural images helps us to deepen our relationship with God. It reminds us that no human language can ever fully capture or describe the Divine Mystery.

What are some of your favorite images of God?

© Justin Horrocks / iStockphoto.com

Article 4: The Second Person of the Trinity: God the Son

The Second Person of the Trinity is God the Son, Jesus Christ, who assumed a human nature for our salvation. Jesus Christ is both truly and fully God and truly and fully man. He has a unique relationship with God the Father: he is the only, and the Eternal, Son of God.

Jesus Is Truly God

Several New Testament passages may help us to understand that Jesus is truly God, who became flesh through the power of the Holy Spirit. For example, the prologue to John's Gospel states:

> And the Word became flesh
> and made his dwelling among us,
> and we saw his glory,
> the glory as of the Father's only Son,
> full of grace and truth.
>
> (1:14)

John's Gospel also contains another often-quoted line about the purpose of the Incarnation: "For God so loved the world that he gave his only Son, so that everyone who believes in him might not perish but might have eternal

Pray It!

Blessed Be God Forever!

"Blessed are you, Lord, God of all creation." The celebrant says these words while praying during the Preparation of the Altar and the Gifts. The prayers he says emphasize that it is through God's goodness that we have the bread and wine to offer. It is because of God's power that they will become the Body and Blood of Jesus Christ. The following prayer is the conclusion to a novena honoring the Body and Blood of Christ. Pray this as a thanksgiving for the great sacrament of Holy Communion:

> O Jesus, since You have left us a remembrance of Your Passion beneath the veils of this Sacrament, grant us, we pray, so to venerate the sacred mysteries of Your Body and Blood that we may always enjoy the fruits of Your Redemption, for You live and reign forever. Amen.

Reign of God
The reign or rule of God over the hearts of people and, as a consequence of that, the development of a new social order based on unconditional love. The fullness of God's Reign will not be realized until the end of time. Also called the Kingdom of God.

The Nativity is a reminder of the Incarnation. Why do you think God chose to enter the world in the form of an infant born in a manger?

life" (3:16). In his Letter to the Philippians, Saint Paul says this of Jesus:

> . . . though he was in the form of God,
>   did not regard equality with God
>   something to be grasped.
>   Rather, he emptied himself,
>   taking the form of a slave,
>   coming in human likeness;
>   and found human in appearance.
>   (2:6–7)

These and other Scripture passages help us to understand that Jesus Christ is the Son of God—a title that signifies his unique and eternal relationship with God the Father. He is truly God's own self made flesh among us.

Jesus Is Truly Man

Jesus is not only truly and fully God but also truly and fully man. He is not only the Son of God but also the Son of the Virgin Mary. Saint Paul writes in his Letter to the Galatians: "But when the fullness of time had come, God sent his Son, born of a woman, born under the law" (4:4). Jesus Christ has a fully human nature. So, he is able to teach us, through his words and actions, how we are to live as sons and daughters of God. Specifically, Jesus teaches us to love one another—even our enemies—as God the Father has loved him and as he has loved us. He teaches us to love the truth, to pray always in faith, and to forgive those who have wronged us. By assuming human nature, Jesus has shown us how to live in a way that reflects the fullness and beauty of the **Reign of God.**

Why Did God Become Incarnate?

The name Jesus, given to him by the angel Gabriel, means "God saves" in Hebrew. This tells us that the

Incarnation is part of salvation history: God's eternal plan to redeem and save humanity. The *Catechism* states that God became incarnate for the following four reasons (see 457–460):

- to save us by reconciling us to himself
- to share divine love with us
- to show us how to be holy
- to enable us to share in God's divine nature

Athanasius, a fourth-century saint, says that "the Son of God became man so that we might become God[2]" (460).

Christ: The Anointed One

Christ is a title given to Jesus, based on the Greek word *christos*, which means "anointed one." The Hebrew equivalent is **Messiah**. In the ancient world, anointing with oil symbolized being chosen by God for some special mission or purpose. For example, in the Old Testament, priests, prophets, and kings were anointed as they prepared to undertake their new role in the community. In the case of Jesus, he is anointed by the Holy Spirit at his human birth, anointed to be our Savior and Redeemer.

For what special mission or purpose do you think God is calling you?

Christ
From the Greek translation of the Hebrew *Messiah,* meaning "anointed." It became the name proper to Jesus because he accomplished perfectly the divine mission of priest, prophet, and king, signified by his anointing as Messiah.

Messiah
Hebrew word for "anointed one." The equivalent Greek term is *christos.* Jesus is the Christ and the Messiah because he is the Anointed One.

Article 5: The Third Person of the Trinity: God the Holy Spirit

The Third Person of the Trinity is the Holy Spirit. In the words of the Nicene Creed, the Holy Spirit is "the Lord, the giver of life, who proceeds from the Father and the Son." The Holy Spirit has been active since the time of Creation, speaking to God's people through the ancient prophets and anointing Jesus for his special mission to redeem and save us.

The Father, Son, and Holy Spirit are distinct Persons, but they are inseparable from one another. From the

Pentecost
The fiftieth day following Easter, which commemorates the descent of the Holy Spirit on the early Apostles and disciples.

beginning of time until the end of time, wherever the Father sends his Son, he also sends his Spirit. The Son and the Holy Spirit share a joint mission to bring us into the Body of Christ as God's adopted sons and daughters. However, the Holy Spirit was not fully revealed until after Jesus' death and Resurrection.

Promised by Jesus, Given at Pentecost

In John's Gospel, we read that when Jesus knew that the hour of his death was near, he promised his disciples that he would ask God to send them an advocate (in Greek, *paraclete*). An advocate is someone who is on our side, to help us, strengthen us, and empower us for holiness. This advocate Jesus promised is the Third Person of the Holy Trinity, the Holy Spirit. Jesus told the disciples that the Spirit would teach them everything they need to know.

After Jesus died and rose from the dead, he made good on his promise. The Risen Lord appeared to the disciples, breathed on them, and said, "Receive the holy Spirit" (John 20:22). Moreover, at **Pentecost**, Jesus sent the Holy Spirit, now fully revealed, to be with his disciples forever—both those who were his earliest followers and those who are his followers today. The Acts of the Apostles describes Pentecost in this way: "And suddenly there came from the sky a noise like a strong driving wind, and it filled the entire house in which they were. Then there appeared to them tongues as of fire, which

© Francis G. Mayer / CORBIS

parted and came to rest on each one of them. And they were all filled with the holy Spirit . . ." (2:2–4).

The Holy Spirit sanctifies the People of God by offering us seven gifts to help us as we strive to live as Christians. Receiving the Gifts of the Holy Spirit means that the mission of Jesus became the mission of the Church. In fact, it becomes *our* mission. Through the Gifts of the Holy Spirit, we are empowered to be true followers of Christ. (See the table "The Gifts of the Holy Spirit" for a list of the Gifts of the Holy Spirit and a brief explanation of how each strengthens us as followers of Christ.) When we allow the Gifts of the Holy Spirit to work in us, we follow the way of Jesus by sharing God's love with our friends and families, being a loving presence to those in need, and preaching the Good News through our words and actions. Because Jesus is no longer physically present here on earth, the **Paraclete** blesses and strengthens our efforts to live as Jesus did: bringing justice, peace, and truth to all those we meet.

Paraclete
A term meaning "advocate" or "helper," used in the Gospel of John to describe the Holy Spirit, the third Divine Person of the Trinity, whom Jesus promised to the disciples as an advocate and counselor.

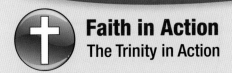

Faith in Action
The Trinity in Action

The Trinity is not simply an abstract concept. Understanding God as Father, Son, and Holy Spirit leads us to an understanding of ourselves and our own human dignity. We are made in the image and likeness of God.

In the twelfth century, one group of religious brothers understood this well. Called the Trinitarians, they were founded by Saint John of Matha to redeem captives and ransom slaves. They not only helped captives and slaves in material and spiritual ways. When necessary, a Trinitarian would offer to trade his own life for the life of a captive!

Why? Because God is our Father, and we are brothers and sisters. Because Jesus, the Son of God, saved us and taught us to love one another, even unto death. Because the Holy Spirit inspires us and helps us to live as images of God in our world!

The Trinitarians still exist today, and include women as well. They still seek out those who "suffer uncommon hardships, especially those who suffer for their faith or who are poor" (*Constitutions of the Order of the Most Holy Trinity*). Many people today are prisoners of invisible forms of slavery: slavery to consumerism, winning at all costs, even at the expense of human dignity, and a "me-first" attitude. In 1998, Pope Saint John Paul II wrote to the Trinitarian Order: "We are on the eve of a new Christian millennium: may this prospect further encourage you to make God's merciful face, revealed to us in the Incarnation of Christ, shine among men [meaning *people*]. Thus, you will become valiant defenders of the dignity of every human being."

The Gifts of the Holy Spirit

Wisdom	Opens our eyes to see God at work, even in our common, everyday experiences.
Understanding	Makes it possible for us to follow the correct course of action in difficult or confusing situations.
Counsel	Also called Right Judgment, helps us to know right from wrong and to choose the good consistently.
Fortitude	Also called Courage; enables us to do the right thing, even when we are afraid.
Knowledge	Empowers us to use our intellect to learn more about our faith.
Piety	Also called Reverence; reminds us that God is God, and enables us to recognize that all we are, all we do, and all we have comes from God.
Fear of the Lord	Also called Wonder and Awe, fills us with a spirit of profound respect as we marvel at God's power and goodness.

For which Gift of the Holy Spirit are you most grateful?

For Review

1. What is monotheism?

2. What three major religions are monotheistic?

3. What does it mean that the three Divine Persons are united? What does it mean that they are distinct?

4. What evidence does Sacred Scripture offer for the existence of the Trinity?

5. What do we acknowledge when we profess that the First Person of the Trinity is Father?

6. In the Gospels, what does Jesus reveal to us about his relation to the Father?

7. What four reasons does the *Catechism* give for the Incarnation?

8. How is the Holy Spirit the advocate for Christians throughout time?

Chapter

2

The Development of Trinitarian Doctrine

Introduction

Have you ever studied something that you know is true but found it took a lot of effort to understand and explain it? The mystery of the Trinity is like that.

For even the most thoughtful theologian, the most distinguished philosopher, or the holiest saint, the Trinity is a complex reality to grasp and express. God revealed the truth of our Trinitarian faith to the very earliest Christians, but it took time for the Church to clarify the depths of this truth. In fact, it took several centuries for early bishops and Church Fathers to develop and agree on language that would best express the subtle nuances of one God in three Divine Persons.

During these early centuries of Church history, varied ideas about the Trinity existed, especially about Jesus' place in it. The early Church sifted through all these ideas—some correct and some incorrect. Their efforts bore fruit in the early Ecumenical Councils. These Councils produced the Nicene Creed and other clear statements of core Catholic truths. They shaped the language and direction of Trinitarian theology for centuries to come. In this chapter, we will take a look at all of these developments.

Article 6: The Early Church Faces Challenges to Apostolic Faith

After Jesus died, rose, and ascended to Heaven, the early Church faced the enormous task of precisely articulating the doctrine about the Trinity and about Jesus and defending those truths against those who challenged them. During these first centuries, bishops and **Church Fathers** worked at these tasks. They often did so in official gatherings called **Ecumenical Councils**. They developed the language that would reflect, as fully as possible, the depth, breadth, and meaning of these **sacred**, revealed truths.

Many people had their own theories about who Jesus was and what his time on earth had achieved. Many of these ideas were heresies, or false teachings. The early Church defended the true teachings passed on from the Apostles against these conflicting and false theories.

Fathers of the Church (Church Fathers)
During the early centuries of the Church, those teachers whose writings extended the Tradition of the Apostles and who continue to be important for the Church's teachings.

Live It!
Take Time to Listen

How can we live a Trinitarian life, in communion with God and with others? Building on our baptismal grace that unites us in love with God—Father, Son, and Holy Spirit—we can work toward mutual respect and love toward one another. Mutual respect and love require that we take time to listen.

Listening is not always easy. If you are preparing for a conversation you sense will be difficult, pray first. Ask the Holy Trinity for help in seeing the other person as a child of God and a brother or sister in Christ. Ask the Holy Spirit to help you listen.

Then focus on the person speaking and give your full attention. Try not to think of what you might say in return. If you don't understand something, ask questions. Make eye contact.

When it is time for you to respond, ask the Holy Spirit to guide you to speak with love and to provide the advice, encouragement, or support the other person needs.

Ecumenical Council
A gathering of the Church's bishops from around the world convened by the Pope or approved by him to address pressing issues in the Church.

sacred
The quality of being holy, worthy of respect and reverence; set apart for God.

The Early Church Develops Trinitarian Language

In his Second Letter to the Corinthians, Saint Paul writes: "The grace of the Lord Jesus Christ and the love of God and the fellowship of the holy Spirit be with all of you" (13:13). Second Corinthians was written in the mid-50s AD. Saint Paul's greeting reflects the early Church's firm belief in the Trinity from the earliest times. As the Church's Trinitarian doctrine developed, the Church Fathers turned to the language of **philosophy** to express the doctrine in a way that would make sense to the people of their time. This language, though often difficult for us to understand, was in common use at that time. Paragraph 252 of the *Catechism of the Catholic Church* explains the following words, which are used to describe Trinitarian doctrine:

Did You Know?

By the hand of Nicholas P. Papas
facebook.com/Nick.Papas.Studio

Saint Irenaeus, Defender of the Faith

Saint Irenaeus (ca. 130–200) was a second-century bishop in what is now Lyons, France. As a prolific writer, he was a key figure in the many controversies that developed as the early Church sought to clarify her Trinitarian faith. His most famous work is a series of books called Against Heresies. In it Irenaeus stresses how crucial it was for the Church to safeguard her apostolic faith. This was the faith that Jesus had shared with the Apostles and that they had passed on to their successors. Irenaeus was particularly concerned about Gnosticism. This was one of the false teachings about Jesus that was circulating in the Church at that time. Irenaeus's courageous effort to defend apostolic faith against Gnosticism and other heresies can inspire us. We too need to speak the truth without fear, trusting always in God's steadfast love. Saint Irenaeus's feast day is June 28.

- The word *substance* is used to name "the divine being in its unity."
- The word *person* (in Greek, *hypostasis*) is used to refer to the Father, Son, and Holy Spirit, each fully God, yet each distinct.
- The word *relation* is used to indicate that the distinction among the three Persons lies in the relationship of each to the others.

Developing this standard vocabulary in speaking and writing about the Trinity enabled the Church Fathers to more easily express the faith of the early Christian community and defend that faith to those who challenged it.

Have you had to learn a foreign language or a computer programming language? What were the difficulties? the rewards?

Article 7: Early Christological Heresies

How can 100 percent man and 100 percent God equal 100 percent Jesus? That just doesn't seem to add up! The mystery of Jesus' being fully man and fully God doesn't make sense as math or science. During the first several centuries of the Church, some **heresies**, or incorrect beliefs, about Jesus, developed. The early bishops and Church Fathers struggled to articulate and defend the mystery of Christ's human and divine natures against these **Christological** heresies.

Some Christological heresies downplayed or denied the divinity of Jesus. For example, Arianism claimed that Jesus was created, just as we were. Arius, its proponent, said that Jesus did not exist before he was conceived in Mary's womb. Arius believed that Jesus was a higher creature than humans but less than God. Nestorianism believed that in Jesus there were actually two persons, one divine and one human. Nestorius argued that it was wrong to say things like "God suffered and died for

philosophy
In Greek this word literally means "love of wisdom." It refers to the study of human existence using logical reasoning.

heresy
The conscious and deliberate rejection by a baptized person of a truth of faith that must be believed.

Christological
Having to do with the branch of theology called Christology. Christology is the study of the divinity of Jesus Christ, the Son of God and the Second Divine Person of the Trinity, and his earthly ministry and eternal mission.

us" or "God was born of the Virgin Mary." These statements would apply to the human person Jesus, but not to the Divine Person. Nestorius was really concerned with people overemphasizing the humanity of Jesus. He would not even allow the Virgin Mary to be known as the Mother of God.

Other heresies played down the humanity of Jesus. Docetism alleged that Jesus' humanity was a sort of disguise—he looked like a human and acted like a human, but inside, he was really just God. For example, Docetists claimed that Jesus didn't really suffer on the cross. They said he *appeared* to be suffering, but he couldn't *really* suffer a human death because he was God. Monophysitism believed that Jesus' divinity fully absorbed his humanity so that, in the end, he was only divine and not human.

Gnosticism, another early Church heresy, claimed that Jesus was not a man at all, but a semidivine being. The name comes from *gnosis*, the Greek word for "knowledge." Gnostics believe that salvation can be reached only by getting special, secret knowledge from God or God's agent, and that God sent Jesus to share this

Primary Sources

The Words of Saint Irenaeus

Saint Irenaeus likens the eternal truth of the Catholic Church to the sun, one light illuminating the world:

[T]he Church, having received this preaching and this faith, although scattered throughout the whole world, yet, as if occupying but one house, carefully preserves it. She also believes these points [of doctrine] just as if she had but one soul, and one and the same heart, and she proclaims them, and teaches them, and hands them down, with perfect harmony, as if she possessed only one mouth. For, although the languages of the world are dissimilar, yet the import of the tradition is one and the same. . . . But as the sun, that creature of God, is one and the same throughout the whole world, so also the preaching of the truth shines everywhere, and enlightens all men that are willing to come to a knowledge of the truth. (Against Heresies, book 1, chapter 10) special knowledge with a select, elite group of people he wanted to save.

Heresies Focusing on Jesus' Humanity	
Heresy	**Beliefs**
Arianism	Jesus was created, just as we were, and he did not exist before he was conceived in Mary's womb. Jesus was a higher creature than humans but less than God.
Nestorianism	In Jesus there were actually two persons, one divine and one human. It was improper to speak of them as one.
Heresies Focusing on Jesus' Divinity	
Docetism	Jesus' humanity was a sort of disguise— he looked like a human and acted like a human, but inside he was really just God.
Monophysitism	Jesus' divinity fully absorbed his humanity, so that, in the end, he was only divine and not human.
Gnosticism	Salvation can be attained only by a select, elite group, by acquiring special, secret knowledge from God.

The Church Defends the Truth

These Christological heresies caused a great deal of division within the early Church. Most of the heresies were incorrect teachings about either Christ's human nature or his divine nature. In response, the Church Fathers needed to present the doctrine of the Incarnation in clear, careful, and balanced teaching. We can benefit from their writings today. They are easily available to those who take the time to find them. The Incarnation is truly a mystery, but that does not mean it is completely beyond our understanding. Rather, it is a mystery of faith because its truth is so deep that we can never exhaust everything that it has to teach us.

Mary, Mother of God: The *Theotokos*

The Church's teachings and beliefs about Jesus are closely related to her teachings and beliefs about his mother, Mary. As early as the New Testament period, Mary was revered as the Mother of Jesus. However, she did not receive the title Mother of God until the Ecumenical Council of Ephesus in 431, when the Nestorian heresy was renounced. This Council affirmed Mary as the

© Bill Wittman / www.wpwittman.com

Theotokos, a Greek word that literally means "God-bearer" but is often translated as "Mother of God." Today both the Roman Catholic Church and the Eastern Orthodox Churches continue to venerate Mary with this title. Honoring Mary as the *Theotokos* acknowledges the unique role she played in our salvation. She brought the presence of God into the world in a way no one else could. Because she is the Mother of Jesus, she is also the Mother of God.

Have you ever had to defend a truth in your own life?

Pray It!

Prayer for Sharing the Truth

Pray the following prayer to seek Jesus' help in your pursuit of the truth, which is not always an easy quest.

Jesus Christ, Son of God and Son of Mary,
Sharing your truth with the world can be difficult and intimidating. Help us to speak and act in accord with your teaching. Guide us in treating all of your children with respect, care, and understanding. Inspire us to overcome any anxiety we might have in sharing your Good News with the world. Teach us to befriend, pray, and sacrifice so that all may know your truth.

Loving God, strengthen us in times we falter and struggle in sharing your Good News. Help us to always remember that you embrace us in your love and forgiveness.
Amen.

Article 8: The Ecumenical Councils of the Early Church

How did the early Church leaders come together to respond to heresies that arose in the early Church? Throughout the Church's history, bishops have met in gatherings called Ecumenical Councils to discuss the challenges facing the Church. A particular focus of the Ecumenical Councils in the early centuries of the Church was the challenges to Christological and Trinitarian doctrines. Seven Ecumenical Councils were held between AD 325 and AD 787. We will discuss the two most important of these; both of which took place in ancient cities located in modern-day Turkey.

Theotokos
A Greek title for Mary meaning "God bearer."

The Council of Nicaea

In AD 325, the Council of Nicaea declared that God the Son is "of the same substance" as God the Father. In other words, Jesus is truly God. Stating and defending this belief countered the heretical claims of Arianism, which maintained that Jesus was more than an ordinary human but less than God.

The Council of Nicaea also produced the first draft of what is now known as the Nicene Creed. You may be familiar with this Creed from praying it at Sunday liturgy. When we pray the Creed, we proclaim that Jesus was "born of the Father before all ages, God from God, Light from Light, true God from true God." These lines, written nearly seventeen hundred years ago, continue to express, with both beauty and clarity, Jesus' identity as the Second Person of the Trinity.

The Council of Chalcedon

Whereas the Council of Nicaea focused on understanding the Trinity, especially the relationship and distinction between God the Father and God the Son, the Council of Chalcedon focused on understanding the inner life of God the Son. In other words, what is the relationship between Jesus' humanity and his divinity? In the year 451, the 350 bishops attending the Council of Chalcedon

Eucharist, the
Also called the Mass or Lord's Supper, and based on a word for "thanksgiving," it is the central Christian liturgical celebration, established by Jesus at the Last Supper. In the Eucharist, the sacrificial death and Resurrection of Jesus are both remembered and renewed. The term sometimes refers specifically to the consecrated bread and wine that have become the Body and Blood of Christ.

solemnities
Important holy days in the Catholic liturgical calendar, such as Christmas, Easter, Pentecost, and All Saints' Day.

Last Judgment
The judgment of the human race by Jesus Christ at his Second Coming. It is also called the Final Judgment.

declared that Jesus' two natures (his human nature and his divine nature) are undivided and inseparable. Jesus is fully man and fully God. He is not half man and half God; nor is he two Persons somehow pushed into one. Jesus, God the Son, is *one* Divine Person with *two* natures. The Council of Chalcedon concluded that Jesus is of the same substance as God the Father when it comes to his divinity, and that he is of the same substance as us when it comes to his humanity.

> **In what ways do you respond to the message of the Gospel of Jesus Christ in your own life?**

Article 9: The Nicene Creed

You've probably studied the Declaration of Independence in one or more of your classes so far. Part of it sums up what people in the British colonies of North America believed in 1776 about their rights. In a similar way, a creed is a summary statement of the beliefs of an individual or a community. The creed Catholics pray most frequently is the Nicene Creed. The formal name for this creed is the Niceno-Constantinopolitan Creed. It is the product of two Ecumenical Councils—the Council of Nicaea held in AD 325 and the Council of Constantinople in AD 381, the latter at which it was promulgated.

Proclaiming Shared Beliefs

Catholics pray the Nicene Creed at Sunday celebrations of the **Eucharist** as well as at **solemnities**, Baptisms, and other special liturgical celebrations. This recitation of the Creed during a liturgy is called the Profession of Faith. Praying the Creed together in this way allows the gathered assembly to "respond to the word of God proclaimed in the readings taken from Sacred Scripture and explained in the homily and that they may also call to mind and confess the great mysteries of the faith" (*General Instruction on the Roman Missal*, 67). It also underscores our unity as one community of faith. We can help and support one another in our efforts to be faithful to the truths we profess together. Moreover, because we belong to a global Church, we are united in faith, through the Creed, with Catholics throughout the world.

The Creed and Baptism

From the early centuries of the Church, the Creed has played an important role in the liturgy of Baptism. Because Baptism is the Sacrament by which one becomes a Christian, it was important for the people being baptized to know and profess the beliefs of the community they were joining. Most Catholics today are baptized as babies, so our parents and godparents promise to raise us according to the faith of the Church as stated in the Creed. Thus praying the Creed each Sunday is a way for us to dedicate ourselves again to the Catholic faith. We renew our commitment to the promises made by us, or by others on our behalf, at our Baptism.

© CURAphotography / shutterstock.com

When we pray the Nicene Creed, we renew our baptismal promises. Read the Creed. Identify what it states about the three Divine Persons of the Trinity and the Church.

Key Concepts in the Nicene Creed

Even if you are familiar with the Nicene Creed, take the opportunity to read it carefully now and find where it expresses these key doctrines of our faith:

- The Creed expresses a Trinitarian faith in God the Father, God the Son, and God the Holy Spirit.
- The Creed identifies Jesus' birth, death, Resurrection, and Ascension as key events in our salvation.
- The Creed states the four "Marks" or characteristics of the Church: the Church is One, Holy, Catholic, and Apostolic.
- The Creed affirms belief in the resurrection of the dead and in the **Last Judgment**.

Using your own words, how would you say the Nicene Creed expresses the essential truths of the Catholic Church?

The Nicene Creed

I believe in one God,
the Father almighty,
maker of heaven and earth,
of all things visible and
invisible.

I believe in one Lord Jesus
Christ,
the Only Begotten Son of
God,
born of the Father before all
ages.
God from God, Light from
Light,
true God from true God,
begotten, not made, consub-
stantial with the Father;
through him all things were
made.
For us men and for our
salvation
he came down from heaven,
and by the Holy Spirit was
incarnate of the Virgin
Mary,
and became man.

For our sake he was crucified
under Pontius Pilate,
he suffered death and was
buried,
and rose again on the third
day

in accordance with the
Scriptures.
He ascended into heaven
and is seated at the right hand
of the Father.
He will come again in glory
to judge the living and the
dead
and his kingdom will have no
end.

I believe in the Holy Spirit,
the Lord, the giver of life,
who proceeds from the Father
and the Son,
who with the Father and
the Son is adored and
glorified,
who has spoken through the
prophets.

I believe in one, holy, catholic
and apostolic Church.
I confess one Baptism for the
forgiveness of sins
and I look forward to the resurrection of the dead
and the life of the world to
come.

Amen.

Article 10: The Trinity: Model for Human Relationships

What does the Trinity have to do with you? For many Catholics the Trinity can seem like an incomprehensible mystery, a distant reality, or an abstract theory. In fact, the Trinity isn't unrelated to our human experience. The Catechism tells us that "there is a certain resemblence between the unity of the divine persons" (1890) and the kind of relationships we should have with one another.

What is this "certain resemblence"? How should our human relationships reflect what we see in the Trinity? The Trinity is a dynamic communion of Persons who dwell together in love and unity. They never cease to reach out with grace, compassion, and mercy to all humanity. Our Triune God is not distant from us, unconcerned with our joys and struggles; rather, our God is involved in human history. Our God is so involved, in

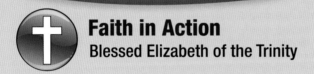

Faith in Action
Blessed Elizabeth of the Trinity

Elizabeth Catez (1880–1906) was born in France. She was the firstborn in her family, and from a young age was known for her terrible temper. After receiving her First Holy Communion, she seemed to be better able to control herself. She grew in her life with God, and developed a special understanding of the mystery of the Holy Trinity.

As a teenager, Elizabeth visited the sick and sang in the parish choir. She taught catechism to the children working in factories. At the age of twenty-one, after declining several offers of marriage, she entered the Carmelite convent in Dijon, France. During her religious life, she wrote about her experiences of God, both in times of light and joy and in times of darkness. She became a spiritual director to many people, helping them to find God along their own paths in life. Her writings were published and have helped to guide others to a deeper knowledge and love of God who is Trinity.

When she died at age twenty-six of Addison's disease (a painful hormone disorder which at that time had no treatment), her last words were, "I am going to Light, to Love, to Life!" She had no doubt that the Holy Trinity she had come to know in her heart during her lifetime would welcome her into the fullness of life in Heaven.

fact, that he became part of human history through the Incarnation of Jesus Christ.

This is the God in whose image we are created, and this is the God with whom we are destined to live forever in Heaven. While we live on earth, we are to live like this God—in relationship with others, not in isolation. Through conversation, service, and one-on-one interaction, we grow as people, discover our gifts and talents, and learn to live in the way God wants us to live. In this way, the Trinity, as a communion of Divine Persons, gives us a foundation for relationships built on unity, truth, and love.

How can you use the Trinity as a model for your own relationships?

- You can be involved in the lives of your family members, even when it is inconvenient.
- You can reach out to a new student at your school.
- You can enlarge your circle of friends and acquaintances to include people that others may have overlooked or excluded.
- You can take on a new role or ministry in your parish community.

God created us to live as a part of a community, supporting, serving, and loving one another. How do you support, serve, and love those in the communities of your family, school, church, and city?

Can you think of other ways?

When we live out our call to community in these and other ways, we are truly following God's plan for humanity. That plan is revealed for us in the mystery of the Holy Trinity: three Divine Persons living forever in unity and love as one.

> **What words come to mind when you think of the word *relationship*?**

For Review

1. What difficult tasks did the early Church face in safeguarding the apostolic faith?

2. What were the two main types of heresies about Jesus in the early Church?

3. Why do we use the title Mother of God to refer to Mary?

4. What did the Council of Nicaea declare about Jesus? What belief about Jesus was the Council defending?

5. What did the Council of Chalcedon affirm about the relationship of the human and divine natures in Jesus?

6. Why do Catholics pray the Nicene Creed at liturgical celebrations?

7. What are some of the key doctrines of the Catholic faith that the Nicene Creed states?

8. In what ways can the Trinity be a model for human relationships?

What exactly is God's gift of Revelation, and how does it fit within the history of salvation? In this unit, we will examine Sacred Scripture and Sacred Tradition as well as the many aspects of God's creation through which we encounter his wisdom and love.

We have been in a loving relationship with God since the beginning of human history. God created us to be in communion with him, and he freely reveals himself to us, offering us the gift of Revelation. When we grow in our relationship with God, we learn to respond to him wholeheartedly, especially when faced with challenging questions about God's existence and the problems of suffering and evil in the world.

Sacred Scripture and Sacred Tradition are our paths to holiness, and they allow us to experience meaningful encounters with God's revealed truth. In the Old Testament, we see the gradual self-disclosure of God, as he reveals his plan of salvation to humanity. Consequently, the New Testament gives us the saving life and work of Jesus Christ. When we learn about the formation of the canon of Sacred Scripture, Apostolic Succession, infallibility, and the lives of the saints, we see the profound transmission of God's Revelation to us, his people.

Even though God is invisible, his work of creation is all around us, all the time. We witness the goodness, power, and glory of God in the everyday experiences of our lives. We know that God is the source of everything, and we know that we can encounter him in daily life, in the faith of others, in science and the natural world, and in the human intellect.

The enduring understandings and essential questions represent core concepts and questions that are explored throughout this unit. By studying the content of each chapter, you will gain a more complete understanding of the following:

Enduring Understandings

1. God has been revealing himself and his plan for our salvation from the beginning of the universe to the Paschal Mystery of Jesus Christ.

2. We can know of God's existence and trust in his plan for human history even though we encounter suffering and evil in our world.

3. We come to know the revealed truth of God through Sacred Scripture and Sacred Tradition.

4. We can discover God in the faith of others, in the beauty and wonder of the natural world, and through our intellectual abilities.

Essential Questions

1. What does the Revelation of God tell us about our place in God's plan for the salvation of humanity?

2. How can we be sure of God's existence and his plan for us when we encounter evil and suffering in the world?

3. What do Sacred Scripture and Sacred Tradition tell us about God's Revelation?

4. How do the faithfulness of others, the natural world, and the human intellect help to inform our understanding of God?

The God-Human Relationship

Introduction

As Christians we believe that God has been engaged in a loving relationship with us since the beginning of human history. He has planted in our hearts the desire to be united with him and has freely offered us the gift of Revelation. Through the life, death, and Resurrection of Jesus Christ, he has saved and redeemed us through the power of the Holy Spirit. When you respond to God in faith, you yourself become a part of this great drama of salvation history.

Responding to God with wholehearted faith can challenge us at times. Although he freely offers us the gifts of faith and reason, we still find ourselves confronted with difficult, complex questions. For example, we may wonder if God really exists. We may question why, if he is a loving God, he allows suffering and evil to exist in the world. We will explore these questions in this chapter, and we will look at ways in which the Church guides us in answering them.

Article 11: What Is Revelation?

Have you ever wanted to get to know someone better? How do you do this? You might really listen to what the person says and watch what he or she does. To really get to know someone means that the person has to share who he or she is in words and deeds. That is what God has done and continues to do throughout **salvation history**.

Revelation is God's self-disclosure to us, which means that God gradually reveals himself and the divine plan of salvation to humanity through deeds and words. God offers "an enduring witness to Himself in created realities" (*Dogmatic Constitution on Divine Revelation [Dei Verbum, 1965]*, 3). This means we can learn about God in the events and experiences of our daily lives, the order and beauty of the natural world, the lives of the saints and other believers, and the wondrous abilities of our human intellect and reason. But God further reveals a type of knowledge that we would not be able to grasp on our own.

salvation history
The pattern of specific events in human history in which God clearly reveals his presence and saving actions. Salvation was accomplished once and for all through Jesus Christ, a truth foreshadowed and revealed throughout the Old Testament.

Revelation Is a Gift

Revelation is a loving gift that God offered to us, not something that he needs to provide. It is his completely free decision to reveal himself to us. To be known by us and to give himself to us, he freely chooses to share his Divine Self with us. This allows us to know God more fully than we ever could on our own. Revelation also empowers us to respond to him with love and devotion. The more you know God, the more you will love him.

How Does Revelation Occur?

Revelation of the divine plan, which also discloses much about who God is, has unfolded slowly, in stages, throughout salvation history. The Old Testament tells the story of how God, over many centuries, reached out to our ancestors in faith, including Abraham, Sarah, Moses, and David. Over time God formed his people into a holy nation. He spoke to them through the prophets Isaiah,

Jeremiah, and Amos, among many others. The New Testament tells the story of God's final and full Revelation in the Person of Jesus Christ, the incarnate Word of God and Son of the Father. Today the Holy Spirit continues to empower the Church to interpret, and shed light on, the mystery of God's Revelation.

In Jesus Christ, Revelation is complete. There is nothing that we need to know for our salvation that wasn't revealed through Jesus' life, teachings, Passion, death, and Resurrection. God's people will continue to grow in understanding of what he has revealed, but there won't be new public Revelation until his plan is fulfilled.

We Cannot *Fully* Know God

If Revelation is complete in Jesus Christ, does that mean we've got God "all figured out"? Unfortunately, no. Though having answers to our many questions about

Did You Know?

Doctors of the Church

© Réunion des Musées Nationaux / Art Resource, NY

When you hear the word *doctor*, you might first think of a person with a medical degree. But the word *doctor* comes from the Latin verb *docere*, meaning "to teach." The Church has named thirty-three theologians Doctors of the Church. All the Doctors of the Church were not only theologians but are also saints. They guide us in understanding and interpreting God's Revelation.

The first four Doctors of the Church were designated in 1295 by Pope Boniface VIII. They were Saint Ambrose, Saint Augustine, Saint Jerome, and Saint Gregory the Great. The three Doctors of the Church named most recently have all been women. In 1970, Pope Paul VI honored Saint Catherine of Siena and Saint Teresa of Ávila with this title. Pope Saint John Paul II bestowed the same honor on Saint Thérèse of Lisieux in 1997.

God might sound appealing, we cannot *fully* know him during our earthly lives. Even with the benefit of Revelation, God is beyond our limited human capacity for thought, words, speech, and understanding. As the *Catechism of the Catholic Church* states, quoting Saint Augustine, a fourth-century bishop and Doctor of the Church: "God remains a mystery beyond words: 'If you understood him, it would not be God'[1]" (230). Even though we cannot *fully* know God while we live on earth, we can certainly experience divine love and mercy when we attune our minds, hearts, and spirits to the many signs of God's active, loving presence in the world.

Are there events in your life that you will never fully comprehend, that give you a sense of the complexity of life and human relationships?

For Saint Augustine, his mother, Saint Monica, was a sign of God's active and loving presence in the world. Who or what is a sign of God's love for you?

Article 12: Sharing in God's Life

Revelation makes it possible for us to respond to God's plan of loving goodness for all people. What is God's plan for us? It is to live in communion with him, to have a share of God's own life, to love as God loves. God has planted in our hearts the desire for him; through Revelation this divine-human bond becomes clear.

We Are Made for God

Human beings are religious by nature and **vocation**. We were created by God and our lives are directed toward God, because our desire for him is indelibly imprinted on our hearts. In other words, we have been created to be in communion with God. We have a built-in longing to be a part of this bond between humanity and divinity.

Nearly every human culture has engaged in some kind of religious behavior, such as prayer, sacrifice, ritual, and meditation. In fact, most of the world's people, in all places and in all times, have believed in, worshipped, and sought out the Divine. This is not a coincidence; rather, it is a sign that we reach the fullness of our humanity only when we heed this built-in bond with our Creator.

God Calls Us to Fullness of Life

God would not place the desire for him within our hearts and then leave us to our own devices to figure out how to reach him. Rather, God has reached out to humanity over and over again throughout history, seeking to connect with us in mutual love. From the very beginning of time, through the age of the **patriarchs**, through the time of the Exodus, and through the era of the Israelite kings

Primary Sources

Not Scattered Away, Gathered Together

In the following excerpt, Saint Augustine explores the immeasurable and inconceivable vastness and totality of God:

Do heaven and earth, then, contain the whole of you, since you fill them? Or, when once you have filled them, is some part of you left over because they are too small to hold you? If this is so, when you have filled heaven and earth, does that part of you which remains flow over into some other place? . . . For the things which you fill by containing them do not sustain and support you as a water-vessel supports the liquid which fills it. Even if they were broken to pieces, you would not flow out of them and away. And when you pour yourself out over us, you are not drawn down to us but draw us up to yourself: you are not scattered away, but you gather us together. (*Confessions*) and prophets, God has revealed himself. His self-disclosure has been fulfilled in the Incarnation of the Divine, Eternal Son, Jesus Christ. The Incarnation is the ultimate work of Divine Revelation. Jesus' saving mission shows us how much God loves us by the act of his becoming one of us in order to save us. In the Letter to the Ephesians, Saint Paul writes of this "plan for the fullness of times, to sum up all things in Christ, in heaven and on earth" (1:10). The Second Vatican Council explains it this way:

> Jesus perfected revelation by fulfilling it through his whole work of making Himself present and manifesting Himself: through His words and deeds, His signs and wonders, but especially through His death and glorious resurrection from the dead and final sending of the Spirit of truth. (*Divine Revelation*, 4)

Today in the ministry and Sacraments of the Church, God continues to offer us his friendship. In Baptism we become adopted daughters and sons of the Divine Father, as we enter into the life and death of Jesus. When we participate in the Eucharist, we share in the sacrifice of Jesus, the Son. When we take part in these Sacraments, and when we engage in prayer and reflection on Sacred Scripture, we do so through the power of the Holy Spirit. We are not acting on our own initiative; rather, we are responding, in faith, to the promptings placed in our hearts by the Triune God.

What are some of the "signs and wonders" that you see at work in your life?

Article 13: God's Plan for Our Salvation

The first and universal witness to God's love for his people is creation itself. If we are open to it, creation makes known to us a loving, caring, and wise God who wants to be in loving union with all his creation, especially human beings. When human sin threatened God's purpose for

vocation
A call from God to all members of the Church to embrace a life of holiness. Specifically, it refers to a call to live the holy life as an ordained minister, as a vowed religious (sister or brother), or in a Christian marriage. Single life that involves a personal consecration or commitment to a permanent, celibate gift of self to God and one's neighbor is also a vocational state.

patriarchs
The ancient fathers of the Jewish people, whose stories are recounted in the Book of Genesis.

Fall, the
Also called the Fall from Grace, the biblical Revelation about the origins of sin and evil in the world, expressed figuratively in the account of Adam and Eve in Genesis.

creation, he responded with a plan for our salvation, a plan that culminates in his new creation in Christ Jesus.

God's plan to save us from sin and death occurs within history, not outside it. In other words, God acts *within* historical events. He uses both the events of the world and the events of our own daily lives to redeem and save humanity. We call the unfolding of God's plan for us salvation history. Salvation history began at the dawn of the universe and continued through all the events of the Old Testament. It culminated in the life, Passion, death, and Resurrection of Jesus. The fullness of God's loving plan for humanity will be revealed at the end of time.

The Promise of the Old Testament

The Old Testament tells the story of God's loving relationship with all humanity—beginning with Adam and Eve. God created us to live in communion with him and to find our happiness in him. Even when Adam and Eve sinned by disobeying God—an event known as **the Fall**—God did not abandon them. Rather, he "buoyed them up with the hope of salvation, by promising redemption" (*Divine Revelation*, 3). As salvation history continued to unfold, God established a covenant with Noah and, later, with the ancient Israelites.

The history of ancient Israel began with God's call to Abraham to leave his and his wife Sarah's homeland and to become the ancestors of God's Chosen People: "I will make of you a great nation, and I will bless you; I will make your name great, so that you will be a blessing" (Genesis 12:2).

Abraham and Sarah's grandson Jacob had a large family, consisting of two wives—Rachel and Leah—twelve sons, and one daughter. When Israel became a nation, the Twelve Tribes would be named for these twelve sons of Jacob.

When the Israelites later became enslaved in Egypt, God brought them to freedom through the leadership of Moses, aided by his brother, Aaron, and his sister,

Miriam. At Mount Sinai, God formed a New Covenant with the Israelites and revealed the Law. This covenant is often called the Sinai Covenant or the Mosaic Covenant.

As salvation history continued, God called kings and priests to be the Israelites' political and religious leaders. He also sent prophets to call the Israelites back to fidelity when they sinned. The prophets offered them the hope of a new and everlasting covenant: "I will place my law within them, and write it upon their hearts; I will be their God, and they shall be my people" (Jeremiah 31:33).

Through these many centuries, God never ceased to share his mercy and love with the people of Israel. They never ceased to be God's Chosen People, and were the first to hear the Word of God.

Jesus Christ: Savior of the World

The New Testament Letter to the Hebrews tells us, "In times past, God spoke in partial and various ways to our ancestors through the prophets; in these last days,

Pray It!

Lesson from Abraham

When you hear about Abraham's relationship with God, you might be tempted to say, "I wish God would speak to me directly and tell me what he wants me to do with my life." God might not come to your house and sit down at the table to tell you what he wishes for you, but he continues to speak to you, and to each one of us. We just have to be willing to listen. Some of the ways we listen to God include praying, being active in our parishes, attending Mass, and reading Sacred Scripture.

Be ready! When you take the time to listen to God, you might be challenged like Abraham to make dramatic changes in your life. Reflect on this passage from Genesis about the covenant with Abraham, and ask God to help you place your trust in him:

> Some time afterward, the word of the LORD came to Abram in a vision:
> Do not fear, Abram! I am your shield; I will make your reward very great.
> . . . [The LORD] took him outside and said: Look up at the sky and count the stars, if you can. Just so, he added, will your descendants be. Abram put his faith in the LORD, who attributed it to him as an act of righteousness. (15:1,5–6)

Salvation History Time Line

Adam and Eve (Genesis, chapters 1–2), Noah (Genesis, chapters 6–9)		**Biblical Prehistory**
Patriarchs and Matriarchs (Genesis, chapters 12, 25–36)		**1850–1750 BC**
Moses (Exodus, chapters 14, 20)		**1290 BC**
Kings and Priests (1 and 2 Samuel, 1 and 2 Kings)		**1250–922 BC**
Prophets		**922–587 BC**
Jesus		**5 BC–AD 30**

he spoke to us through a son, whom he made heir of all things and through whom he created the universe" (1:1–2). In other words, the Revelation of God's loving plan in history finds its fulfillment in the Incarnation. Indeed what better way to reveal the divine plan to us than by becoming one of us? The life, Passion, death, and Resurrection of Jesus—the Eternal Son of God Made Flesh—is God's definitive effort to save us, to reveal the truth, and to bring us to the fullness of life.

> **When you find that something is fulfilling, how would you describe it?**

Article 14: Encountering God with the Eyes of Faith

If you have ever wondered whether God really exists, you are not alone. This question has captivated the imaginations of the greatest religious thinkers. It can be hard to accept something we can't see with our eyes, and trusting in a spiritual reality requires self-surrender. We don't believe in God only because it makes good sense to do so; rather, we believe because he is trustworthy. Nevertheless, he has given us several sources that can help to assure us of his existence.

Encountering God in Sacred Scripture

In the Gospels, we learn of Jesus' sending the Twelve Apostles on a mission: "He summoned the Twelve and gave them power and authority over all demons and to cure diseases, and he sent them to proclaim the kingdom of God and to heal [the sick]" (Luke 9:1–2). After Jesus' death and Resurrection, these Twelve Apostles—with many other disciples as their coworkers—continued this mission. They preached the Good News of God's Reign through their words and actions. Eventually the witness of these very early followers of Jesus—those people who had been commissioned by Christ himself—was preserved in the writings of the New Testament. The New

martyrdom
Witness to the
saving message of
Christ through the
sacrifice of one's
life.

Testament is a rich and varied collection of Gospels,
epistles, sermons, speeches, parables, and accounts of
Jesus' miracles. Like the Old Testament, because it was
written through the inspiration of the Holy Spirit, it is a
privileged place for us to encounter God's strong, reliable,
and active presence in our lives.

The Witness of Faith-Filled People

The testimony of those with a strong belief in God
can inform our own approach to the question of God's
existence. God offers the same gift of faith to all people,
but sometimes we hear of people who have responded
to that gift with extraordinary trust despite trials, suffering, and persecution, some even accepting **martyrdom** for
their faith. Their stories can be especially powerful and
enriching for our own faith. The willingness of so many
people—both in ancient times and in modern times—to
die as martyrs for their Christian faith can challenge us
to reconsider our own doubts.

In addition to the accounts of saints and martyrs
whose example can lead us to greater discipleship, many
of us are blessed with living examples of people whose
unshakable faith deepens our own faith in God. You
might be inspired by the faith of your parents, grandpar-
ents, or other family members, or of teachers, priests, or
members of your parish community. Regardless of who
the models of faith are in your lives, these people can
help you to root your life more firmly in faith.

Knowing God through Reason and Conscience

Saint Anselm of Canterbury is known for his description
of theology as "faith seeking understanding." This statement means that although faith is a sure and certain gift
of God, we are able to use our human faculties to understand our faith more fully. Indeed God created us with
human reason and a moral conscience. God wants us to
use these gifts to explore our religious questions, including the question of his existence. When we truly listen to

the message inherent in creation and to our conscience, we discover that God can indeed be known and understood by witnessing the created world through the use of our own human reason. In other words, our brains and our faith are not on parallel tracks that will never intersect. Our reason and intellect can nourish our faith in God's existence, for the deeper our knowledge of God's truth runs, the greater our faith in his gifts becomes.

Try to bring these different sources—Sacred Scripture, the witness of other believers, and human reason—to your prayer. They will help you to truly grow in your knowledge and experience of God. This does not

Faith in Action
Saint Maximilian Kolbe of Auschwitz

© Bill Wittman / www.wpwittman.com

Saint Maximilian Kolbe was born in Poland in 1894. He was ordained a Franciscan priest as a young man. When Hitler invaded Poland in 1939, Kolbe spoke out against Nazi oppression. He protected Jews from persecution. His arrest in 1941 brought him to Auschwitz, the largest of the Nazi death camps.

One day, after some prisoners tried to escape from the camp, ten men were chosen at random to be starved to death. One of the ten, Franciszek Gajowniczek, protested that he had a family who would be devastated by his death. In a courageous act of self-sacrifice, Kolbe volunteered to take Gajowniczek's place and was sent to the starvation bunker. When he was found still alive after ten days with no food or water, he was killed by lethal injection. Kolbe's unwavering faith in Jesus led him to accept terrible suffering, knowing the greater good that it would lead to. At Auschwitz, someone once asked Kolbe whether his sacrifices for others "made sense in a place where every man was engaged in a struggle for survival." He answered: "Every man has an aim in life. For most men, it is to return home to their wives and families, or to their mothers. For my part, I give my life for the good of all men" (*Blessed Maximilian*, OFM, Conv.).

Saint Maximilian Kolbe's feast day is August 14. He trusted in the reality of God's love, mercy, and protection even in the worst circumstances imaginable.

theodicy
From the Greek words for "God" and "justice," referring to the study of evil and suffering in the world, which seems contrary to the existence of a presumably good God.

free will
The gift from God that allows human beings to choose from among various actions, for which we are held accountable. It is the basis for moral responsibility.

mean you will never doubt God's existence again. Such questions and concerns are normal and natural parts of the human condition. It does mean you will have the resources to investigate your questions with honesty, clarity, and humility.

> **Who are some of the people in your life that lead lives of extraordinary faith and strength?**

Article 15: Evil and Suffering and a Good and Powerful God

Drought, famine, and earthquakes. Violence, disease, and war. Stories of suffering, near home and in faraway places, are not hard to come by. If God is all-powerful and all-good, how can there be so much suffering in the world? Human attempts to answer this age-old question are called **theodicy**. In many ways, the whole Christian story seeks to answer this question, and every part is in part an answer to the question. Let's consider four key elements of the Church's answer to the question.

The World Is Yet Imperfect

Our world is far from perfect. This should be obvious to anyone with any awareness of current events. First, natural disasters like floods, droughts, and earthquakes continue to happen throughout the world. These events are not punishment from God or a sign of divine anger or displeasure; they are simply part of the laws of nature. The more perfect exists alongside the less perfect for now, until God's ultimate plan for the world is fully revealed. God did not create the world as a fixed, fin-ished reality. Rather, he has put us on a journey toward ultimate fulfillment, the ultimate perfection of our souls when they rest in him.

Because we are part of the real world, human beings continue to sin and commit evil acts. Because God cre-ated us with **free will**, we have the option to sin. God respects our freedom. He never forces us to choose the good, even though suffering for ourselves or others often results when we sin. This means we continue to live in an imperfect world. However, by learning to use our free will wisely, we participate in God's work of spreading the Reign of God throughout the world.

Suffering Can Be Redemptive

Because Jesus' death redeemed, or saved, humanity from sin, we view suffering, especially when endured on behalf of others, as redemptive. Because God suffered in the Person of Jesus, he is truly with suffering people in a very special way. Our suffering unites us with the crucified Christ, and our efforts to alleviate the suffering of others allow us to serve the very Body of the Crucified Lord.

The Paschal Mystery Gives Us Hope

The Church's theodicy is rooted not only in Jesus' death on the cross but also in his Resurrection. Because we were baptized into Christ's death, we will share in his Resurrection: we also will live again after we die. The

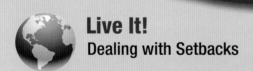

Live It!
Dealing with Setbacks

How well do you unite sufferings in your personal life with Jesus' redemptive acts of love? Whether setbacks are large or small, they are an opportunity to unite personal suffering with that of Jesus. For example, you might be disappointed that a test you expected to ace goes badly, or that a date you were sure you'd get didn't happen, or that a game you hoped your team would win turned out to be a disaster. At such times you can either mope and complain or offer your frustrations up in prayer.

At times you might also be blindsided by larger sufferings, such as a friend betraying you, or a major illness afflicting you or someone you love.

When you experience any suffering—whether great or small—how do you respond? How might you respond differently, in a way that will lead to good coming from your suffering? Reflect on how you respond to setbacks in your life, and make a commitment to unite your suffering with that of Jesus, who willingly accepted suffering for our redemption.

Paschal Mystery
The work of salvation accomplished by Jesus Christ mainly through his Passion, death, Resurrection, and Ascension.

Resurrection is not just about life after death. It is also about the **Paschal Mystery**, the centerpiece of Christian faith. The Paschal Mystery shows us that suffering, sin, and evil will never have the last word. Just as God brought the hope and joy of the empty tomb out of the agony and torment of the cross, so will he bring forth new life and hope out of the most desperate and seemingly hopeless situations today.

We See Only Partially

Because God is good and gracious, he always wills and desires what is best for us. It is easy to believe this when life is good, but experiences of pain and loss challenge us to trust that "all things work for good for those who love God" (Romans 8:28). In times like this, we are invited to place our confidence in God's plan for humanity, even though it is difficult for us to understand why suffering must be a part of that plan. Through faith we can be certain that though God allows evil, he also causes good to come from every evil, but in ways we will only fully understand in eternal life. Suffering and evil are never good in themselves, but God's powerful love and mercy can transform the worst suffering or the deepest evil into something good.

Natural disasters, such as Hurricane Katrina, are an unfortunate part of our lives. When we are grounded in our faith, we have the strength to persevere and have our suffering transformed into something good.

© Alex Neauville / shutterstock.com

Suffering reminds us that we cannot see the "big picture" that God can see. In his First Letter to the Corinthians, Saint Paul contrasts the perspective on life we have now, while we are on earth, with the clearer, more complete view we will have in Heaven. He writes: "At present we see indistinctly, as in a mirror, but then face to face. At present I know partially; then I shall know fully, as I am fully known" (13:12).

Encounters with suffering and evil are difficult and distressing. Still, we can trust that somehow, in a way we cannot yet fully understand, the hand of God is at work. God is bringing the world to the state of perfection for which he created it.

> **In what ways do you rely on God during times of personal pain and loss?**

For Review

1. If we can know about God through our own reason and observation, why did God make Revelation available to us?

2. Throughout history humans have been seeking God. Why do we have that inborn drive?

3. What is salvation history?

4. In what ways is God's loving plan in history fulfilled in the Incarnation?

5. What sources of information can help to assure us that God really exists?

6. Given that faith is a sure and certain gift of God to believe in him, why should we try to use our reason to reach him?

7. What is theodicy? What are the key elements of the Catholic approach to theodicy?

Sacred Scripture and Sacred Tradition

Introduction

As you have learned, we are created in love by God and we are redeemed in his mercy. Furthermore, we grow in holiness through our meaningful encounters with God's revealed truth. Both the Old and New Testaments offer profound wisdom and numerous opportunities to strengthen our faith as they recount the stories of God's covenant love, first with the ancient Israelites and later with the Church. Sacred Tradition, the process of sharing and handing down all that God has communicated, also offers us a path to holiness. As you will learn in this chapter, both Sacred Scripture and Sacred Tradition direct us to Jesus Christ, the true Word of God, who is also the complete and final Revelation of God.

You may wonder whether this Deposit of Faith— that is, the truth revealed by God through Sacred Scripture and Sacred Tradition—could really be of divine origin. The Church has faithfully preserved and shared the truth of Christ's original mission with generations of believers from the time of the Apostles to our present age. This heritage of faith assures us that God indeed dwells in and with the Church.

It is through both Sacred Scripture and Sacred Tradition that God is revealed and his truth is known to us. The Church also furthers our understanding of God's truth by relying on Apostolic Succession and papal infallibility to help us understand her teachings.

Article 16: God's Revelation through Sacred Scripture: The Old Testament

inspired
Written by human beings with the guidance of the Holy Spirit to teach faithfully and without error the saving truth that God willed to give us.

The Old Testament is the story of God's covenant relationship with the ancient Israelites. Through this collection of sacred, **inspired** writings, we learn the gradual process of God's self-disclosure to humanity, which ultimately points to the fullness of his Revelation in Jesus Christ. The accounts in the Old Testament communicate great wisdom and insight as they reveal God's plan for our salvation.

The Old Testament: An Ancient Sign of God's Love

When Christians read the Old Testament, they do not leave out Jesus. Rather, we read the Old Testament in full awareness of Jesus as the crucified and Risen Christ. The life, death, and Resurrection of Jesus Christ do not make the Old Testament dated or unnecessary. Instead the Old Testament—divinely inspired by the Holy Spirit—is an essential part of Sacred Scripture and is of infinite value to all Christian believers. As Saint Paul wrote in his Letter to the Romans, "For the gifts and the call of God are irrevocable" (11:29), meaning that God is always faithful. His relationship with the ancient Israelites, the ancestors of today's Jews, endures forever. God's commitment to Abraham and all his descendants, even to the present day, will never end. Thus the inspired books of the Old Testament—which contains books that are also Scripture of the Jewish people—will always be a privileged way for people of faith, both Jews and Christians, to encounter God.

The Jewish Roots of Christianity

Christians enrich their faith lives through familiarity with the stories, characters, and themes of the Old Testament because Christianity is rooted in Judaism. Think of the image of a family tree. The family begins at the base of the tree trunk. Then it grows in many directions,

Gentile
Someone who is not Jewish.

represented by the branches. Saint Paul used this image to demonstrate the relationship of Judaism to Christianity. In his Letter to the Romans, written to **Gentile** Christians, he said, "you . . . have come to share in the rich root of the olive tree, . . . consider that you do not support the root; the root supports you" (11:17–18). In Saint Paul's analogy, Judaism is the original tree and the Gentile Christian communities are the branches that were later grafted onto the tree. Just as a transplanted branch could never survive without the support of the original tree's root, Christianity would not be with us today without its foundation in the roots of Judaism.

When we understand the Old Testament as the root of our Christian faith, we are reminded that Jesus, as a member of a Jewish family, grew up studying the Old Testament and learned its stories. Joseph and Mary taught Jesus about the patriarchs, Moses and the Law, and about the kings and prophets of Israel. The story of God's covenant with ancient Israel became a part of Jesus'

Did You Know?

The Old Testament in Catholic Liturgy

© Bill Wittman / www.wpwittman.com

Did you know that about half of the Scripture readings proclaimed at Sunday Eucharistic liturgies are taken from the Old Testament?

At a typical Sunday Mass, Catholics hear four passages from Scripture: the First Reading, the Responsorial Psalm, the Second Reading, and the Gospel. Two of these are usually from the Old Testament—the First Reading and, of course, the Responsorial Psalm, which is taken from the Book of Psalms.

The Responsorial Psalm is usually sung rather than read. The Book of Psalms is often called the prayer book of ancient Israel. It has also been a cornerstone of Christian prayer for many centuries.

At the next Sunday Mass, pay careful attention to the Scripture readings. What is God revealing in the Old Testament and the Gospel proclamation? What psalm is sung? What new insights into Judaism, Christianity, and the person of Jesus do these ancient texts offer you?

identity and mission. Thus when we as Christians study the Old Testament, we gain great insights into the person and saving work of Christ himself.

> **What specific insights about God's love for us have you learned from reading the Old Testament?**

Article 17: God's Revelation through Sacred Scripture: The New Testament

The Old Testament tells the story of God's saving work among many generations of ancient Israelites. The books of the Old Testament show the development and progress of God's covenant relationship with the Israelites, spanning many hundreds of years. In contrast, the New Testament covers a much shorter period of time. The books of the New Testament focus on the saving life and work of one person: Jesus, the Eternal Son, sent by the Father to redeem us in the Holy Spirit.

The Life and Teachings of Jesus

Have you ever read a book about a famous person, maybe a sports star, actor, or other celebrity? What did this person do to earn fame, fortune, or accolades? Did she or he perform great deeds or help large numbers of people? There is one story of a famous person who is truly deserving of fame and accolades and so much more. When we learn about the life of Jesus Christ, true God and true man, we learn of greatness beyond human understanding.

The books of the New Testament are rooted in the historical life and teachings of Jesus of Nazareth. Jesus was born to Saint Joseph—his earthly Father—and the Virgin Mary. As an adult, Jesus began his public ministry. Although the New Testament is not a complete, biographical account of the life of Christ, it does faithfully transmit "all that Jesus did and taught until the day he was taken up" (Acts 1:1–2).

Oral Tradition

Many people are surprised to learn that no part of the New Testament was written while Jesus was alive. For approximately twenty years after Jesus' death and Resurrection, little, if anything, was written about him. Instead his disciples shared their experiences of Jesus through oral tradition, or by "word of mouth." They even traveled to distant cities in the Roman Empire to share what was already being called the Good News—the Gospel—of Jesus Christ: the fulfillment of God's saving plan. The journeys of the early disciples are called the missionary campaigns because these believers demonstrated their faith in Jesus and encouraged others to accept the message of the Gospel.

The Epistles

The earliest writings in the New Testament are the Epistles, or letters. In fact, the Epistles of the New Testament predate even the four Gospels and are among the oldest Christian documents in existence. The first New Testament letters were written by Saint Paul, beginning around the year AD 51. A prolific writer and early disciple of Jesus, Saint Paul had encountered the Risen Lord in a vision on the road to Damascus. He was the most well-known person to join in the missionary campaign in the decades just after Jesus' death and Resurrection. He traveled to cities like Corinth, Thessalonica, Philippi, and Rome, and to the region we now know as the Middle East. After leaving those cities for new missionary destinations, he wrote letters to the Christian communities he had left behind. These letters are preserved in the New Testament. They offer us marvelous insights into the early Church and the faith that led Saint Paul and his followers to take incredible risks for the sake of the Gospel message.

The Gospels

The Gospel of Mark, the shortest and earliest Gospel written, dates from about AD 70. It was followed by the

Gospels of Luke, Matthew, and finally John, which were probably written around the year AD 95. The Gospels do not offer a complete record of the life of Jesus; they are not biographies. The **Evangelists** wrote for certain early communities of both Gentile and Jewish Christians. Each chose the teachings, parables, and miracles of Jesus that would be most useful for nurturing the faith of the communities for whom he was writing. As the Vatican II document *Dogmatic Constitution on Divine Revelation (Dei Verbum*, 1965) states, "The sacred authors, in writing the four Gospels, selected certain of the many elements which had been handed on, either orally or already in

Evangelists
From a Greek word meaning "messenger of good news," the title given to the authors of the Gospels of Matthew, Mark, Luke, and John.

Faith in Action
Madonna House

Madonna House in Combermere, Canada, is a center of lay apostolic life. Members of Madonna House live and work as a community, offering programs for guests who seek to deepen their understanding of the Catholic faith. Madonna House was founded by Catherine de Hueck Doherty (1896–1985). As a Russian immigrant of aristocratic ancestry, Catherine settled in Canada, where she experienced the hardship of a broken marriage and of being a single parent. Through it all, Catherine's faith in God remained strong, and she eventually dedicated her life to him through service to the poor. This led her to open Madonna House, a place she described as "a house of hospitality . . . where people are received, . . . simply as people. They are loved."

The seed of Catherine's call to serve the poor was "The Little Mandate"—words that Catherine believed she received from Christ. She described these words as a "distillation of the Gospel." The Little Mandate became the heart of the spirituality of the members of Madonna House. The Little Mandate is a reminder to all of us that Sacred Scripture is not just for reading. Sacred Scripture is a guide for life. Among the teachings summarized in the Little Mandate are the following:

Arise—go! Sell all you possess. Give it directly, personally to the poor.
Take up My cross (their cross) and follow Me, going to the poor, being poor, being one with them, one with Me.
Little—be always little! Be simple, poor, childlike.
Preach the Gospel with your life—*without compromise!* Listen to the Spirit. He will lead you.

canon of Scripture
The books of the Bible officially recognized by the Church as the inspired Word of God.

written form; others they synthesized or explained with an eye to the situation of the churches" (19). The books they wrote—the four Gospels—have always been treated with a special reverence by Christians. As *Divine Revelation* explains: "It is common knowledge that among all the inspired writings, including those of the New Testament, the Gospels have a special place, and rightly so, because they are our principal source for the life and teaching of the incarnate Word, our Saviour" (18).

Formation of the Canon of Scripture

The collection of seventy-three books that make up the Bible is called the **canon of Scripture**. Twenty-seven of the books compose the New Testament. These twenty-seven books are not the only writings about Jesus Christ that existed during the years after his death and Resurrection. Many other writings—including other books about Christ's life—claimed to be authentically inspired texts. The early Church Fathers determined which books were divinely inspired and canonical (that is, part of the sacred canon), based on the following criteria:

- **Apostolic origin** The book is based on the preaching and teaching of the Apostles and their closest companions.

- **Community acceptance** The book is universally accepted and received by all major Christian communities in the Mediterranean world.

- **Use in early Christian worship** The book was being used in Christian liturgical celebrations—most important, when the faithful gathered for the Eucharist.

- **Consistency** The book's message is consistent with other Christian and Hebrew, or Jewish, writings. The writer was an Apostle or close associate of an Apostle.

What book of the New Testament do you find yourself most drawn to? Why?

Article 18: God's Revelation through Sacred Tradition

Some Christians mistakenly rely on only Sacred Scripture for God's Revelation. Catholics, however, recognize the authority of both Sacred Scripture and **Sacred Tradition**. Sacred Scripture and Sacred Tradition both come from God, so they are not separate or contradictory. Rather, they are two ways of transmitting Divine Revelation.

What Is Sacred Tradition?

Does your family tell certain stories over and over again, passing them down through the years? Maybe the stories are about how your relatives came to this country or how your parents first met. Something like this happens with accounts of God's actions in the Church.

In Jesus Christ, the Eternal Son, God the Father revealed himself to humanity. He entrusted this Revelation to the Apostles. Christ commanded the Apostles to preach the Gospel to the ends of the earth; to share the fullness of his revealed truth so that all might be saved (see Matthew 28:19–20). Inspired by the Holy Spirit, the Apostles did this, in both preaching and writing. The Apostles' teaching authority was passed on to the popes and bishops who succeeded them (the **Magisterium**) so that the apostolic teaching would be handed down to all generations until Christ comes again in glory. This living transmission of the Good News of Jesus Christ is called Sacred Tradition, or sometimes the Apostolic Tradition. It is distinct from Sacred Scripture. It may be helpful to consider this order of events to better understand the process of Sacred Tradition:

- The Apostles witnessed Jesus' life, teachings, death, and Resurrection. Jesus charged them to share this Good News (which can also be called Revelation, the Word of God, or the Gospel) with all people. In Jewish Scriptures (which will become the Old Testament), they saw many stories and prophecies pointing to Christ, which they now understood more clearly.

Sacred Tradition
The process of passing on the Gospel message. Sacred Tradition, which began with the oral communication of the Gospel by the Apostles, was written down in Sacred Scripture, is handed down and lived out in the life of the Church, and is interpreted by the Magisterium under the guidance of the Holy Spirit.

Magisterium
The Church's living teaching office, which consists of all bishops, in communion with the Pope, the bishop of Rome.

- Inspired and strengthened by the Holy Spirit, the Apostles first shared the Good News with those people to whom they preached.
- Later the Apostles and others wrote about the Good News in the form of Gospels and letters.
- These writings became the New Testament canon.
- Through the centuries until the end of time, the Magisterium interprets and teaches the Word of God to the whole world.

Each step of this process is guided by the Holy Spirit. The bishops, in communion with the Pope, authentically interpret the Word of God in its written form and in the form of Sacred Tradition.

The Unity of Scripture and Tradition

Because Tradition and Scripture are both "flowing from the same divine well-spring" (*Divine Revelation*, 9), they work together to achieve the same goal. The Second Vatican Council identified Tradition and Scripture as the two primary ways the Church imparts God's revealed truth: "Sacred Tradition and sacred Scripture make up a single sacred deposit of the Word of God, which is entrusted to the Church" (10). Together, Tradition and Scripture hand down the Gospel. They both reveal God to us, so we must respect both: "Both Scripture and Tradition must be accepted and honored with equal devotion and reverence" (9).

Tradition versus *tradition?*

So what's the difference between *Tradition*, with a capital *T*, and *tradition*, with a lowercase *t*? *Tradition* with a capital *T*, as in *Sacred Tradition*, is the process of sharing God's authoritative Revelation in the Church. Sacred Tradition is a *living* process. This means it is ongoing and never ending, because new generations always need to hear the Gospel message.

In contrast, *tradition* with a lowercase *t* refers to a custom. For example, does your parish community sing "Silent Night" at Midnight Mass on Christmas? Do you wear a medal of your patron saint, or pray the Rosary during the month of October? These are all examples of Catholic traditions. They are not part of God's authoritative Revelation, so they can be changed or altered to suit different circumstances, time periods, and cultures. In other words, because singing "Silent Night" is a *tradition*—rather than part of *Tradition*—it is okay to sing a different song at Christmas Mass.

> **In what ways do you see Sacred Tradition fitting together with Sacred Scripture?**

Article 19: Passing On God's Revelation

You may have wondered, how can we be sure the beliefs and teachings of the Church come from God? How do we know that someone didn't just make up all this? Understanding Apostolic Succession and papal infallibility can help us with this question.

Apostolic Succession: Appointed by Christ

The Church teaches today the same Word of God that Jesus entrusted to his Apostles. When Jesus chose the Apostles, he commissioned them to share in his ministry of preaching the truth and proclaiming the Reign of God. As we read in Mark's Gospel, Jesus "went up the mountain and summoned those whom he wanted and they came to him. He appointed twelve [whom he also named apostles] that they might be with him and he might send them forth to preach and to have authority to drive out demons" (3:13–15). Jesus called these Apostles to share in his mission during his earthly life. He also commissioned them to continue his mission after his death, Resurrection, and Ascension. Jesus said to the disciples while they were gathered on the mountain in Galilee: "All power in heaven and on earth has been given to me. Go, therefore, and make disciples of all nations,

Apostolic Succession
The uninterrupted passing on of apostolic preaching and authority from the Apostles directly to all bishops. It is accomplished through the laying on of hands when a bishop is ordained in the Sacrament of Holy Orders as instituted by Christ. The office of bishop is permanent, because at ordination a bishop is marked with an indelible, sacred character.

baptizing them in the name of the Father, and of the Son, and of the holy Spirit, teaching them to observe all that I have commanded you. And behold, I am with you always, until the end of the age" (Matthew 28:18–20). This is called the Great Commission. The Apostles, in turn, shared the mission that Christ had entrusted to them with their designated successors, who passed it on to their successors, and so forth, even to the present day. Consequently, the truth that Jesus shared with the first Apostles continues to be preached today through their successors, the bishops of the Church. This entire process is called **Apostolic Succession**.

The Pope, who is the Bishop of Rome, and all the bishops of the Church, are the modern-day successors of the Apostles. Vatican II's *Dogmatic Constitution on the Church (Lumen Gentium,* 1964) states this clearly: "The apostolic tradition is manifested and preserved throughout the world by those whom the apostles made bishops and by their successors down to our own time" (20). Christ continues to teach through the Magisterium, the official teaching authority of the Church. In this way, he keeps his promise to the Apostles, for Christ is with us until the end of time (see Matthew 28:20).

Live It!
Becoming Friends of God

The Church reminds us that we are all called to holiness—that is, to be saintly people. But how can you do this in your everyday, ordinary life? A great first step is to work at building a friendship with God. Get to know him better through daily spiritual practices such as the Eucharist, prayer, and Sacred Scripture reading. Make a commitment to accomplish your studies and other activities with and for God. Strive to please God in all that you do. And as with any friend you cherish, help others get to know and love him too, through your example and word.

Infallibility: Certainty of Faith and Morals

Jesus has guaranteed that all his followers—everywhere and throughout time—would continue to have access to the truths necessary for their salvation by giving his Church a share in his own infallibility. The doctrine of papal **infallibility** was held by the faithful for many years, but it was formally declared at the First Vatican Council in 1870. *Infallible* means "without error." This doctrine means that statements of the Pope are always true in certain situations. The Pope is infallible when he teaches a doctrine related to faith or morals. The Pope is *not* speaking infallibly every time he speaks—such as in making a remark about the weather! Rather, the Holy Spirit guides the Pope and keeps him from error when he speaks *ex cathedra* about matters essential to our salvation. Literally, *ex cathedra* means "from the chair," and it tells us that the Pope is speaking in his official role as authoritative teacher.

infallibility
The gift given by the Holy Spirit to the Church whereby the pastors of the Church, the Pope and the bishops in union with him, can definitively proclaim a doctrine of faith and morals without error.

Pray It!

Prayer for Unity

The need for interreligious dialogue and prayer is taken seriously by the United States Conference of Catholic Bishops (USCCB). In fact, a section of the USCCB website is devoted to ecumenical affairs; it highlights ongoing events and news regarding the importance of interfaith dialogue and the fostering of Christian dialogue.

The following prayer is taken from the Week of Prayer for Christian Unity, which in 2008 commemorated the hundredth anniversary of the Prayer Octave for Christian Unity. Originally introduced to cover the days between the feasts of Saints Peter and Paul, this eight-day series of prayers occurs every year and is an international ecumenical event focused on Christian communion and unity. In the prayer, we express our human need for connection and sharing, as we ask God to give us the strength to find common cause with others.

Lord, you desire truth deep down within us: in the secret of our hearts, you teach us wisdom. Teach us to encourage one another along the road to unity. Show us the conversion necessary for reconciliation. Give to each of us a new, truly ecumenical heart, we pray you. Amen.

ex cathedra
A Latin term literally meaning "from the chair," referring to pronouncements concerning faith or morals made by the Pope, acting with full Apostolic authority, as pastor and teacher of all Christians.

ecumenism
The movement to restore unity among all Christians, the unity to which the Church is called by the Holy Spirit.

What about individual bishops other than the Pope? They cannot speak infallibly by themselves, but the *whole body* of bishops (which includes the Pope) can share in the gift of teaching infallibly on matters of faith and morals. They do so when they speak together with one voice, especially in an Ecumenical Council.

Because of Apostolic Succession and papal infallibility, all Catholics throughout time, whether in the third century or the twenty-first, whether in Korea or Guatemala or France, share one faith that goes all the way back to Christ himself. The God who, in Jesus, promised to be with us "until the end of the age" (Matthew 28:20) has guaranteed that all of us will continue to have access to the truth until Christ comes again in glory.

The Catholic Church and Other Religions

Doctrines such as Apostolic Succession and papal infallibility can be hard for non-Catholics to understand. Despite this, it is important to seek unity among Christians and with all people of goodwill, without compromising the truths of faith. In recent years the Catholic Church has made huge strides in building bridges with other Christians and with people of other faiths, including the following efforts:

- The Vatican II *Decree on Ecumenism (Unitatis Redintegratio*, 1964) stressed that the Sacrament of Baptism unites all Christians: "All who have been justified by faith in baptism are incorporated into Christ" (3).

- Also among the writings of Vatican II is the *Declaration on the Relation of the Church to Non-Christian Religions (Nostra Aetate*, 1965). It speaks of the "high regard" in which the Catholic Church holds other faiths. These often "reflect a ray of that truth which enlightens all" (2). (See the sidebar "Primary Sources: *Declaration on the Relation of the Church to Non-Christian Religions [Nostra Aetate, 1965].")*

- Pope Saint John Paul II built on the views expressed at Vatican II. He began **interreligious dialogue** with the Jewish community and was the first Pope since Saint Peter to visit a synagogue. He was also the first Pope to pray at the Western (Wailing) Wall in Jerusalem.

- During his papacy, Pope Benedict XVI visited Jewish communities throughout the world and also dialogued with Muslims.

- Pope Francis has also increased the signs of interreligious understanding and tolerance. At the liturgy celebrating Holy Thursday, the Pope washed the feet of twelve juvenile inmates. Among the children were a Muslim boy and two girls, one of whom was also a Muslim. Additionally, when Pope Francis was installed as pontiff, many leaders of the Islamic world attended the Mass.

interreligious dialogue
The efforts to build cooperative and constructive interaction with other world religions.

Primary Sources

Declaration on the Relation of the Church to Non-Christian Religions (Nostra Aetate, 1965)

A section of Relation of the Church to Non-Christian Religions specifically addresses Jewish-Catholic relations, often a deep-seated source of tension, misunderstanding, and pain. The excerpt below helps us to understand the Church's stance toward the Jewish people:

> Although the Church is the new people of God, the Jews should not be presented as rejected or accursed by God, as if this followed from the Holy Scriptures. All should see to it, then, that in catechetical work or in the preaching of the word of God they do not teach anything that does not conform to the truth of the Gospel and the spirit of Christ.
>
> Furthermore, in her rejection of every persecution against any man, the Church, mindful of the patrimony she shares with the Jews and moved not by political reasons but by the Gospel's spiritual love, decries hatred, persecutions, displays of anti-Semitism, directed against Jews at any time and by anyone. (4)

Efforts to dialogue with people of other religions do not alter or water down the Catholic Church's mission to pass on God's revealed truth. Rather, these ecumenical and interfaith efforts are an essential part of our mission. As Catholics we are called to be channels of unity, makers of peace, and witnesses to the truth in every time and place.

> **What are some examples of how Apostolic Succession and papal infallibility connect us as a people of faith?**

For Review

1. What is significant about Christianity being rooted in Judaism?

2. Why do the Gospels have a special place among all of Sacred Scripture?

3. What criteria did the early Church Fathers use to determine which books formed the canon of the New Testament?

4. Name the two primary ways the Church passes on Revelation and explain how these ways are related.

5. Explain the difference between *Tradition* with a capital *T* and tradition with a small *t*.

6. How do we know that the beliefs and teachings of the Church really come from God?

7. What is the attitude of the Church toward other religions?

Discovering God in Creation

Chapter 5

Introduction

Do you have favorite authors or film directors? You probably don't know them personally, but you may know something about them because of the themes, characters, and settings of their books and films.

We can know something of God in the same way. "Ever since the creation of the world, his invisible attributes of eternal power and divinity have been able to be understood and perceived in what he has made" (Romans 1:20). Saint Paul shares a powerful truth with us with these words. Our God is invisible, but we need look no further than creation to glimpse his goodness, power, and glory. "Creation" includes many things— our daily experiences, the people with whom we share our lives or who inspire us through their holiness, the natural world, and our own intellectual abilities. Because we believe that God is the Source of all that is, there is nothing that *cannot* speak to us of his wisdom and love. Throughout this chapter we will explore the many ways we can encounter God and how we can grow in our awareness of his faithful presence throughout all of creation.

Article 20: Discovering God in Our Daily Lives

We can discover God's goodness and glory not only in Sacred Scripture and Sacred Tradition but also in the events and experiences of our everyday lives. In fact, our Divine Father wants to be known by us. For this reason, the Holy Spirit enables us to transform our daily experiences into powerful encounters with God's wisdom and love.

Faith in Action
Venerable Catherine McAuley of Dublin

Design by Judy Ward, RSM; from the original painting by Cloy Kent; Used with permission from Mercy Iowa City.

When we become more aware of the Revelation of God in our everyday experiences, amazing things can happen.

Catherine McAuley was born in Dublin, Ireland, in 1778. She was a Catholic in a country largely controlled by Protestants. Her father, who died when Catherine was only five, was known for his generous service to the poor. Catherine's mother died fifteen years later. Following her mother's death, Catherine lived with various relatives, some of whom were non-Catholic and had little tolerance for Catherine's faith. In 1803, Catherine was invited to live with the Callaghans, a childless couple. Upon Mr. Callaghan's death in 1822, Catherine inherited a large fortune.

She now had the means to live a life of luxury, but she never forgot her father's example, or the suffering poor of Dublin. She used her fortune to build a home to provide religious, educational, and social services to women and children. The home came to be called the House of Mercy.

In time Catherine and her first coworkers took religious vows and became the first Sisters of Mercy. This religious order continues to serve the poor—especially women and children—throughout the world.

Catherine McAuley encountered God in the poor. Her openness to his will and to the action of the Holy Spirit changed the course of her life and enabled her to serve God and his people in exceptional ways.

"Find God in All Things"

Saint Ignatius of Loyola was a sixteenth-century Spanish priest who founded the Society of Jesus, or the Jesuits. He told those who sought his spiritual counsel to "find God in all things." He meant that every experience of our lives can make us aware of God's presence if we devote time and energy to reflecting on our experiences. God is not confined to certain places, like church buildings, or to certain times, like when we close our eyes to pray; rather, Saint Ignatius tells us, God infuses *all* places and *all* times.

There are no experiences—good or bad—that cannot teach us and lead us into closer communion with God. For example, from the pain of suffering, we can learn compassion for others. From the struggle of making a difficult decision, we can learn to trust in God's guidance. From the joy of success, we can learn gratitude for what God makes possible. Through all the events of our lives, God works on us like a potter works on clay, shaping and molding us into the people we were created to be. Through the prophet Jeremiah, God tell us, "Indeed, like clay in the hand of the potter, so are you in my hand" (Jeremiah 18:6).

> **What are the details in your life that show God's continual presence?**

Article 21: Discovering God in the Faith of Others

We are never alone as we seek to live in fidelity to the truth that the Divine Father has revealed through his Son, Jesus. Thanks to the Holy Spirit, the faith of other believers is a powerful witness and support for us. We can look to both those who have gone before us and those with whom we share our lives today.

domestic church
A name for the first and most fundamental community of faith: the family.

The Example of the Early Church

When Jesus sent out his followers to preach and heal in his name, he never asked them to fulfill this mission alone. Instead Jesus encouraged his disciples to work together to help fulfill his mission. Jesus wanted his followers to live and work as a dedicated community, together demonstrating Christian brotherhood and service to all people. After Jesus' death and Resurrection, his disciples continued to follow his example and his instruction by creating communities of faith. The Acts of the Apostles describes how the early Christians drew strength from their life in community:

> They devoted themselves to the teaching of the apostles and to the communal life, to the breaking of the bread and to the prayers. . . . Every day they devoted themselves to meeting together in the temple area and to breaking bread in their homes. They ate their meals with exultation and sincerity of heart, praising God and enjoying favor with all the people. (2:42,46–47)

Although these early Christians were not walking an easy road—they would be ridiculed, misunderstood, and persecuted—their shared life of faith enabled them to persevere in holiness.

The Importance of Family

Among those people who sustain our lives of faith by revealing God to us, our family is of foundational importance. The *Catechism of the Catholic Church* (*CCC*) refers to the family as the **domestic church**, because the family is the foundation of the Christian life and where we first learn about our faith. As we mature, our family members can encourage our growth in faith and stand by us during times of doubt and confusion. Family is truly one of God's wondrous gifts to us.

Communal Prayer

Remember, we are never alone in our search for God. What if family or friends let us down? We still have the whole Communion of Saints—that is, the whole community of the faithful in Heaven and on earth—with whom to share both our joys and our struggles. Indeed Catholicism is fundamentally communal, not individualistic. This is especially clear in our lives of prayer. Though private prayer is meaningful and important, communal prayer—especially Eucharistic liturgy—is central to our Catholic identity. Celebrating the Eucharist tells us that we are together the Body of Christ. We are united by our Baptism, strengthened by the presence of Jesus in his precious Body and Blood, and sent out to be the life and light for the world.

Prayer is not always a silent and solemn act. Retreats, diocesan and national youth gatherings, and World Youth Days are opportunities for young people to gather and share in joyful praise and song.

© Bill Wittman / www.wpwittman.com

Pray It!

The Communion of Saints in the Eucharist

When we gather for Mass, we join our prayers with those of others gathered and with the Communion of Saints. The next time you attend Mass, pay special attention to the Eucharistic Prayer. You will notice that we pray for a wide range of people. We pray for the entire Church, the Pope and our local bishop, and all of the bishops and clergy, as well as all of those who have died.

When you are at Mass, really focus on praying for all the groups mentioned in the Eucharistic Prayer. Also call to mind family and friends whom you want to include privately in these general prayers. In this way, you join your prayer with the prayer of the whole Church.

The passage below is an excerpt from a Eucharistic Prayer that you can meditate on when you want the help and fellowship of the community of saints.

To us, also, your servants, who, though sinners, hope in your abundant mercies, graciously grant some share and fellowship with your holy Apostles and Martyrs: with John the Baptist, Stephen, Matthias, Barnabas, (Ignatius, Alexander, Marcellinus, Peter, Felicity, Perpetua, Agatha, Lucy, Agnes, Cecilia, Anastasia) and all your Saints: admit us, we beseech you, into their company, not weighing our merits, but granting us your pardon, through Christ our Lord. (*Roman Missal*)

canonized
A deceased
Catholic's having
been publicly
and officially
proclaimed a saint.

What a tremendous gift to be part of this worldwide community of believers.

Whom do you look to as a real-life example of a faith-filled life?

Article 22: The Saints: Our Models of Holiness

Although God is active in the life of every person, we can especially perceive him at work in the lives of the saints, holy men and women of every time and place. Christ's Church is a Communion of Saints, a gathering of holy people, some of whom are living on earth, and some of whom are living with God in Heaven. Those people whom the Church has officially **canonized** as saints have led lives of exemplary holiness. However, the saints were at one time just people who lived in the midst of difficulties, uncertainty, and suffering. Despite these circumstances they made extraordinary choices to put their faith into action, and their lives can teach us to do the same.

Many of the saints were misunderstood during their own lifetimes, their holiness being recognized only much later. For example, the family of Saint Thomas Aquinas didn't approve of his decision to become a priest. They even kidnapped him to try to get him to change his mind! The father of Saint Francis of Assisi was similarly perplexed when his son announced his decision to renounce the family's business in favor of a simple life of preaching and begging. Saint Katharine Drexel, a nineteenth-century heiress from Philadelphia, used her vast inheritance to found schools for African Americans and Native Americans. Her friends and family members thought she was wasting her money—and her time. In these and other trying situations, the saints persevered in holiness by staying faithful to God and by taking great risks for the sake of the Gospel.

The Saints: Our Intercessors and Companions

Although the saints are not physically present on earth—they live with God in Heaven—we often seek their help and ask for their prayers. Catholics, however, do not worship the saints. Only God is worthy of worship and adoration, and only he can answer our prayers. When we pray to the saints, we simply ask them to pray with us and for us. Many saints are traditionally considered to be the patrons of specific issues or causes. Have you ever prayed that Saint Anthony of Padua would help you to find something you lost? Then you know he is the patron of lost items. You may also know that Saint Jude is the patron of desperate situations, and Saint Valentine is the patron of lovers. But did you also know that Saint Martha is the patron of waiters and waitresses? that Saint Clare is the patron of television? There is even a patron saint of the Internet—Saint Isidore of Seville.

Praying to the saints and knowing their stories is like having an extended family—people we can turn to for advice, look to for inspiration, and ask to accompany us as we face new challenges each day. Saint Gregory of Nyssa once said that the true goal of the Christian life is to become God's friend. The saints have truly been friends of God throughout the centuries, and by their witness they invite us also to befriend God.

What individual saints do you look to for guidance?

Saint Francis is the patron saint of animals, families, and the environment. Saint Clare is the patron saint of healthy eyes, television, and telephones. Research the patron saints for activities you like to do or causes that are important to you.

© Alinari / Art Resource, NY

Article 23: Discovering God in the Natural World

Have you ever found peace while sitting on the beach at sunset, awe while hiking through a lush forest, or amazement while flying over snow-capped mountains? Then you have come to know God in the natural world. Even small things—a plant growing on a window ledge, a bird chirping a morning song, a dog wagging its tail—can reveal the beauty and wonder of nature and can move us to prayer and praise.

God, Creator of the Natural World

Think about it: How could something as immense as the universe, as astounding as a volcano, or as complex as a human being come from anything but a divine source? Through nature we can know that God is the origin and Creator of all that is. Listening to the voice of creation reveals to us that God is the cause of everything, the beginning and the end of all that we know.

God did not *have* to create the world; rather, in great wisdom and love, he freely chose to bring the universe into being. Psalm 104 states:

> How varied are your works, LORD!
> In wisdom you have made them all;
> the earth is full of your creatures.
> (Verse 24)

Moreover, all creatures of the earth, because of their divine origin, reflect God's glory. Elephants and dolphins, roses and redwood trees, mushrooms and moss, planets and stars and human beings all share together in the beauty, truth, and goodness of God's creation.

The Role of Science

Does belief in the divine origin of the universe mean that Catholics are against scientific inquiry? Of course not! The *Catechism* states that there can be no real discrepancy between faith and reason; both are gifts to us from God (see 159). Addressing the topic of science in particular, the *Catechism* quotes the Vatican II document *Pastoral*

*Constitution on the Church in the Modern World (Gaud-
ium et Spes,* 1965): "The humble and persevering inves-
tigator of the secrets of nature is being led, as it were, by
the hand of God . . . for it is God, the conserver of all

Did You Know?

Saint Thomas Aquinas and the Five Proofs

© Alinari Archives / CORBIS

Saint Thomas Aquinas (1225–1274) was an Italian Dominican priest. He is considered to be one of the greatest Catholic theologians who ever lived. His powerful intellect allowed him to gain respect as the author of many works and as a clear thinker and respected university lecturer.

Aquinas was thought to be innovative in his time. He used the writings of the pagan Greek thinker Aristotle in his own writings on theology. Aquinas's *Summa Theologiae*, a synthesis of major theological topics of his day, is still considered a classic of Western thought. In the *Summa Theologiae*, Aquinas laid out five logical arguments for the existence of God. These reasoned arguments were a major innovation in the fields of philosophy and theology. They are sometimes referred to as "proofs" but they shouldn't be confused with the modern notion of scientific proof.

- **The First Mover** Because the universe is constantly in motion and everything we know is always changing, there must be a First Mover, someone who has set everything in motion and guides the course of the universe.
- **Causality** When we look at the cycle of life around us, we see that everything is caused by something else, something outside of itself, since nothing can create itself. This First Efficient Cause or Ultimate Cause is God.
- **Contingency** Similar to causality, contingency is based on the fact that things come into existence because of something else. God is the only one who creates but is not created. He is the Necessary Being that gives life to all beings.
- **Perfection** It is easy to see that our world is imperfect. However, how do we *know* imperfection? The answer is that we know imperfection because we have a sense of what perfection is—God.
- **Intelligent Being** We see that our world is one of order and that even things without intelligence are guided and achieve their ends. One then must assume that a great designer or architect is directing everything in the universe. This intelligent designer is God.

theology
Literally, "the study of God"; the academic discipline and effort to understand, interpret, and order our experience of God and Christian faith.

things, who made them what they are[1]" (CCC, 159). In other words, the fact *that* God brought the universe into being is a key religious truth, but science can inform us as to *how* this may have been accomplished. In helping us to explore the many wonders of the universe, science can also reveal God's glory to us in new and amazing ways. It can move us to awe and reverence at the work of our Creator.

What in the natural world most dramatically demonstrates to you the beauty and wonder of God?

Article 24: Discovering God through the Human Intellect

What image do you associate with God? Perhaps you picture a voice booming from out of a cloud, the heavens parting, or a choir of angels and other heavenly beings. Though Sacred Scripture does recount stories of people who experienced God's Revelation of himself in such ways, we don't need visions to know something about God. We need look no further than our human reason

Primary Sources

Saint Thomas Aquinas: Is God in All Things?

The following excerpt from the *Summa Theologiae* demonstrates the power of Aquinas's philosophical argument by offering an answer to the question, Is God in all things?

I answer that, God is in all things; not, indeed, as part of their essence, nor as an accident, but as an agent is present to that upon which it works. . . . Now since God is very being by His own essence, created being must be His proper effect; as to ignite is the proper effect of fire. Now God causes this effect in things not only when they first begin to be, but as long as they are preserved in being; as light is caused in the air by the sun as long as the air remains illuminated. Therefore as long as a thing has being, God must be present to it, according to its mode of being. . . . Hence it must be that God is in all things, and innermostly. (Part 1, question 8, article 1) and intellect, for "the one true God, our Creator and Lord, can be known with certainty from his works, by the natural light of human reason[2]" (CCC, 47).

The Gift of Human Intellect

The Church has a long tradition of urging us to use our minds to grow in understanding our faith. In fact, Saint Anselm of Canterbury's classic definition of **theology** is "faith seeking understanding." Saint Anselm understood that God gave us the gift of our human intellect to understand and know him more fully. We can use this gift to study Sacred Scripture, read about the lives of the saints, learn Church teaching, and engage in intellectual inquiry related to our faith. Taking responsibility to do such things is part of what it means to be a mature Catholic and enables us to know and love God more deeply.

© Falconia / shutterstock.com

Our intellect and our ability to reason are two of the greatest gifts God has given us.

How Can We Speak about God?

Although we can know something of God through our human reason and intellect, the language we use to express that knowledge can never fully capture the Divine Mystery. In fact, the words we choose to describe the wonder of the Creator always fall short of his true mystery. This is why there is such a great diversity of representations of God in Sacred Scripture. No single image could ever fully express who he is. These images are drawn from the created world, "for from the greatness and the beauty of created things / their original author, by analogy, is seen" (Wisdom 13:5). Thus Scripture depicts God through images of nature, such as light, rock, fire, and water. Scripture also refers to God with images of humanity, such as potter, shepherd, king, mother, and husband. Each of these ways of speaking of God gives us meaningful insight into his goodness and

glory. No description of God is ever complete and no representation of him through symbols from the created world is intended to be taken literally. God is not literally a rock, a shepherd, a king, or anything but God. He is "the inexpressible, the incomprehensible, the invisible, the ungraspable[3]" (CCC, 42).

When have you used reason and your intellect to better understand God's Revelation?

Live It!
Using Your Mind to Study Religion

Our minds are a gift from God, who wants us to use them well. He especially wants us to use our minds to learn about him and his relationship with humanity. When we use our intellect to learn about our faith, we can grow closer to God.

Here are some pointers that can help you to grow closer to God through the study of your faith:

- Take your theology classes seriously.
- Seek to grasp what is presented in class and apply it to your life.
- Pray about subject matter that you find particularly powerful or that confuses you.
- Strive to make the faith really your own.

For Review

1. What did Saint Ignatius of Loyola mean when he said to seek to "find God in all things"?

2. Why is communal prayer important?

3. Why is there no real disagreement between faith and science?

4. What can we learn from the lives of the saints? How can the saints help us?

5. How can we use the gift of human intellect God gave us to know him better?

6. Why does Sacred Scripture use such a wide variety of images to represent God?

Jesus: The Definitive Revelation of God

Jesus Christ, the Divine Son of God, took on flesh and became man. This is the great mystery known as the Incarnation, when Jesus as God's Word Made Flesh became truly man while remaining truly God. In this unit, we shall see how Jesus Christ the Son of God was conceived by the Virgin Mary through the power of the Holy Spirit. He took on human flesh and became a man, like us in all ways except sin, and he did this in order to offer us salvation. The Son of God became one of us to share in our humanity and by doing so, gave us the chance to unite with him in his divinity. Through the Incarnation, God's ancient and covenant relationship with humanity was fully realized and is still alive today.

In studying the Incarnation, we see that the two natures of Jesus—divine and human—are always fully present at the same time, for he is true God and true man. When we look at Jesus' actual life as a man amidst the political and cultural landscape of Palestine in the first century, we realize that he lived a deeply religious life. Jesus experienced all the beauty and anguish of human existence; he enjoyed friendships, but he also experienced suffering. After exploring the earthly life of Jesus, we will move on to view his divine nature as expressed in the doctrine of the Incarnation and by his role as Lord and Redeemer.

The enduring understandings and essential questions represent core concepts and questions that are explored throughout this unit. By studying the content of each chapter, you will gain a more complete understanding of the following:

Enduring Understandings

1. The doctrine of the Incarnation is one of the distinctive marks of Christian faith.

2. Christ continues to be present in the world through his Body, the Church.

3. By our Baptism we are called to share in Jesus' mission by living out our Christian vocation.

Essential Questions

1. What does the doctrine of the Incarnation say about Christianity?

2. Why do we say that the Church is Christ's Body in the world?

3. How does our Christian vocation relate to the mission of Jesus Christ?

Chapter

6

The Incarnation

Introduction

The doctrine that the Son of God assumed a human nature to become Jesus of Nazareth is one of the distinctive marks of Christian faith. Our God took on human flesh, being conceived in Mary's womb, in order to save us from sin and death. The Incarnation truly united humanity with God, for in sharing our humanity, he allowed us to share in his divinity.

When we speak of the Incarnation, which will be the focus of this chapter, we often speak of Jesus as the Word Made Flesh (see John 1:14). This image helps us to remember that the Incarnation is the fulfillment of a long relationship God had initiated with humanity and, in particular, with the people of Israel, many centuries earlier. God made a covenant with Abraham and all his descendants. Finally, in the fullness of time, he sent his only Son to earth. God's covenant relationship with the Jews, the first people to receive, accept, and live by his Word, is still valid even to the present day. However, because of the Incarnation, God's Word is fully, definitively, and uniquely present as Jesus Christ.

Article 25: What Is the Incarnation?

The Incarnation means that Jesus Christ, the Son of God, became human to accomplish our salvation. That the Son of God actually came in the flesh to save us from sin and death is an important mark of our Christian faith. Let's spend some time exploring this great and miraculous mystery.

By the Power of the Holy Spirit

Luke's Gospel tells us how the Incarnation occurred through the power of the Holy Spirit. The angel Gabriel announced to Mary that she would give birth to a son who would be called Jesus—a name which means "God saves." Mary responded with a question: "How can this be, since I have no relations with a man?" (1:34). Gabriel

Did You Know?

The Sacred Heart of Jesus

© Mark Strozier / iStockphoto.com

Have you ever thought deeply about the reality of the Incarnation? As a real human being, Jesus ate, drank, laughed, and cried. He had a human body just like ours, with hands, feet, and a heart. Did you know that devotion to the Sacred Heart of Jesus powerfully reminds us of the truth of the Incarnation—that the Son of God walked among us as an actual flesh-and-blood man?

Prayer to the Sacred Heart of Jesus began in the Middle Ages, but it was Saint Margaret Mary Alacoque, a Sister of the Visitation living in seventeenth-century France, who made this devotion popular. Jesus appeared to **Saint Margaret Mary** in visions. He told her that she had been chosen to spread devotion to his Sacred Heart, especially through celebration of the Eucharist on the first Friday of each month. Like many saints and visionaries, Alacoque's ideas were not accepted during her lifetime. In 1856, nearly two hundred years after Saint Margaret Mary's death, Pope Pius IX placed the Solemnity of the Sacred Heart on the Church's liturgical calendar. The Solemnity continues to be celebrated each year on the third Friday after Pentecost. This year let this feast day remind you of the awesome gift of God's saving presence among us as one who, though he was divine, loved all with a human heart.

told Mary: "The holy Spirit will come upon you, and the power of the Most High will overshadow you. Therefore the child to be born will be called holy, the Son of God" (1:35). This passage helps us to understand that Jesus was conceived by the Holy Spirit in order to begin his saving work among us. The action of the Holy Spirit in Mary gave humanity the great gift of "Emmanuel," God with us (see Matthew 1:23).

From All Eternity

Jesus' conception in Mary's womb began the *earthly* existence of the Son of God. His *heavenly* existence is eternal—that is, without a beginning or an end. The opening words of John's Gospel tell us:

> In the beginning was the Word,
> and the Word was with God,
> and the Word was God.
> He was in the beginning with God.
> (1:1–2)

The angel Gabriel's announcement to Mary that she would give birth to Jesus is known as the Annunciation. The Feast of the Annunciation, celebrated each year on March 25, honors Mary's courageous "yes" to God.

At a certain point in history, more than two thousand years ago, the Word of God "became flesh / and made his dwelling among us" (John 1:14). When the Son of God became flesh, he did not stop being God. He had always been God, but now he was a man as well. To put it another way, he had always been the Son of God, but now he was also the Son of Mary. Therefore the Incarnation is the mystery of the union of the human and the divine in one Divine Person—Jesus Christ.

Over the years various heresies, or incorrect beliefs, have denied the fullness of the Incarnation. For example, some people mistakenly think Jesus started out as a human and then somehow became God over the course of his life. Others err in thinking that Jesus was not God at all but was just a really special person God chose, at some point in his life, for a special mission. However, Jesus Christ, the Eternal

© Bill Wittman / www.wpwittman.com

Son of God and the Second Divine Person of the Trinity, was always God—before, during, and after his life on earth. By his very nature, Jesus was God eternally. He was the Son of God before his conception in the womb of the Virgin Mary, and remained so after his death, Resurrection, and Ascension.

> **What do you think makes the Incarnation a mystery?**

Article 26: Mary's Role in the Incarnation

In order for the Incarnation to occur, the Eternal Word of God needed a human mother. This woman, prepared from all eternity for this role, was Mary of Nazareth, the Blessed Mother. Her willingness to say yes to God's gracious plan made our salvation possible. In her very body, the Holy Spirit completed all the preparations for Christ's coming.

Because she is the Mother of Jesus Christ, the Eternal Son of God Made Man who is God himself, Mary is also truly the Mother of God, which in Greek is translated as *Theotokos*. This is a title of honor the Church has bestowed on Mary. Devotion to Mary centers on her unique role in salvation history and on three important doctrines about her.

Mary's Immaculate Conception

The Solemnity of the Immaculate Conception of Mary is celebrated on December 8, a **holy day of obligation**. Many people make the mistake of thinking that we celebrate Jesus' conception on this day. In fact, the Immaculate Conception celebrates the day on which *Mary* was conceived in the womb of her mother, Saint Ann. Because Mary was to fulfill the

holy day of obligation
Feast day in the Liturgical Year on which, in addition to Sundays, Catholics are obliged to participate in the Eucharist.

One of the many titles Mary has that reflects her special place in the life of Jesus and the Church is Queen of Heaven. What other titles for Mary are you familiar with?

© Bill Wittman / www.wpwittman.com

Original Sin
The sin by which the first humans disobeyed God and thereby lost their original holiness and became subject to death. Original Sin is transmitted to every person born into the world, except Mary and Jesus.

absolutely unique role of carrying the Eternal Son of God into the world, God allowed her to be conceived without **Original Sin**. This is why her conception is described as immaculate. She was redeemed from the first moment of her life and remained free from all **personal sin** throughout her life.

Mary's Perpetual Virginity

Jesus was conceived in Mary's womb through the power of the Holy Spirit. Luke's Gospel states this clearly: "The holy Spirit will come upon you, and the power of the Most High will overshadow you" (1:35). Therefore Mary became pregnant with Jesus while remaining a virgin. Mary remained a virgin throughout her life, as a sign of her total dedication to serving God as "the handmaid of the Lord" (Luke 1:38).

Although Jesus was Mary's only biological child, Mary is a spiritual mother to all of us. The Second Vatican Council's *Dogmatic Constitution on the Church (Lumen Gentium,* 1964) reminds us of this fact and what

Live It!
Holy Days of Obligation and the Liturgical Calendar

In the course of the Liturgical Year, the whole mystery of Christ unfolds, from his Incarnation and Nativity through his Ascension into Heaven, to Pentecost and our expectation of his return in glory. The Church's cycle of prayers and Scripture readings recalls the important events from Christ's life and his work of salvation. We recall these events on Sundays and on the Church's holy days of obligation. Along with all the Sundays of the year, there are six holy days of obligation. On these days we are obliged to participate in the Eucharist. Make a commitment to attend Mass on these holy days:

- Christmas (December 25)
- Solemnity of the Blessed Virgin Mary, the Mother of God (January 1)
- Ascension of the Lord (forty days after Easter)
- Assumption of the Blessed Virgin Mary (August 15)
- All Saints' Day (November 1)
- Immaculate Conception of the Blessed Virgin Mary (December 8)

it means. It states that "the Catholic Church, taught by the Holy Spirit, honors her [Mary] with filial affection and piety as a most beloved mother" (53). As any attentive mother, Mary can pray with us and for us. She acts as our advocate, comforter, companion, and friend.

Several passages in the New Testament refer to Jesus' brothers and sisters (see, for example, Mark 3:32 and Galatians 1:19). Given that Mary remained a virgin her whole life, what are we to make of these passages? There are several possible explanations. The *Catechism of the Catholic Church* (*CCC*) states that "the Church has always understood these passages as not referring to other children of the Virgin Mary" (500). The individuals referred to in Scripture are "close relations of Jesus, according to an Old Testament expression[1]" (500). Eastern Catholics and Orthodox Christians have traditionally believed that Joseph was a widower when he married Mary and that the people referred to as Jesus' siblings are in fact Joseph's children from his former marriage. Both explanations help us to understand these Scripture passages in light of the Church's firm and constant teaching on Mary's perpetual virginity.

Mary's Assumption

Mary had the great honor and blessing of carrying the physical presence of the Eternal Son of God into the world in her own body. Therefore, when she died, God

personal sin
Any deliberate offense, in thought, word, or deed, against the will of God.

Pray It!

Ten Simple Words

In the Gospel of Luke, after the angel Gabriel shares with Mary that she will give birth to Jesus, Mary responds by saying: "Behold, I am the handmaid of the Lord. May it be done to me according to your word" (1:38). This response shows Mary's willingness to do what God is asking of her.

The next time you pray, consider simply praying, "May it be done to me according to your word." This simple prayer can change your life. If you mean what you pray, these ten simple words will open you up to all that God desires for you.

did not allow her body to decay. God brought her whole being—body and soul—into Heaven. Roman Catholics celebrate this event as the Solemnity of the Assumption. This is another holy day of obligation. Eastern Catholics and Orthodox Christians call it Mary's Dormition (or "falling asleep"). Both groups celebrate this special end to Mary's earthly life on August 15.

Mary, Seat of Wisdom

Many of the Church's titles for Mary are rooted in what the Church believes about Christ (see CCC, 487). For example, because Jesus is the Word Made Flesh, we have the beautiful image of Mary as the Seat of Wisdom.

In the Old Testament, wisdom is personified as a woman who invites all people to share in her life and to dine at her table. For example, in the Wisdom of Ben Sira (sometimes called Ecclesiasticus or Sirach), we read:

> Wisdom sings her own praises,
> > among her own people she proclaims her glory.
> In the assembly of the Most High she opens her mouth,
> > in the presence of his host she tells of her glory:
>
> . . . .
>
> Come to me, all who desire me,
> > and be filled with my fruits.
> You will remember me as sweeter than honey,
> > better to have than the honeycomb.
> > > > (24:1–2,19–20)

There are countless images of Mary, both classical and contemporary. What do you think the artist of this stained-glass piece was trying to communicate about Mary?

Because the Old Testament figure of Wisdom is female, the Catholic Church "has often read the most beautiful texts on wisdom in relation to Mary[2]" (CCC, 721). This, along with our belief that God's Word, made flesh in Mary's womb, is full of wisdom for us, has given Mary the title Seat of Wisdom.

What does Mary's dedication to serving God inspire you to do?

© Bill Wittman / www.wpwittman.com

Article 27: Jesus: The Word Made Flesh

The Gospel of John tells us:

> And the Word became flesh
> and made his dwelling among us,
> and we saw his glory,
> the glory as of the Father's only Son,
> full of grace and truth.
>
> (1:14)

This "Word" (in Greek, *Logos*) is the Eternal Son of God. The Word is with God the Father in Heaven for all eternity, along with the Holy Spirit. At a particular point in history, the Word became incarnate (flesh) in Mary's womb.

God Prepared Humanity for the Incarnation

The Old Testament tells the history of God's self-revelation to humanity. It shows how God guided, corrected, challenged, and comforted us after sin had damaged our original friendship with him. God spoke to Abraham, telling him to leave his home and journey with his wife, Sarah, to a new land as the ancestors of the Chosen People (see Genesis 12:1). God gave the ancient Israelites the Law at Mount Sinai. He made clear his desires and expectations (see Exodus, chapter 20).

God sent the prophets, placing in their mouths and on their hearts the very word he wished them to speak.

The prophets called the Israelites back to fidelity to the Covenant (see, for example, Jeremiah 1:4). Through these many centuries, God drew closer and closer to his people, until, in the fullness of time, "God sent his Son, born of a woman, born under the law, to ransom those under the law, so that we might receive adoption" (Galatians 4:4–5). Thus, throughout the history of the ancient Israelites, God prepared humanity for the ultimate self-revelation, the Incarnation of the Word—the coming of his Son—and for the development of the Church.

Jesus Perfects the Law

In the Gospel of Matthew, Jesus said to his disciples: "Do not think that I have come to abolish the law or the prophets. I have come not to abolish but to fulfill. Amen, I say to you, until heaven and earth pass away, not the smallest letter or the smallest part of a letter will pass from the law, until all things have taken place" (5:17–18). This passage helps us to understand that Jesus fulfilled, and did not replace, God's Law, given to the ancient

Primary Sources

Saint Hippolytus of Rome on the Incarnation: The Word Made Flesh Deifies Us

The following passage on how the Incarnation deifies us—that is, makes us like God—is taken from a treatise by the third-century Church Father Saint Hippolytus of Rome:

We know that the Word assumed a body from a virgin and, through a new creation, put on our old nature. We know that he was a man, formed from the same substance as we are. If he were not of the same nature as ourselves, his command to imitate him as a master would be a futile one. If he was of a different substance, why does he command me, naturally weak as I am, to do as he did? How can he be good and just?

When you have learned to know the true God, you will have a body immortal and incorruptible, like your soul; you will gain the kingdom of heaven, you who lived on earth and knew the king of heaven; freed from passion, suffering and disease, you will be a companion of God and a co-heir with Christ, for you have become a god.

Israelites. *Fulfilled* means that Jesus perfected the Law, revealed its ultimate meaning, and redeemed any sins people had committed against it. We know that Jesus did not replace the Law, because God's covenant with the Israelites, today known as Jews, is still active and valid. God's fidelity to the people he has chosen endures forever.

These are just some examples of how the Old Testament prepares us for the coming of Christ, whose saving work and mission are clearly revealed in the New Testament. Both Testaments reveal that the Divine Word of God is fully present in a unique, definitive way in the Person of Jesus Christ.

What images come to mind when you hear the phrase "the Word Made Flesh"?

Article 28: The Union of God with Humanity

The Incarnation brought humanity and God closer together than we would ever otherwise be able to be. Because of the Incarnation, we are able to see God's human face, to renew our relationship with God, and even to share in his divine nature.

Jesus, the Revealer and Mediator

The Incarnation was an absolutely singular, unique event. Never before (and never since!) had God assumed human nature. Therefore Jesus, as God Made Flesh, fulfills two unique roles.

First, Jesus reveals God the Father to us. In John's Gospel, Jesus states: "Whoever has seen me has seen the Father" (14:9). Because he is the Divine Son of the Father, Jesus is truly the human face of God among us. Are there times when you wonder what God would do, say, or think? You simply need to look to the actions, words, and thoughts of Jesus, as recorded in the New Testament and as interpreted by the Church through the centuries.

Second, Jesus is the one and only mediator between humanity and God. He is like a bridge that connects earth with Heaven, making God accessible to us even though we had lost God's friendship through sin. The Incarnation and all the subsequent events of Jesus' life, especially his death and Resurrection, give us a new and certain path to God and to salvation.

Sharing in the Divine Life

Because Jesus shared in our lives, we are able to share in God's life. Saint Paul's Letter to the Colossians states, "For in [Jesus] dwells the whole fullness of the deity bodily, and you share in this fullness in him, who is the head of every principality and power" (2:9–10). The Second Letter of Peter makes the same point, saying, "he has

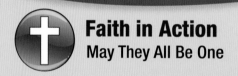

Faith in Action
May They All Be One

In 1943, a group of young women, led by Chiara Lubich 1920–2008), together discovered the heart of the Gospel and began to live it: "God is love" (1 John 4:8). Yet, the God of love was no abstract notion. In Jesus, God has taken on our humanity. Accepting the God of love meant working for the unity of the entire human race. The unity of all became the life's work of this group, who called themselves *Focolare.* This word, in Italian, means "hearth" or "family fireside," the gathering place for all in the household.

"That they may all be one" (John 17:21) is the mission of the Focolare movement. As Chiara Lubich said, "We were born for these words, for unity, to give a contribution to its realization in the world."

The Focolare movement emphasizes living in unity with others of all religious convictions. The specific ways members of the Focolare support one another and live out their mission of unity differ according to various situations. In some places, the Focolare, both men and women, have established "little towns" in which they live and work together. The Focolare movement sponsors its own publishing company, New City Press, and also publishes an English-language magazine, *Living City*, which promotes the ideals of the Focolare movement: unity and communion. In 1997, in honor of her life's work, Chiara Lubich won the Templeton Prize for progress in religion and peace.

bestowed on us the precious and very great promises, so that through them you may come to share in the divine nature" (1:4).

Sharing in the divine life of God means we are drawn into communion with the Trinity. During our time on earth, we are profoundly united with God through our Baptism, through our sharing in the Eucharistic feast, and through our participation in the other Sacraments of the Church. We are invited to cooperate with God's plan for our lives and to participate actively in our salvation. During our life after death, we will experience the **Beatific Vision**, enjoying God's presence and glory forever.

Many of the early Church Fathers were truly awed by the gift God gave us in the Incarnation. In their writings, they pondered with amazement the idea of God's inviting us to share in the divine nature. The words of Saint Athanasius, a fourth-century saint and Church Father, are often quoted in this regard: "The Son of God became man so that we might become God[3]" (CCC, 460). A version of this idea has even found its way into our liturgy. The next time you are at Mass, listen closely to the prayers the priest offers as he prepares our gifts of bread and wine. Although these words are not audible, you may hear the priest pray: "By the mystery of this water and wine / may we come to share in the divinity of Christ / who humbled himself to share in our humanity" (*Roman Missal*).

Beatific Vision
Directly encountering and seeing God in the glory of Heaven.

collects
Prayers offered by the person leading an assembly in communal prayer.

The Christmas Liturgy: Celebrating the Incarnation

The prayers of the Christmas liturgy reflect core truths about the Incarnation in moving and poetic language. Consider these brief excerpts from the **collects** and other prayers of the liturgies of Christmas, quoted from the *Roman Missal*:

- "Grant, we pray, that we, who have known the mysteries of his light on earth, / may also delight in his gladness in heaven."
- "May [we] be found in the likeness of Christ, / in whom our nature is united to you."
- "May we serve you all the more eagerly / for knowing that in [the coming festivities] / you make manifest the beginnings of our redemption."
- "We pray, / that we may share in the divinity of Christ, / who humbled himself to share in our humanity."

These prayers of the liturgy deepen our understanding of the mystery of the Incarnation and our appreciation of this wondrous gift.

In what concrete ways are we closer to God because of the Incarnation?

For Review

1. What is the Incarnation?

2. What is the significance of the Incarnation for us?

3. What is Mary's role in the Incarnation?

4. Define *Theotokos* and explain the significance of this term.

5. Jesus comes to fulfill, not to replace, the Law God gave to the Israelites. What does this mean?

6. Describe two unique roles that Jesus, as God Made Flesh, fulfills.

7. What does it mean that we are able to share in the divine life of God?

The Two Natures of Jesus: Human and Divine

Introduction

Sacred Scripture and Sacred Tradition teach that Jesus Christ is true God and true man. Exploring various aspects of Jesus' life will equip us to understand more completely how God and humanity came together in an absolutely unique way in Jesus of Nazareth.

Key features of Jesus' life that are worthy of our study and investigation include his friendships, his emotions, and his religious life as a faithful Jew. These features remind us that Jesus lived a fully human life, complete with both joys and challenges. It is also crucial to grasp that Jesus lived, taught, and ministered in the political and cultural world of the Roman Empire. The meaning of many of his teachings becomes clearer when considered against this backdrop.

Learning as much as we can about Jesus' earthly life enriches our appreciation of the Incarnation. It sheds light on the many titles devout Christians, through the centuries, have applied to the One who lived and died on earth in order to save us.

sanctify
To make holy; sanctification is the process of responding to God's grace and becoming closer to God.

Article 29: Jesus: A Human Mind, a Human Heart

The doctrine of the Incarnation affirms that Jesus was truly man—human like us. As the Vatican II document *Pastoral Constitution on the Church in the Modern World (Gaudium et Spes,* 1965) states: "He worked with human hands, he thought with a human mind. He acted with a human will, and with a human heart he loved" (22). Jesus was truly like us in all things except sin.

The Joys and Trials of Human Nature

Jesus experienced both the blessings and the difficulties of normal life, just as we do. Jesus had close friends and family members with whom he developed genuine relationships. The Gospels tell us that he shared meals and celebrations with those people. He attended the wedding feast at Cana (see John 2:1–11). He had dinner at the home of Martha, Mary, and Lazarus (see Luke 10:38–42). Jesus also enjoyed visiting the homes of those who were misunderstood or cast out by society, such as Simon the Pharisee (see Luke 7:36–50) and Zacchaeus the tax collector (see 19:1–10). Like us, Jesus delighted in the spirit of friendship that is kindled when people gather around a table to share a meal.

Jesus also experienced frustration, hunger, pain, fatigue, suffering, and sorrow. He knew all the circumstances that can make life hard. For example, following his forty days of fasting in the desert, Jesus was weakened by hunger and thirst, making him a target of temptation by the Devil (see Matthew 4:1–11). Later in his life, Jesus cried when he heard that his dear friend Lazarus had died (see John 11:35). Most obviously, in his Passion and death, Jesus felt genuine pain—psychological fear and emotional anxiety in the garden at Gethsemane and physical torment on the cross.

Jesus' fully human life—with all its joys and struggles—**sanctifies** every part of our own lives. Because of the Incarnation, the blessings of our lives—like friends, family, and the beauty of nature—are signs of God's presence. In addition, our struggles, trials, and difficulties are ways for us to grow in trusting and loving God. Our faith in the Incarnation enables us to embrace every good day and every bad day of our earthly lives as unique opportunities to grow in holiness.

Jesus Experienced Faithful Friendship

In the Gospels, we meet Martha, Mary, and Lazarus, three siblings who lived together in Bethany, a town not far from Jerusalem. In the Gospels, Jesus often visited the home of these dear friends.

Martha showed great hospitality toward Jesus as a guest in her home (see Luke 10:38–42). She confessed her faith in him as "the Messiah, the Son of God, the one who is coming into the world" (John 11:27).

Mary faithfully absorbed Jesus' words, sitting at his feet in the traditional posture of a disciple listening to her teacher (see Luke 10:38–42). Later, as Jesus prepared for death, she anointed his feet with perfumed oil and dried them with her hair (see John 12:1–8).

Lazarus remained silent in these stories, but Jesus' raising him to life after he had been dead four days is one of the most dramatic miracles in all of the New Testament (see John 11:1–44).

In his relationship with Martha, Mary, and Lazarus, Jesus experienced one of life's greatest joys: friendship. Friends are one of God's great gifts to us. It seems that Jesus himself knew that "faithful friends are a sturdy shelter / . . . are beyond price / . . . are life-saving medicine" (Ben Sira 6:14–16).

© Holy Transfiguration Monastery, Brookline, MA. Used with permission.

© Brooklyn Museum / Corbis

Jesus' human heart felt joy, happiness, temptation, and pain. This picture depicts Jesus' being tempted by the Devil after forty days of fasting. How does it help you to know that Jesus also experienced temptation?

circumcision
The act, required by Jewish Law, of removing the foreskin of the penis. Since the time of Abraham, it has been a sign of God's covenant relationship with the Jewish people.

Jesus Never Stops Being God

In exploring the mystery of Jesus as man, we must not forget that at no point did Jesus cease to be God—not in his birth, life, emotions, friendships, or death. Even as he lived on earth, Jesus remained at all times the Son of God, the Second Divine Person of the Trinity. As the *Catechism of the Catholic Church* (*CCC*) states, "In his soul as in his body, Christ thus expresses humanly the divine ways of the Trinity[1]" (470).

> **Why do you think it is important to remember that Jesus was a man, and not just God?**

Article 30: Jesus: A Faithful Jew

We cannot comprehend Jesus' earthly life without focusing our attention on his religious identity as a faithful Jew. During his time on earth, Jesus lived the life of a Jew obedient to the Law of God.

Raised in a Jewish Home

The very earliest stories of Jesus' infancy make clear that Mary and Joseph brought him up in accordance with Jewish laws and traditions. For example, Jesus was circumcised on the eighth day after his birth (see Luke 2:21). From the time of Abraham and Sarah, **circumcision** has been the physical sign of God's covenant with the people of Israel. The circumcision of Jesus is an important sign of his connection to the descendants of Abraham, the people of the covenant. Furthermore, Jesus' circumcision demonstrates his obedience to the Law and his lifelong commitment to live as an observant, faithful Jew.

Later Mary and Joseph brought Jesus to Jerusalem to present him at the Temple (see Luke 2:22–38). In this action, they followed the law of Exodus: "Consecrate to me every firstborn; whatever opens the womb among the Israelites, whether of human being or beast, belongs to me" (13:2). Mary and Joseph also followed the law of Leviticus, which required the sacrifice of a lamb and a turtledove forty days after the birth of a baby boy (see 12:6–8). Interestingly, Mary and Joseph adhered to a variation on the law for poor families by bringing a second turtledove instead of a lamb.

Jesus' Practice of His Jewish Faith

In the Gospels, Jesus celebrated Jewish holidays, such as the Feast of the Passover (see John 2:13); the Feast of Tabernacles, or Sukkoth (see 7:2); and the Feast of the Dedication, or Hanukkah (see 10:22). Jesus often traveled to Jerusalem to mark these occasions.

Jesus also frequently demonstrated his knowledge of the Hebrew Scriptures (Old Testament). For example, look at what happened when he was tempted by the Devil (see Luke 4:1–13). He used direct quotations from the Book of Deuteronomy to refute every point the Devil made. Another time Jesus was talking with a group of **scribes** and **Pharisees**. He referred to the Hebrew stories of Jonah the prophet and Solomon the king (see Matthew 12:38–42). In order to teach the **Sadducees** about resurrection, he drew on the story of Moses and the burning bush (see Mark 12:18–27). Clearly Jesus was very familiar with the Scripture of his people, for he had immersed himself in these ancient texts in his prayer and study.

One Gospel story that allows us a vivid glimpse into Jesus' religious life as a Jew occurs in Luke 4:16–22. In this passage, Jesus engaged in the customary practices of the Jewish people by going to the synagogue on the Sabbath. (A synagogue is a Jewish place of worship; the Sabbath is the Jewish day of prayer and rest.) There Jesus read from the scroll of the prophet Isaiah—one of the books of the Hebrew Scriptures—and taught the people.

scribes
Jewish legal scholars or teachers of Jewish law. In the New Testament they are associated with the Pharisees and the High Priests as opponents of Jesus.

Pharisees
A Jewish sect at the time of Jesus known for its strict adherence to the Law.

Sadducees
A Jewish sect at the time of Jesus known for its strong commitment to the Temple in Jerusalem.

Together with many other Gospel stories, this passage offers us a compelling portrait of Jesus, a faithful Jew and religious teacher.

> **Why do you think it was important for Jesus to follow Jewish religious law and custom?**

Article 31: Jesus' Life in First-Century Palestine

Knowing a little bit about the historical world Jesus lived in can enrich our understanding of his life on earth. It can also help us to better understand many of his teachings.

Historical Background

Jesus lived in Palestine, which was the name the Greeks had given to the land of Israel. In fact, the influence of Greek culture was still felt in the time of Jesus, even

Did You Know?

Bethlehem University

© Madzia71 / iStockphoto.com

The "little town of Bethlehem" still exists today. It is a small city of about twenty-five thousand people. Although most of the people who live in Bethlehem are Muslims, Palestinian Christians make up about 2 percent of the population. Many Christian families can trace their Christianity back to apostolic times. The heart of Bethlehem is the Church of the Nativity, marking the place where Christ was born. You may also be surprised to learn that Bethlehem has a local university sponsored by the Lasallian Christian Brothers. Founded as a coeducational institution in 1973, its mission is to provide quality higher education to the people of Palestine—both Christian and Muslim.

Because of the unstable political situation between Israel and Palestine, the people of Bethlehem live in a difficult situation. Yet both the teachers and students at Bethlehem University know that they are preparing, in the best way possible, for a better future.

though the Roman occupation of Palestine had begun in 63 BC. By Jesus' lifetime (approximately 4 BC–AD 30), Rome controlled the whole Mediterranean basin, from modern-day France and Spain in the west, to the Black Sea and the Caspian Sea in the northeast, to northern Africa in the south. At the time of Jesus' birth, the Roman emperor allowed local kings to rule regions in his stead, provided the local kings remained loyal to Rome. At the time of Jesus' birth, this king in Palestine was Herod. He was known as Herod the Great because of his political skills, although his reputation for cruelty and violence was formidable. You might remember the story known as "Massacre of the Innocents," in which Herod killed all the baby boys in the region because he had heard about the birth of a new king of the Jews: Jesus (see Matthew 2:16–18).

After Herod's death in 4 BC, his three sons were each given a section of Palestine to rule. One of the sons, Herod Antipas (sometimes just called Antipas to avoid confusing him with his father), ruled Galilee, the region where Jesus' hometown of Nazareth is located. Philip ruled the northeastern part of Palestine. Archelaeus ruled Judea, Samaria, and Idumea, regions of Palestine in which many events in Jesus' life occurred. However, Archelaeus was such an unskilled ruler that the Romans eventually replaced him with one of their own officials, called a procurator. You probably know the name of the procurator of this region at the time of Jesus' death: Pontius Pilate.

The Realities of the Roman Occupation

Jesus and his companions lived under the rule of a foreign power. The presence of Roman authority was a constant reality, a backdrop to their every activity. They used Roman money and encountered Roman soldiers on the streets. They paid taxes to the emperor as well as local tolls charged on traded goods and for the use of ports, markets, and roads. This money funded useful government building projects but also served to widen the gap

pluralistic
Characterized by the presence of many different ethnic, religious, or cultural groups.

between the rich and the poor. Although the Romans were officially tolerant of the many different people they ruled, they also did not hesitate to put down rebellions, often with violence and cruelty. They used the threat of torture and violence to discourage people from challenging Roman power. One of these threats was crucifixion. Crosses with dead and decaying bodies on them lined the road into Jerusalem. The sight was a clear message from the authorities, meant to deter any potential opposition.

Roman Religion

Official Roman religion, which Roman citizens were expected to practice, was based on worship of the emperor as a god. However, by the time of Jesus, many other religious traditions had found their way into Roman culture. These included the Greek gods and goddesses of Mount Olympus and the Egyptian cult of Isis. Even in this **pluralistic** context, Jews existed within the empire as a religious minority.

Live It!
Christ in Society

Jesus encountered opposition to his teachings. Within the Jewish community, many did not recognize him as the promised Messiah and did not see that his teachings fulfilled the Law. Jesus also came in conflict with Roman leadership and culture.

Similarly, as a follower of Jesus in a world that sometimes values individual freedom over faithfulness to God's will, you may face criticism or opposition because of your faith. You should not lose heart. We have a positive and joyful message to pass on. Pray, set a good example, and talk with your friends. Get involved in action groups, the media, or leadership positions. Rely on the Gifts of the Holy Spirit to overcome the resistance you will face, and bring Christ more into your school, parish, and neighborhood.

How Understanding Jesus' Social Context Helps Us

We have taken a brief look at the historical, cultural, and political background of Jesus' time. This kind of study can help us to grasp the importance of key aspects of his life and teachings. For example, we see how cruel Herod the Great really was. We can then marvel that Jesus, even as a baby, barely escaped death at the hands of an oppressive ruler. We find out that tax collectors were hated as agents of the Roman occupying forces. We can then appreciate the shock of Jesus' asking tax collectors, like Matthew (see Matthew 9:9) and Zacchaeus (see Luke 19:1–9), to share in his ministry. We learn how the Romans valued violence and militarism and practiced political and economic oppression. We can then grasp the extent to which Jesus challenged Roman society. For example, in the **Beatitudes**, he proclaimed as blessed the peacemakers, the meek, and the persecuted (see Matthew 5:5,9–10). Jesus also focused his ministry on people on the edges of society. He reached out to women, those who were sick, and those who were poor. Jesus did not compromise in his faithfulness to his mission to begin the Reign of God. This brought him into constant conflict with both political and religious leaders.

> **Why is it important to know the political and social history of the region in which Jesus was born?**

Beatitudes

The teachings of Jesus that begin the Sermon on the Mount and that summarize the New Law of Christ. The Beatitudes describe the actions and attitudes by which one can discover genuine happiness. They teach us the final end to which God calls us: full communion with him in the Kingdom of Heaven.

Article 32: Jesus: Union of the Human and the Divine

At the time appointed by God the Father, the only Son of God, the Eternal Word—that is, the Word and substantial Image of the Father—became incarnate. Without losing his divine nature, he assumed a human nature. In other words, the Son of God, the Second Person of the Trinity, did not stop being God in order to become the man Jesus of Nazareth. Christ was at all times *one* Divine Person with *two* natures. Christians call this the

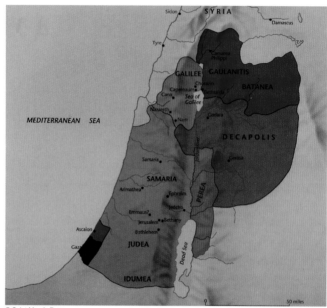

© Saint Mary's Press

This map shows the division of Palestine between the sons of Herod after his death in 4 BC. Archelaeus inherited the areas of Samaria, Judea, and Idumea. Herod Antipas inherited Galilee and Perea. Philip inherited the regions of Gaulanitis and Batanea in northeastern Palestine.

hypostatic union

The union of Jesus Christ's divine and human natures in one Divine Person.

hypostatic union. The Greek word *hypostasis* refers to the underlying reality. The two natures of Jesus Christ do not simply exist one alongside the other; instead they are joined so completely that both are always fully present.

Early Church Councils and the Hypostatic Union

Heretical beliefs about Jesus circulated during the early centuries of the Church. These heresies included Arianism, which said that Jesus was a kind of in-between creature; he was more than a man but less than God. Another was Nestorianism, which said that in Jesus existed *two separate persons,* one divine and one human. In response to these and other mistaken beliefs, Church councils were convened to define and clarify official Christian teachings about Jesus.

The fourth Ecumenical Council was held at Chalcedon in the year AD 451. It officially established the doctrine of the hypostatic union. The bishops who convened for that event issued a decree summarizing the agreements they had reached.

> We confess that one and the same Christ, Lord, and only-begotten Son, is to be acknowledged in two natures without confusion, change, division, or separation. The distinction between the two natures was never abolished by their union, but rather the character proper to each of the two natures was preserved as they came together in one person (*prosopon*) and one hypostasis.[2] (CCC, 467)

A later Ecumenical Council was held in the city of Constantinople in AD 553. It further explained this teaching. The gathered bishops maintained that *God* did everything that the *human Jesus* did, including suffering and dying on the cross for us. Because Jesus' divine and human natures cannot be separated, it was not only the human Jesus who endured pain and agony for our redemption; it was also God. The decree produced by the Council of Constantinople states, "He who was crucified in the flesh, our Lord Jesus Christ, is true God, Lord of glory, and *one of the Holy Trinity*[3]" (CCC, 468).

Primary Sources

The Tome of Leo

In 449, Pope Leo I (Pope 440–461) issued a letter reflecting on the person of Christ. Known as the *Tome of Leo,* the document outlines the dual nature of Jesus Christ. This letter was affirmed at the Council of Chalcedon, thereby becoming a definitive statement on the Incarnation and the hypostatic union. Below is a brief excerpt:

> [T]he Son of God comes down from his heavenly throne and enters the depths of our world, born in an unprecedented order by an unprecedented kind of birth. . . . The Lord of the universe veiled his measureless majesty and took on a servant's form. The God who knew no suffering did not despise becoming a suffering man, and, deathless as he is, to be subject to the laws of death. . . . And the fact that the birth was miraculous does not imply that in the lord Jesus Christ, born from the virgin's womb, the nature is different from ours. The same one is true God and true man.

Why the Hypostatic Union Matters to Catholics

Because Jesus is one Divine Person, a union of a fully human nature and a fully divine nature, we know and experience Jesus' divinity *through* his humanity. We come to know Jesus, God Made Flesh among us, through knowing Jesus the man. The whole of Jesus' earthly life, including his emotions, friendships, values, and priorities, reveals God to us in a unique and powerful way.

Here's the even more amazing part. When we are baptized as Christians, we are baptized *into Christ* (see Romans 6:3). We become part of Christ's own Body, the Church. Therefore, because of the hypostatic union, we can experience God not only through Jesus' humanity but also through our own humanity. The hypostatic union makes our joys and pains, our triumphs and struggles reveal God, for us and for all those with whom we share our lives.

> **The term *hypostatic union* is a complex and difficult concept to grasp immediately. In your own words, how would you explain it?**

Pray It!

A Scripture Reflection: The Vine and Branches

The following passage from the Gospel of John communicates to us the divine nature of Jesus and his invitation to us for salvation and union with the Father. Read the passage, and then reflect on the questions that follow.

> Remain in me, as I remain in you. Just as a branch cannot bear fruit on its own unless it remains on the vine, so neither can you unless you remain in me. I am the vine, you are the branches. Whoever remains in me and I in him will bear much fruit, because without me you can do nothing. (15:4–5)

Jesus invites you to remain in him. How do you respond to that invitation? What does it mean to you to understand Jesus as the vine and yourself a branch of that vine? How does Jesus enable you to "bear much fruit"?

Article 33: Jesus: Lord and Redeemer

Lord and Redeemer are two titles often given to Jesus, both in the New Testament and in later writings of the Church Fathers. Understanding the meaning of these two titles can aid our study of Jesus' mission and identity.

Jesus, Our Lord

To understand the significance of calling Jesus "Lord," we need to back up a little. In the Old Testament, most of which was originally written in Hebrew, God reveals the divine name to Moses as YHWH. In Hebrew this name is an unpronounceable form of *to be,* which is often translated as "I am who I am" or "I will be who I will be." Out of respect for the holiness of God's name, both ancient and modern Jewish readers use a different term whenever they see *YHWH*. They use the word *Adonai*, meaning "Lord." When the Old Testament was translated into Greek, the word *Kyrios,* "Lord," was used for the name YHWH. Thus, in the New Testament, giving the title *Kyrios* to Jesus indicates his divinity. When people address Jesus as Lord, it demonstrates not only profound respect and trust, but also the fact that Jesus is God. Practically speaking, believing in Jesus as our Lord means that all the honor, glory, and reverence we offer to God the Father are due to Jesus as well.

The divine name YHWH, which God revealed to Moses (see Exodus 3:14), can be literally translated "I am who I am" or "I will be who I will be." What does this divine name say about the nature of God?

© David Lees / CORBIS

Jesus, Our Redeemer

We also need to back up a little bit to understand the title Redeemer as it applies to Jesus. In the Roman world, a ransom was the price paid to buy the freedom of a slave. The person who paid the ransom was known as a redeemer. Guided by the Holy Spirit, the early

Christians began to reflect on the meaning and significance of the death of Jesus, borrowing this language from the Roman world (remember, they were living in the Roman Empire). They were also aware of Old Testament prophecies promising that God would save the people from their sin; see especially some of the promises in Isaiah (43:1–4, 53:1–12). So the early Christians taught that Jesus had "paid the price" to "ransom" us from our slavery to sin; therefore, Jesus is truly our Redeemer.

Jesus' death redeemed us from sin (and from death, the consequence of sin) because of the hypostatic union.

Faith in Action
Finding God in All Things

© Rochdale Art Gallery, Lancashire, UK / The Bridgeman Art Library

A *spirituality* is a way of understanding God and how he works in one's own life. Often a spirituality is connected to a religious order and its particular spiritual path, as in "Franciscan spirituality" or "Benedictine spirituality."

Jesuit, or Ignatian, spirituality is based on the life and directives of **Saint Ignatius Loyola**, the founder of the Society of Jesus (or Jesuits). Saint Ignatius taught that the aim of life is to find God in all things. He wanted the priests and brothers of his order to be contemplatives in action—to bring work and prayer together while serving others.

Their model in this way of life is none other than Jesus Christ, true God and true Man, who united in himself both prayer and action, the human and the divine. By following Christ and by meditating on the Gospels, Jesuits use the good human things of this world to bring people closer to Christ and help them to become their own best selves as human persons. Through following the path of Saint Ignatius Loyola and his *Spiritual Exercises* (a series of prayerful meditations based on the Gospels), Jesuits help others to see God at work in their own ordinary human lives.

Because of the Incarnation, our world, created as good, has been graced by the presence of God in human flesh. Following Christ in all good things and rejecting all that does not lead to Christ is the path of Jesuit spirituality. But Jesuit spirituality is not just for Jesuits! We can all pray for the grace to find God in all things, and to follow the way of Christ in our own everyday lives.

Remember that the hypostatic union means that Jesus is one Divine Person with two natures—one human and one divine—fully and completely united. Because Jesus, as the Second Person of the Blessed Trinity, fully assumed our human nature, he was able to redeem that nature through his suffering and death on the cross. What if Jesus had not been fully human? What if, for example, he only seemed to be human? What if he were God wearing a sort of human disguise, like a costume? Then he would not have been able to redeem us. As the early Church Father Saint Gregory of Nazianzen famously stated, "What was not assumed [in Christ] was not redeemed; whatever is united to God is saved." Jesus completely embraced our human condition, even unto death. He forever united humanity with God and made salvation possible.

Jesus as Suffering Servant

Each year on Good Friday, the day on which Christians commemorate Jesus' Passion and death, we hear a reading from the prophet Isaiah, which includes these lines:

> Yet it was our pain that he bore,
> > our sufferings he endured.
> We thought of him as stricken,
> > struck down by God and afflicted,
> But he was pierced for our sins,
> > crushed for our iniquity.
> He bore the punishment that makes us whole,
> > by his wounds we were healed.
> . . . .
> Because of his anguish he shall see the light;
> > because of his knowledge he shall be content;
> My servant, the just one, shall justify the many,
> > their iniquity he shall bear.
> > > > > (53:4–5,11)

This passage is one of four in the prophecy of Isaiah called servant songs (the others are 42:1–7, 49:1–6, and 50:4–9). These songs praise the virtues of an unnamed person who serves God faithfully. He brings justice to the nations even at the cost of great personal suffering.

Biblical scholars have long debated the original identity of this "servant." They wonder if it refers to a specific individual or perhaps collectively to the people of Israel, who had always been invited to serve God faithfully. Early Christians, many of whom were devout Jews, read these passages in light of the life, death, and Resurrection of Jesus. They detected clear parallels between Jesus and the servant. Because they had come to believe in Jesus as their Lord and Redeemer, they interpreted these passages as testimony to the salvific power of Jesus' death, an interpretation that is part of the Church's Tradition.

> **What do the two titles *Lord* and *Redeemer* say to you about who Jesus is?**

For Review

1. Name some examples from Sacred Scripture that illustrate Jesus' experiencing both the blessings and frustrations of normal life.

2. How do the Gospels help us to understand Jesus' religious life as a faithful Jew?

3. How did Roman rule in Palestine affect Jesus and the Jewish community?

4. What is the hypostatic union?

5. Why is the hypostatic union important to us today?

6. What does it mean to call Jesus "Lord" and "Redeemer"?

7. How is Jesus a "suffering servant"?

Jesus and the Church

Introduction

Each year at the end of the Easter season, the Church celebrates Pentecost. This feast marks the day when the Holy Spirit came upon the followers of Jesus, enabling them to preach and baptize with the power of Christ. Even today Jesus continues to pour out the Holy Spirit on the Church.

The Church is Christ's own Body in the world. Christ acts through the Sacraments, which he instituted, bringing us into closer communion with one another and with him. Through the Eucharist, especially, Jesus is present in his Church. He continues his teaching ministry through the Magisterium, or teaching office, of the bishops and the Holy Father. Jesus acts through all the members of the Church as they respond to his will for their lives.

Each of us, in Baptism, has become a member of the Body of Christ and has been given a share in his divine mission as priest, prophet, and king. When we serve others in the name of Jesus, we help to bring his healing, liberating, and redeeming presence to a world in great need of holiness and grace.

Article 34: Pentecost and the "New Age" of the Church

After his Resurrection, Jesus appeared to his Apostles and made this promise: "But you will receive power when the holy Spirit comes upon you, and you will be my witnesses in Jerusalem, throughout Judea and Samaria, and to the ends of the earth" (Acts 1:8). The Apostles waited in Jerusalem, along with some of the women disciples, for the Spirit that Jesus had promised. Here's how the story continues:

> And suddenly there came from the sky a noise like a strong driving wind, and it filled the entire house in which they were. Then there appeared to them tongues as of fire, which parted and came to rest on each one of them. And they were all filled with the holy Spirit and began to speak in different tongues, as the Spirit enabled them to proclaim.
>
> Now there were devout Jews from every nation under heaven staying in Jerusalem. At this sound, they gathered in a large crowd, but they were confused because each one heard them speaking in his own language. They were astounded, and in amazement they asked, "Are not all these people who

Primary Sources

The Holy Spirit

During a Christmas address to the members of the Roman Curia in 2008, Pope Benedict XVI spoke about God's presence in our lives and he speaks to us, if only we take the time to listen:

We saw once more the grandeur of something which we take too much for granted in our daily lives: the fact that God speaks, that God answers our questions; the fact that, with human words, he speaks to us personally. We can listen to him; hear him, come to know him and understand him. We can also realize that he can enter our life and shape it, and that we can emerge from our own lives to enter into the immensity of his mercy.

Thus, we realized once again that, in his Word, God is speaking to each one of us, that he speaks to the heart of everyone: if our hearts are alert, and our inner ears are open, we can learn to listen to the word he personally addresses to each of us. ("Address of His Holiness Benedict XVI to the Members of the Roman Curia for the Traditional Exchange of Christmas Greetings," December 22, 2008) are speaking Galileans? Then how does each of us hear them in his own native language?"

(2:2–8)

This event is called Pentecost. It is named for the Jewish feast day on which these events took place. In the Old Testament, Pentecost celebrated God's gift of the Torah, or the Law, to the people of Israel. Now, in the New Testament, Pentecost takes on a new meaning: God gives the Holy Spirit to his Apostles, the community soon to be known as the Church.

The Church: Christ's Presence in the World

The Church was revealed to the world on the day of Pentecost. The Church was founded by Christ, in his preaching, in his healing, and in the saving work of his death, Resurrection, and Ascension. But at Pentecost, the Spirit that had anointed Jesus was now poured out on to the entire Church. The Church became Christ's presence in the world.

We are living in the age of the Church, a time when Christ continues his ministry, not as a historical man living in a particular place and time, but rather through the Church, which is now his true Body. For us today, Christ lives and acts in and with his Church in ways that address our age.

When have you felt the presence of the Holy Spirit?

Article 35: Jesus Fulfills His Mission in the Church

After Jesus died, rose, and ascended into Heaven, he was no longer physically present to his followers. However, he gave his disciples, both then and now, the gift of his ongoing presence in the Church, a presence that although not physical is nonetheless real. At Pentecost the followers of Jesus experienced the power of the Holy Spirit. They understood that this power would enable them to continue the work of Jesus through the Church. Gradually the Holy Spirit revealed to the early community of believers that the Church is the true Body of Christ in the world, whose mission is to continue Jesus' ministry. The Church began to understand itself as a Body whose head, and true leader, was Christ himself.

The Church: The Means and Goal of God's Plan

The Holy Trinity—Father, Son, and Holy Spirit—has a plan for the world, and the goal of the plan is the Church. This doesn't mean that the visible Church as we see it today is that goal. The Church today is a gathering of people brought together by God, but a full communion has yet to be achieved. The Church's journey toward perfection will be completed only when the Kingdom of God is fully realized and all the faithful are gathered together in unity with one another and with God in Heaven.

The Father created the universe out of love for his people and for their communion with the divine life. He sent his Son, Jesus Christ, to forgive sin and make this communion possible. After Jesus had inaugurated the Church and all his work on earth was completed, the Holy Spirit was sent to pour forth gifts upon the Church so that she can continue Jesus' mission of announcing the Good News and making disciples. The Church is the means by which God accomplishes his goal for us, for it is the salvation of our souls that is the ultimate end and the ultimate goal of his great plan.

How do you see the Church today as a continuation of the ministry of Jesus?

Article 36: Four Marks of the Catholic Church

Through the power of the Holy Spirit, Christ has given the Church four characteristics, or marks: One, Holy, Catholic, and Apostolic. The Church is the Body of

Christ; it embodies the same characteristics as Christ himself. Though the Church does not perfectly embody these characteristics, Christ gave us the **grace** to grow in attaining them more completely.

The Church Is One

The Church is One in the Lord, Jesus, who founded the Church, has bestowed a unity and common identity upon all the baptized. We are One in the faith that we share and that has been passed down from the apostolic age to the present day. We are also one in Baptism, the Sacrament that unites all Christians. The Second Vatican *Council's Decree on Ecumenism (Unitatis Redintegratio,* 1964) states that "all who have been justified by faith in baptism are incorporated into Christ" (3). This is why we do not baptize those from other ecclesial communities (such as Presbyterians or Methodists) who convert to

grace
The free and undeserved gift that God gives us to empower us to respond to his call and to live as his adopted sons and daughters. Grace restores our loving communion with the Holy Trinity, lost through sin.

Did You Know?

Images of the Church

© David Barnet / Illustration Works / Corbis

Vatican II's document *Church* contains a wide variety of images of the Church that speak beautifully and poetically of the profound reality of the gathered people of God. Here are some examples of this vivid imagery:

- The Church is a flock, led by Christ, the Good Shepherd, who gave his life for his sheep.
- The Church is a cultivated field, a fruitful vineyard planted by God in which Christ, the true vine, sustains all the branches.
- The Church is a building made of living stones, constructed by Christ on the foundation of the Apostles.

All of these images are only metaphors, of course. Christians are not literally sheep, Christ is not literally a vine, and stones are not alive. However, these symbols speak to us of the great mystery of the Church more deeply than literal language ever could.

Catholicism: they are already united with Christ in faith. As long as they were baptized with water "in the name of the Father, and of the Son, and of the Holy Spirit," the Catholic Church embraces them as fellow Christians. Christ's mission is to unite all people in himself; united with Christ through the Church, we are also united with one another.

The Church Is Holy

As the Body of Christ in the world, the Church is holy because Christ is unfailingly holy. This mark of the Church does not, however, guarantee the holiness of all the members of the Church. In fact, all members of the Church, including all religious men and women, must acknowledge the fact that they are all sinners. In recent years, the Church has been made acutely aware of this. Many allegations of sexual abuse of children by priests and other Church officials have surfaced. It has been painful for us to realize, firsthand, that perfect holiness is something not yet achieved by the Church. Despite the grave failings of certain individuals in the Church, the presence of Christ makes it possible for the Church to continue to bring sanctifying grace to the world. The Church is united with Christ, she is sanctified by him, through him, and with him. And it is this sanctification by Christ that allows the Church herself to be a sanctifying force in our world.

The Church Is Catholic

The Church is Catholic, or universal, in two ways. First, Christ's presence in the Church makes her Catholic; the Church is a body that is unified under one head, Jesus Christ. The Church will be Catholic in this way until the day of Christ's coming again in glory. Second, the Church has a universal mission to the whole human race. The Good News of Jesus Christ is for everyone, not just a select few. As members of Christ's Body, we share in Christ's mission to bring all people into unity with him. Though we respect those from other religious traditions, we accept Christ's mandate to "Go, therefore, and make disciples of all nations" (Matthew 28:19).

The Church Is Apostolic

The Church is Apostolic. She is "built upon the foundation of the apostles and prophets, with Christ Jesus himself as the capstone" (Ephesians 2:20). With the help of the Holy Spirit, the Church endeavors faithfully to hand down the teaching of the Apostles in every age and circumstance. Moreover, the members of the Church continue to be instructed by the Apostles through their successors, the bishops.

> **How did Jesus demonstrate through his teachings that the Good News is for everyone and not just for a chosen few?**

Sacrament
An efficacious and visible sign of God's grace, instituted by Christ and entrusted to the Church, by which divine life is dispensed to us. The Seven Sacraments are Baptism, the Eucharist, Confirmation, Penance and Reconciliation, Anointing of the Sick, Matrimony, and Holy Orders.

Article 37: The Seven Sacraments: Encounters with Christ

Although Christ has ascended into Heaven, he has not left us alone. He is present to us in the **Sacraments** that he established in order to freely give us his grace. When we participate in the Sacraments, the Holy Spirit makes Christ present to us, and we enter into a closer communion with Christ and one another. Once united by the Sacraments, we become the Body of Christ, allowing him to live in us and work through us. We share in Christ's saving work by our participation in the Sacraments, which are true encounters with the living Christ and offer us real grace.

The Sacraments are classified into three categories:

- Sacraments of Christian Initiation (Baptism, Confirmation, the Eucharist)

- Sacraments of Healing (Anointing of the Sick, Penance and Reconciliation)

- Sacraments at the Service of Communion (Matrimony, Holy Orders)

consecrate
To declare or set apart as sacred or to solemnly dedicate to God's service; to make holy.

Eucharistic species
The gifts of bread and wine after they have become Christ's Body and Blood.

Matrimony, or Marriage, is one of the Seven Sacraments. How is Matrimony a visible sign of God's presence and love?

All Seven Sacraments allow us to experience Jesus' ongoing presence with his Body, the Church, which is both a living entity and a life-giving entity.

The Sacraments: Visible Signs of God

While we live here on earth, God's presence is hidden from us. We cannot see God directly the way we will when we live with him in Heaven. However, through the Sacraments, we experience the invisible presence of God in very visible, tangible ways. In the waters of Baptism, in the Sacred Chrism (blessed oil) used in Confirmation, in the words of Absolution said by the priest during Penance and Reconciliation, and in the bread and wine that become Christ's Body and Blood in the Eucharist, all of our senses are engaged by God's love and grace. The actual objects, words, gestures, and actions used in each Sacrament function as sacramental symbols that bring us God's healing, powerful love. As human beings we need these physical signs of the presence of God, who never stops reaching out to us.

The Sacraments: Signs of Salvation

The Sacraments, as symbols and rituals, actually put us in touch with God's power. The Sacraments, most especially the Eucharist, bring into the present moment the saving action of Christ. Jesus has already accomplished the work of redemption through his death, Resurrection, and Ascension. It is the Sacraments that bring this saving work into our individual lives, thus offering us new life in Christ.

For example, the waters of Baptism do not merely remind us of our new birth in Christ, for we are *really reborn* in the cleansing waters of this Sacrament. The words of Absolution said by the priest during the Sacrament of Penance and Reconciliation (Confession) are not just comforting words. We are *really forgiven* when we hear the words of the priest during this Sacrament

© Bill Wittman / www.wpwittman.com

of Healing. The Eucharist is not just a mental reminder, representation, or symbol of Jesus Christ. The bread and wine *really become* Christ's Body and Blood in the Sacrament of the Eucharist. The **consecrated** bread and wine, the **Eucharistic species**, are the *Real Presence* of Jesus, broken and poured out for the life of the world. Although all the Sacraments celebrate important moments in life, they are much more than that. The Sacraments empower us to bring the healing power of Jesus' ministry into our everyday lives and to persevere, in faith, through any struggle we may face.

The Sacraments			
Sacrament	**Essential Sacramental Symbol**	**Minister**	**Repeated?**
Baptism	Water poured over or immersed in water while saying, "I baptize you in the name of the Father, and of the Son, and of the Holy Spirit"	Bishop, priest, deacon, or anyone in an emergency	No
Confirmation	Laying on of hands and anointing with Chrism (sacred oil) while saying, "Be sealed with the gift of the Holy Spirit"	Bishop or a designated priest	No
Eucharist	Wheat bread and grape wine and the works of Consecration	Priest	Yes
Penance and Reconciliation	Laying on of hands and the words of Absolution (forgiveness)	Priest	Yes
Anointing of the Sick	Anointing with the Oil of the Sick accompanied by the liturgical prayer of the priest	Priest	Yes
Holy Orders	Laying on of hands and the prayer of Consecration asking for the gifts specific to that order	Bishop	No
Matrimony	Exchange of marriage vows	A baptized man and woman who are free to marry, assisted by a priest or deacon who receives their consent and gives them the Church's blessing	No, unless a spouse dies

Confirmation is one of the Sacraments you might soon be preparing for (or have recently received). When we prepare for Confirmation, we select as a sponsor an adult member of the Church who will help to guide and support us. What traits do you think are important in a sponsor?

The Ministry of Jesus Christ

Though Catholic sacramental celebrations are always led by a minister of the Church (usually a priest, but sometimes a bishop or deacon), in all of the Sacraments, it is really Jesus Christ who sanctifies us. For example, it is Christ who baptizes, Christ who confirms, and Christ who gives us his own Body and Blood in the Eucharist—the same Christ who once walked this very earth, living among us as a man, and showing us the way to true unity with God and with one another. Through our regular participation in the sacramental life of the Church, we affirm our identity as members of Christ's Body. As part

© Bill Wittman / www.wpwittman.com

of the ministry of Jesus, we are strengthened in holiness and given a preview of our ultimate salvation.

See the table "The Sacraments" in article 37 for more about the Seven Sacraments.

What do the Sacraments mean to you? What Sacraments have you already experienced in your life?

liturgy
The Church's official, public, communal prayer. It is God's work, in which the People of God participate. The Church's most important liturgy is the Eucharist, or the Mass.

Article 38: Jesus' Presence in the Sacrament of the Eucharist

Jesus is uniquely present whenever we celebrate the Eucharist. The Eucharistic **liturgy**, or Mass, is the central liturgy of the Church. *Eucharist* is a Greek word that means "thanksgiving." When we celebrate the Eucharist, we give thanks for all that God has done for us, especially for the Paschal Mystery—Christ's work of salvation accomplished mainly through his Passion, death, Resurrection, and Ascension. Jesus instituted the Eucharist to perpetuate his sacrifice on the cross throughout the ages, until his return in glory—a sacrifice we offer with him at every celebration of Mass. The Second Vatican Council's document *Constitution on the Sacred Liturgy (Sacrosanctum Concilium*, 1963) says that Christ is present to us in four ways at a Eucharistic liturgy. He is present in the assembly, in the priest, in the Word, and, most especially, in the Eucharistic species. The Eucharist is the heart and summit of the Church's life, because in it Christ unites his Church and all her members with his sacrifice on the cross, offered to God the Father. By this sacrifice Christ pours out the graces of salvation on his Body, the Church (see *Catechism of the Catholic Church*, 1407).

When we participate in the Eucharist, we take part in the heart and summit of the Church's life. Active participation enables us to more fully experience the presence of Christ. How can you more actively participate in the Mass?

Christ Present in the Gathered Assembly

In Matthew's Gospel, Jesus said that "where two or three are gathered together in my name, there am I in the midst of them" (18:20). Therefore Christ is present in the assembly of people when they pray and sing at a Eucharistic liturgy. The next time you are at Mass, think about this: all the people sitting around you are

© Bill Wittman / www.wpwittman.com

members of Christ's own Body, as are you. In our prayers during Mass, we are all joined to Christ and to one another. This unity and sense of communion is especially apparent at the sign of peace.

Christ Present in the Priest

Christ is present in a unique and particular way in the bishop or priest, who celebrates a Eucharistic liturgy. As the celebrant leads the liturgy, he makes the redemptive sacrifice of Christ's death present again for our salvation. Christ works through the priest to bring the saving power of his sacrificial death and Resurrection into our lives.

© Bill Wittman / www.wpwittman.com

Christ Present in the Word

The Church document *Sacred Liturgy* states that Christ "is present in his word since it is he himself who speaks when the holy Scriptures are read" (7) during the Mass in the Liturgy of the Word. Christ truly speaks to us through these ancient texts. If we listen carefully and prayerfully, we can gain wisdom, guidance, courage, and peace.

Christ Present in the Eucharist

Jesus is present in a real, substantial, and unique way in his Body and Blood once the bread and wine have been consecrated. The Catholic doctrine of the Real Presence means that the consecrated elements of the Eucharist still taste and look like bread and wine, but they are truly the Body and Blood of Jesus. This is one important aspect of belief where other ecclesial communities are not fully united with the Catholic Church. Some believe that Christ is present only symbolically in the bread and wine. Others teach that the bread and wine are simply reminders of Jesus, the way a treasured gift from a loved

Pray It!

Eucharistic Adoration

Eucharistic adoration is a type of prayer in which one meditates before the Blessed Sacrament, either privately or during a communal prayer, such as the Benediction. The Blessed Sacrament is the consecrated host, which is the Real Presence of Jesus. Adoration allows us time to simply be with Jesus in a very real way. It also deepens our appreciation for the Mass.

Find out when your parish provides opportunities for Eucharistic adoration and plan to spend one hour in adoration of the Blessed Sacrament. You can use the following prayer to help you focus on growing your relationship with Jesus through participation in Eucharistic Adoration:

Lord, Jesus, thank you for the gift of yourself in the Eucharist. As I kneel before you, open my mind and heart to your loving presence in my life. Help me to respond to you with love, and allow your grace to strengthen me. Accompany me always that I may be an instrument of your love and mercy to others.

one might bring that person to mind. Catholics, however, recognize that although the bread and wine retain their physical forms, they have truly become Jesus' real Body and Blood. Thus we always treat the Eucharist with the utmost care, respect, and reverence.

> **How does knowing that Jesus is truly present in the Eucharist affect your understanding of the liturgy?**

Article 39: Jesus Teaches through the Church

Think of the best teachers you've ever had. What was great about them? Did they really know their subject matter? Could they explain difficult concepts clearly and well? Did they truly care about the students? Jesus displayed every one of these traits and more. He was, in fact, the greatest of all teachers.

In the four Gospels, Jesus was called "Teacher" forty-five times. (The Hebrew word for teacher is *rabbi.*) Jesus certainly earned the title of teacher because he frequently taught the crowds who followed him from place to place. For example, if we look at the Sermon on the Mount, beginning in Matthew, chapter 5, we see Jesus teaching about anger, prayer, divorce, and the Golden Rule. In Mark, chapter 6, we find Jesus teaching the crowd out of genuine concern for them: "When he disembarked and saw the vast crowd, his heart was moved with pity for them, for they were like sheep without a shepherd; and he began to teach them many things" (verse 34). We find another example in Luke, chapter 4, when Jesus taught the people in the synagogue at Nazareth, the town where he had grown up. The assembly was so impressed that "all spoke highly of him and were amazed at the gracious words that came from his mouth" (verse 22).

"[Jesus] said to them again, 'Peace be with you. As the Father has sent me, so I send you'" (John 20:21). Jesus entrusted his disciples to carry on his teaching mission. Through Apostolic Succession this mission has been entrusted to the Church today.

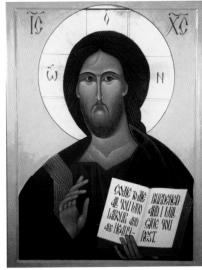

© Bill Wittman / www.wpwittman.com

Similarly, in Matthew, chapter 7, after hearing one of Jesus' parables, "the crowds were astonished at his teaching, for he taught them as one having authority, and not as their scribes" (verses 28–29).

Jesus Entrusts the Church with His Ministry

Today Church leaders are able to speak with authority, just as Jesus did, because the Church is Christ's Body. The Magisterium, the official teaching voice of the Catholic Church, is made up of the Pope and the bishops, the successors of Peter and the Apostles, who speak with one global, unified voice. The Magisterium issues pronouncements on matters of Catholic doctrine, as well as on certain moral questions.

Live It!
Participate in the Liturgy

"Mass is boring!" Have you ever said this out loud or thought it to yourself? You are not alone. This feeling is not uncommon among young people. Adults also sometimes find Eucharistic liturgies boring.

The liturgy is the work of the whole Christ, head and body. Thus the assembly of people gathered for liturgical prayer should be engaged in "full, conscious, and active participation" (*Sacred Liturgy*, 14). Here are a few suggestions for how you can do that. You can be assured that when you take these actions, you will find Mass more engaging, and not boring!

- Sing and make the appropriate spoken responses, like "Amen" and "Thanks be to God."
- Pray the words of the liturgy by focusing your attention on the Scripture readings and prayers.
- Read and reflect on the Scripture readings before going to Mass.
- Become a liturgical minister, like an altar server, lector, cantor, or Eucharistic minister.
- Recognize the great gift the Eucharist offers to us. Though we cannot expect that every liturgical celebration will be exciting, we can expect that every liturgy will offer us abundant grace and the Real Presence of Christ. Mere excitement aside, the gift of the Eucharist as celebrated in Holy Mass is a marvelous truth.

When the bishops exercise their ministry of teaching, they follow the example of Christ the Teacher, the one who gave the Apostles and their successors the authority to teach in his name. The bishops are our teachers who, like Christ, preach the faith to the people, who in turn put their faith into practice. The Magisterium is entrusted with passing down and interpreting the truth revealed by God through Sacred Scripture and Sacred Tradition.

When the Pope issues a pronouncement *ex cathedra*, his words are considered to be infallible—that is, without error. The bishops, when speaking with one unified voice together with the Pope, also share in this gift of infallibility. As Vatican II's *Dogmatic Constitution on the Church (Lumen Gentium, 1964)* states, the bishops, although not individually, "nevertheless proclaim Christ's doctrine infallibly whenever, even though dispersed through the world, but still maintaining the bond of communion among themselves and with the successor of Peter, and authentically teaching matters of faith and morals, they are in agreement on one position as definitively to be held" (25). The infallibility of the Magisterium includes all Church doctrine, including moral doctrine, without which the truths necessary for salvation could not be preserved. As a gift of Christ to the Church, infallibility gives us the ability to find the truth we need for our salvation until the glorious return of Jesus Christ.

What qualities do you think make a teacher great?

Article 40: Jesus' Ministry through the Community of Faith

Our Baptism makes us members of Christ's own Body. As a result we share in Christ's mission as priest, prophet, and king. Have you ever been to a liturgy at which the Sacrament of Baptism was celebrated? You may recall hearing this prayer just before the person was anointed: "The God of power and Father of our Lord Jesus Christ has freed you from sin and brought you to new life through water and the Holy Spirit. He now anoints you with the chrism of salvation, so that, united with his people, you may remain for ever a member of Christ, who is Priest, Prophet, and King" (*The Rite of Baptism*, 62).

As the community of baptized people who bear the name of Christ, we participate in the ongoing ministry of Christ to the world through the particular vocation to which God has called us. All Christian vocations are oriented to service, whether through ordained ministry, as a member of the **laity**, or through the consecrated life.

Ordained Ministry: Bishops, Priests, and Deacons

Ordained ministry as a bishop, priest, or deacon is conferred through the Sacrament of Holy Orders. Bishops

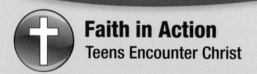

Faith in Action
Teens Encounter Christ

Is there a place for teens and young adults in the Church? There certainly is! The Teens Encounter Christ (TEC) movement is a movement of Catholic spirituality, designed for older adolescents and young adults. For over forty-seven years, Teens Encounter Christ has introduced teens to Christ in a group setting. But these gatherings are not silent retreats, which is why they are called "encounters." During a weekend encounter, teens and young adults concentrate their prayers and activities on the Paschal Mystery of Christ—his life, death, Resurrection, and Ascension—and what this means personally to each participant.

During an encounter, teens and young adults are guided by trained adult mentors, who are in turn guided by bishops and priests knowledgeable in theology and spirituality. In fact, each local TEC group must be approved by the local bishop.

Teens Encounter Christ helps teens and young adults to realize that they, in themselves, are gifts of God. In turn, they are encouraged to ask themselves the following questions: How can I thank the Lord for his goodness to me? How can I give back to God and to my faith community? How is Christ inviting me to follow him in my life?

The teen years are often full of questions. TEC helps teens to discover the answers!

are in charge of a particular geographical region of the Church called a diocese or archdiocese. Deacons and priests assist the bishop in caring for the needs of the Church within that region. You are probably most familiar with priests, who serve at your parish and perhaps at your school. A priest's unique role is the one he plays in sacramental ministry, especially presiding at Eucharistic liturgies and celebrations of the Sacrament of Penance and Reconciliation. Many priests have promised to serve God's people in obedience to a bishop within a certain diocese. These are called diocesan priests. Other priests are members of religious orders, such as the Jesuits, the Franciscans, or the Dominicans, and thus are not tied to one diocese. Religious order priests may serve in many parts of the world, usually in places where their religious order has established its ministry. Through this community of ordained men, Christ the Healer, Liberator, and Redeemer continues his work of salvation.

laity
All members of the Church with the exception of those who are ordained as bishops, priests, or deacons. The laity share in Christ's role as priest, prophet, and king, witnessing to God's love and power in the world.

The Laity: Marriage, Parenthood, and Single Life

The vast majority of Christians live out their baptismal call to service as members of the laity. Technically a layperson is anyone who is not ordained, but this term is commonly used to refer to anyone who is neither ordained nor a member of a religious order.

Laypeople who are called to marriage serve God through a loving, self-sacrificial relationship with their spouse, and, if God wills that they become parents, through raising their children. Other laypeople are called to a dedicated (or committed) single life, which allows them the freedom to help their parents, siblings, and other family members, and to engage in works of charity and justice. Through the care and generosity of the laity, Christ, who was perfect love for our salvation, continues his work.

evangelical counsels
The call to go beyond the minimum rules of life required by God (such as the Ten Commandments and the Precepts of the Church) and strive for spiritual perfection through a life marked by a commitment to chastity, poverty, and obedience.

Consecrated Life

Some Christian laity are called to live the consecrated life. The consecrated life is a permanent state of life that is marked by the following three lifelong commitments, which are also called **evangelical counsels**:

- commitment to *poverty*, to limit their ownership and use of material possessions, focusing on people instead of things

- commitment to *chastity*, to serve only God with their whole hearts, minds, and souls, refraining from marriage and from romantic relationships

- commitment to *obedience*, to listen carefully to God's will for their lives and to serve wherever they are needed

© Bill Wittman / www.wpwittman.com

Just as each one of us is unique, we are each called to our own unique vocation. Whether we are called to married, ordained, consecrated, or single life, we share a common mission to be Christ for the world.

There are many different ways of living out the consecrated life. Some people are called to live as hermits, separating themselves from all the cares and distractions of the world so they can completely commit themselves to prayer, penance, and meditation. Others are called to live as consecrated virgins or consecrated widows, still living in the world but devoting themselves to a life of prayer, penance, and service. Such people are consecrated to God by their diocesan bishop, in an approved liturgical rite.

However, the majority of those living the consecrated life serve as members of a religious order (sometimes called a religious community or congregation) where they are often called Sister or Brother. You may know some of the hundreds of Catholic religious orders that exist today, such as the Marianists, the Sisters of Mercy, the Daughters of Charity, the De La Salle Christian Brothers, and the Fathers and Brothers of the Holy Cross. The ministry of most religious orders focuses on meeting some particular need, such as education, health care, or service to the poor. Furthermore, all members of religious orders take public **religious vows** to live the evangelical counsels.

Through the faithful service of those who live out the consecrated life, Christ, the Compassion of God poured out for the life of the world, continues his work of salvation.

> **What do you think are the main challenges of living a consecrated life? What might be the rewards?**

religious vows
The promises made by members of religious communities to follow the evangelical counsels of poverty, chastity, and obedience.

For Review

1. Describe the significance of Pentecost for the Church.

2. The Church is both the means and the goal of God's saving plan. What does this mean?

3. What are the four characteristics, or marks, of the Church? What does each tell us about the Church?

4. What three categories are used to classify the Seven Sacraments?

5. How do the Sacraments bring the saving action of Christ into our lives?

6. Name four ways Jesus is present in a celebration of the Eucharistic liturgy.

7. What does the Catholic doctrine of the Real Presence mean?

8. What is the Magisterium?

9. What are the vocations through which Christians share in the ministry of Christ?

Jesus: The Definitive Revelation

What do the life and work of Jesus reveal about God's plan for humanity? Why are we created in the image of God? What does the Church teach us about the dignity of life and the stewardship of creation?

Jesus offers us a model and a vision of authentic humanity. Jesus shows us how we can be *really* human, how we can serve both God and others through our humanity. From Sacred Scripture we know that we were created in God's own image, for as God says in chapter 1 of Genesis: "Let us make human beings in our image, after our likeness" (1:26). The fact that we are created in the divine image of our creator means that all of humanity shares an inherent dignity and a duty to care for all creation.

Not only are we created in the image of God, but we are also created to be happy here on earth as well as eternally in Heaven. Through the Sacrament of Baptism, we become God's adopted children, receiving sanctifying grace and sharing in the life of the Trinity. We learn through the example of Jesus that we must be faithful and persistent in our prayer life, even during times when we feel like God may not be listening.

Christ teaches us that we must grow in holiness; we must not be complacent in our call to serve God and one another. Jesus offers us his Sermon on the Mount as the ultimate model for the ethical and spiritual life of a fully realized Christian life. He also gives us his parables and the Greatest Commandments as examples of how to live in the world and reveals to us the importance of the Last Judgment, true discipleship, and the Works of Mercy.

The enduring understandings and essential questions represent core concepts and questions that are explored throughout this unit. By studying the content of each chapter, you will gain a more complete understanding of the following:

Enduring Understandings

1. Jesus reveals God's plan for us by giving us a vision of authentic humanity.

2. Because we are created in the image of God, we have an inherent dignity and a duty to respect life.

3. Through Baptism we become God's adopted children, destined to live forever in Heaven.

4. Our call to holiness is revealed through the teachings of Jesus found in the Gospels.

Essential Questions

1. What does Jesus reveal to us about living authentic human lives and about God's plan for us?

2. What are our responsibilities toward life as individuals created in God's image?

3. How do we respond to our baptismal call?

4. How do the Gospel teachings of Jesus help us to be holy?

Chapter 9

Jesus Reveals a Vision of Authentic Humanity

Introduction

What does it mean to be authentically human? As human beings what are our responsibilities and duties to one another and the rest of creation? Questions such as these have been asked throughout time—ever since we first discovered and developed our capacity for thought. All cultures and societies have had their own perspectives on these basic issues of human identity.

As Catholics we answer such questions in light of our faith in Jesus Christ. All of Christ's life, his teachings, his actions, his miracles, his death, and his Resurrection teach us who we are and how we are to live in the world. Because the Eternal Son of God fully assumed human nature, we can look to him for a vision of authentic humanity. Jesus invites us to follow his example of a humble life devoted to prayer and service. He also calls us to use our God-given gifts of intellect and free will as we seek to love all people, including our enemies, and to care responsibly for all creation.

Article 41: Jesus Teaches Us How to Be Authentically Human

We know that Jesus Christ, the Eternal Son of God, became man and lived an earthly life as part of human society. All of Christ's life was a continual teaching—his speeches, his miracles, his prayers, his interactions with his disciples, his love for people, his special care for the poor, his total sacrifice on the cross for the redemption of all people, and his Resurrection. The events of Jesus Christ's life are the realization of the Word of God and the fulfillment of Revelation.

We Are Made in the Image of God

In order to live an authentically human life, we must be aware of our identity as a people made in God's image. As we see in chapter 1 of Genesis, "God created mankind in his image; / in the image of God he created them; / male and female he created them" (Genesis 1:27). Even though we are made in the image of God, we do not look physically like God, the way a child resembles his or her parents. Nor does this mean that we necessarily act or think like God; we sin and make mistakes. Rather, being made in God's image means we have a fundamental dignity and that we are predestined to reproduce the image of God's Son made man, for "He is the image of the invisible God, / the firstborn of all creation" (Colossians 1:15). Though humanity was originally created in the image and likeness of God, Jesus Christ as the incarnate Word and our Savior shares his divinity with us.

Jesus responded to the dignity of others. He never treated people as mere things; instead he always treated them as individuals made in God's divine image. Jesus sought out and ministered to many people whose dignity was not recognized by their society. He healed lepers, treated sinners with respect, and reached out to **Samaritans** and to Gentiles, all of whom were looked down upon by the Jews of Jesus' time. When Jesus ministered to the people whom society cast aside, he made it

Samaritan
An inhabitant of Samaria, in the central hill country of Palestine. The Samaritans rejected the Jerusalem Temple and worshipped instead at Mount Gerizim. The New Testament mentions the Jewish rejection of Samaritans in both the Parable of the Good Samaritan (see Luke 10:29–37) and the account of Jesus' speaking with the Samaritan woman at the well (see John 4:1–42).

clear that all people have an inherent, or built-in, dignity given to them by their Creator.

The Perfect Man: Jesus, Our Model for Being Human

Not only did Jesus teach us about the inherent dignity of all persons, but he also personally embodied all that is good in our shared humanity. Therefore "in all of his life Jesus presents himself as *our model.* He is 'the perfect man',[1] who invites us to become his disciples and follow him. In humbling himself, he has given us an example to imitate, through his prayer he draws us to pray, and by his poverty he calls us to accept freely the privation and persecutions that may come our way[2]" (*Catechism of the Catholic Church [CCC]*, 520). Let's explore each of the points mentioned here as we try to understand how exactly Jesus is the ideal model of humanity for all of us:

- **Humility** The Son of God humbled himself firstly by assuming human nature. However, one clear example of Jesus' humility in his earthly life occurs in John's Gospel. At the Last Supper, he washed the disciples' feet (see 13:1–20). Washing feet, a traditional sign of service and hospitality, was normally performed by a slave. Yet Jesus, as both teacher and master, took on the task of a servant, giving his disciples a striking example of humble service and a vision of God's Reign. Indeed Jesus explicitly told the disciples, "If I, therefore, the master and teacher, have washed your feet, you ought to wash one another's feet. I have given you a model to follow, so that as I have done for you, you should also do" (13:14–15).

- **Prayer** In praying numerous times throughout the Gospels, Jesus modeled for us a life firmly grounded in a direct and personal relationship with God the Father. Jesus also taught us to pray in the words of the Lord's Prayer, or the Our Father (see Luke 11:2–4, Matthew 6:9–13).

- **Poverty** From his birth in humble surroundings to his death on the cross, Jesus lived and died in material poverty. For much of his public ministry, Jesus did not even have a permanent home: "Foxes have dens and birds of the sky have nests, but the **Son of Man** has nowhere to rest his head" (Matthew 8:20). Jesus thus challenges us to consider our relationship to material things and our willingness to do without certain physical comforts.

Son of Man
A messianic title from the Book of Daniel, used to describe a figure who receives authority over other nations from God; the only messianic title in the Gospels used by Jesus to describe himself.

Saint Paul Tells Us to Imitate Christ

Saint Paul's letter to the Philippians contains a beautiful early Christian hymn about the humility of Jesus and our call to imitate it. It reads, in part, as follows:

> Have among yourselves the same attitude that is also yours in Christ Jesus,
>> Who, though he was in the form of God,
>>> did not regard equality with God something to be grasped.
>> Rather, he emptied himself,
>> taking the form of a slave,
>> coming in human likeness;
>> and found human in appearance,
>> he humbled himself,
>> becoming obedient to death, even death on a cross.
>> (2:5–8)

This passage powerfully expresses Christ's humility. Because the Son of God willingly gave up his right to remain "in the form of God" (2:6), we must be willing to put aside our own selfish needs and engage in loving, generous service of others, especially when this work is unglamorous or difficult. We may never receive rewards or recognition for our labor, but we will know that we are following in the path of Jesus, the One whose life of humble, obedient service and selfless, sacrificial death brought salvation to all the world.

What are some of Christ's teachings that reveal his human nature?

Article 42: The Gifts of Intellect and Free Will

The vision of authentic humanity revealed for us by Jesus includes the gifts of intellect and free will.

The Gift of Intellect

As human beings created in the image of God and imbued with a unique intellect, we have the capacity to think and reason logically and to learn about the world around us. Furthermore, we maintain the ability to make wise decisions and to think about the consequences of our actions. Of all God's creation, only human beings have the ability to develop the wonderful gift of an intellect. Paragraph 15 of Vatican II's *Pastoral Constitution on the Church in the Modern World (Gaudium et Spes,* 1965) describes the human intellect as a "sharing in the light of the divine mind." It praises human "attempts to search out the secrets of the material universe," and points to the progress we have made "in the empirical sciences, in

Live It!
Serving with Your Mind

One way you can follow the will of God right now is by being the best student you can be. God gave you intellectual abilities so you could be fully human and give glory to him. How can you do this for God? One way to serve God is by developing your mind as best you can and by using your intellectual abilities to serve others.

You can begin to develop your intellect by realizing and appreciating how your academic studies relate to God's plan. The pursuits of science, which explore the nature of the universe, for example, profoundly demonstrate to us the wonderful order and beauty of God's creative work. The study of literature, history, and the other humanities reveal the drama of how human beings, the summit of creation, have used their God-given freedom and intellect to do good or evil.

As you concentrate on your academic studies and develop your intellectual gifts, strive always to glorify God and to serve others through your knowledge, talents, and abilities.

technology, and in the liberal arts." Indeed when people conduct research to discover the cure for a disease, when they think carefully about how to bring peace between two warring nations, or when they plan and create a beautiful work of art, they are using their God-given intellectual powers.

Paragraph 15 of *The Church in the Modern World* also makes clear that through the power of the Holy Spirit, we are able to use our intellectual abilities to pursue "truths of a higher order": the truths of divine wisdom. Wisdom "gently draws the human mind to look for and to love what is true and good." Ultimately, wisdom leads us to God: "We are led through visible realities to those which are invisible."

conscience
The "inner voice," guided by human reason and Divine Law, that enables us to judge what is good and what is evil. To make good judgments, one needs to have a well-formed conscience.

The Gift of Free Will

God desires that we make good, moral decisions. Through God's grace we are able to respond to him and recognize the good, even before we make a moral decision, for he gives each of us the gift of a **conscience** to help us choose rightly. However, God has also given us the gift of freedom, or free will, to make our own decisions and choose our own path in life. This means God cannot force us to act a certain way. Think about it: Could you force someone to love you? Love, as a gift freely offered to another person, is not something that we can force on, or demand from, others. It must be given and accepted willingly. Similarly, God cannot force us to love him or to make decisions that please him. This is up to us, and it is our free will that allows us to choose. Even though God wills that we try our very best to live in loving harmony with other people and with all creation, the choice is ultimately our own. If we allow ourselves to be open to divine grace, the Holy Spirit will help us to use our free will wisely, with strength and courage.

Even Jesus, when death was upon him, was free to choose whether to follow through with what God the Father wanted of him. In the Gospel of Mark, chapter 14, Jesus prays in the Garden at Gethsemane for guidance and assurance during his suffering: "Abba, Father, all things are possible to you. Take this cup away from me, but not what I will but what you will" (verse 36). Here Jesus demonstrates perfect obedience to God the Father, modeling how we should freely choose to surrender to God's will and his desire for our lives.

What are some positive aspects of the gifts of intellect and free will? What about the challenges?

Article 43: Created to Love

Through his life, death, and Resurrection, Jesus revealed that we were created to love. We have been created to love God, and, because we love him, we are to also love our neighbor, who was likewise created in God's image.

Did You Know?

Catholic Colleges and Universities: Nurturing the Gift of Intellect

© Andresr / shutterstock.com

You may have attended a Catholic elementary school. You now attend a Catholic high school. Did you know you can continue your Catholic education in college? The Catholic Church holds the intellectual pursuit of academic knowledge and spiritual wisdom in high esteem. The heart of the Catholic intellectual life is found in Catholic colleges and universities. Catholic universities have flourished in Europe since the Middle Ages. The first Catholic institution of higher education in the United States—Georgetown University—was founded in 1789. Today in the United States, 245 Catholic colleges and universities enroll more than 600,000 students each year.

Every Catholic college or university is unique, but they all view our intellectual abilities as gifts from God. This understanding of the divine origin of the human intellect informs the approach to every academic subject, from art to biology, from physics to philosophy. Indeed developing our abilities in a wide variety of fields of study is a gift we can offer back to the God who has given so much to us.

No other creature on earth can offer to the Creator the response of faith and love that we can.

How Jesus Loved

Jesus loved others in every aspect of his earthly ministry. As a teacher, he showed this immense love by speaking the truth, even when people would not listen to him or

Faith in Action
Julian of Norwich (c. 1342–c. 1413)

© Private Collection / The Stapleton Collection / The Bridgeman Images

In May of 1373, during the Middle Ages, a young English woman named Julian was suddenly stricken by a strange illness. Thinking she was dying, she was shown a crucifix and afterward recovered. After her recovery, Julian wrote down sixteen revelations (or interior visions) she had seen while she was ill. Julian's reflections on these mystical revelations became the first book in the English language ever written by a woman. The book, *Revelations of Divine Love,* has since become a hallmark of English medieval mysticism.

In *Revelations of Divine Love,* Julian focused on the great mysteries of Christianity. Specifically, some of her revelations revealed details of events in the life of Jesus Christ, particularly scenes from his Passion and death. Julian wondered deeply about the meaning of these events. She received and wrote the following answer: "'Would you learn to see clearly your Lord's meaning in this thing? Learn it well: Love was his meaning. Who showed it to you? Love. . . . Why did he show it to you? For Love. . . .' Thus I was taught that Love was our Lord's meaning" (chapter 86). Much of Julian's writing is concerned with understanding and responding to God's love.

It was through the humanity of Jesus that Julian learned the true meaning of God's love for us. Through meditating on the Gospels and asking Jesus to be with us, we too can touch his love and compassion, perfectly human and perfectly divine.

Julian (her name is sometimes rendered as Juliana) was most likely a Benedictine nun from Norwich, England, and may have lived as an anchoress (a religious woman vowed to live in seclusion). Perhaps due to her obscure life, Julian of Norwich was never officially beatified by the Church, but she has long been regarded as a great Christian mystic.

threatened him with violence. As a healer he demonstrated his love for humanity by making the lame walk, the blind see, the deaf hear, and the dead live again. As the Word of divine mercy incarnate, Jesus sought out and loved those whom society had excluded and forgotten, like those who were poor, the Samaritans, and women. Jesus welcomed people like this—people with little power, influence, or worldly success—to be his friends and followers.

Most of all, Jesus gave us his love through his death on the cross. In fidelity to the will of his Divine Father, Jesus Christ willingly sacrificed himself so that all people might be free from sin and death. When we follow the example of Jesus' self-sacrificial love, we are well on our way to full, authentic humanity. In fact, when we follow Jesus' examples of how to love, we will become the people God has always desired us to be.

Loving Others as Jesus Did

Jesus invites us to love him and one another because God the Father first loved him. It follows that as God, the First Divine Person of the Blessed Trinity, loves Jesus, so Jesus loves his disciples, and so we are to love one other. In the

Pray It!

Care for Others

Jesus Christ is the ultimate example of the empathetic individual. Did you know that the word *empathy* is derived from two words, a Greek term meaning "affection" or "passion," and another word meaning "to suffer"? In the following prayer, we are encouraged to leave our selfish concerns aside and begin to truly live for others:

Dear Jesus,

Encourage us to care less about things and more about other people. Teach us to be willing to make sacrifices so we can use our time and money to help those in need. Help us to forget our own comfort so we can more readily provide for the relief of others. May your life inspire us to be generous and compassionate at all times. In your name we pray. Amen.

Gospel of John, chapter 15, Jesus states, shortly before his arrest:

> As the Father loves me, so I also love you. Remain in my love. If you keep my commandments, you will remain in my love, just as I have kept my Father's commandments and remain in his love. I have told you this so that my joy may be in you and your joy may be complete. This is my commandment: love one another as I love you. No one has greater love than this, to lay down one's life for one's friends. . . . This I command you: love one another." (Verses 9–13,17)

Laying down one's life for one's friends might seem extreme and unrealistic, but this sentiment is at the heart of Christian love. Many popular songs lead us to think that love is merely a happy, warm feeling. In reality love is fundamentally a choice we make. When we choose to truly and authentically love other people as Christ did, we choose to love them even when they disappoint us or even when we realize they are not perfect. Like Jesus we choose to seek their good, even at the expense of our own comfort or sometimes even our own lives.

Jesus invites us to develop a love for one another that is so all-encompassing it includes love even for our enemies: "But I say to you, love your enemies, and pray for those who persecute you, that you may be children of your heavenly Father, for he makes his sun rise on the bad and the good, and causes rain to fall on the just and the unjust" (Matthew 5:44–45). With the help of the Holy Spirit, we can make the choice to love those who have hurt us greatly, for we must recognize that these people are loved by God too. If we could only see our enemies as God does, how differently would we treat one another?

How do you show God that you love him?

Article 44: The Call to Be Stewards of Creation

Jesus and his disciples lived closely tied to the natural world. The followers of Christ were farmers, fishers,

stewards
People who are put in charge of managing, caring for, and protecting something, such as money or personal property.

stewardship
The careful and responsible management of someone or something that has been entrusted to a person's care. This includes responsibly using and caring for the gifts of creation that God has given us.

and shepherds—people whose livelihood depended on the land and the sea. In his parables, Jesus told stories about planting seeds, losing sheep, gathering a harvest, and hauling in a catch of fish, all activities familiar to his listeners. Jesus knew that humanity and the natural world are deeply interconnected, and it is through this connection that our call to care for creation responsibly is revealed.

The Creator's Gift

According to the *Catechism*, God, as the Creator of all the earth, "willed the diversity of his creatures and their own particular goodness, their interdependence, and their order" (353). According to the design of God, "*each creature possesses its own particular goodness and perfection,*" reflecting "in its own way a ray of God's infinite wisdom and goodness" (339). The vast universe in which we make our home is God's gracious gift to us, for he "destined all material creatures for the good of the human race" (353). When we take care of the natural world and allow it to sustain us in life, we enable all of creation to share in the glory of the One who is the Source of all being.

The Goods of the Earth: Intended for All

We are used to thinking of the things we own as "mine." My room, my clothes, my smartphone, and so on. It is easy to get possessive and forget that all the material things we own ultimately come from God. He allows us to own and use them, but he wants us to also be aware of the rights and needs of others.

Because the earth is the first of God's many gifts to humanity, the goods of the earth—like land, water, air, food, and other natural resources—are the rightful property of all people and are destined for the whole human race. The earth is divided among all people to assure the security and dignity of human lives. To deny anyone access to the goods of the earth is to steal, which is a violation of the Seventh Commandment. All people have a right to private possessions and property acquired in a just way, for guaranteeing their own personal freedom and dignity and meeting their own basic needs and the needs of those in their care. However, we must balance this right to private property with the right of all people to have their basic needs met and to live in dignity. We must follow principles of justice and charity in the administration and distribution of earthly goods. Because God is the ultimate source of all we have, we are obligated to make sure that all people enjoy a share in the many good things of the earth.

Stewardship of Creation

In the Creation accounts in Genesis, God blesses the newly created man and woman, saying to them: "Be fertile and multiply; fill the earth and subdue it. Have dominion over the fish of the sea, the birds of the air, and all the living things that crawl on the earth" (1:28). Sometimes people mistakenly think the word *dominion* gives us permission to do whatever we want to creation—that it is here simply for us to use and enjoy. However, we are not free to be arbitrary or destructive in our use of creation; rather, we are to be **stewards** of all life, including human life, and of the earth itself.

God has graciously given us the natural world as a precious gift, and has entrusted us with **stewardship** of creation, a responsibility to care for and protect all the good he has created. Stewardship is a sacred obligation and a sacred relationship between humanity and creation. God has entrusted us with this beautiful and wondrous world that sustains us in life, so we must not abuse, exploit, destroy, or harm it in any way. Rather, we must safeguard its resources and use them for the benefit of all peo-

We each share in the responsibility to care for God's creation. What actions can you and your family take to help nurture and care for the environment?

© magicinfoto / shutterstock.com

ple now and in future generations. This spiritual respect for our world helps us to see that the care of creation is a crucial part of our vocation. God has commanded us to care for that which is his gift to us.

We need to truly fall in love with nature, allowing its beauty to touch our hearts and stir us to action. Only then can stewardship bring us satisfaction, joy, and a renewed sense of our own place in the universe. In the words of Psalm 8:

> When I see your heavens, the work of your fingers,
>   the moon and stars that you set in place—

. . . .

Primary Sources

"The Canticle of the Sun," by Saint Francis of Assisi

A long tradition has associated *Saint Francis of Assisi* with creation. In his famous poem "Canticle of the Sun," Saint Francis reveals his close relationship with creation by praising "brother sun," "sister moon," "brother fire," and "sister water." Here is an excerpt from the poem:

Praise be You, my Lord, through Sister Moon
and the stars, in heaven you formed them
clear and precious and beautiful.

Praised be You, my Lord, through Brother Wind,
and through the air, cloudy and serene,
and every kind of weather through which
You give sustenance to Your creatures.

Praised be You, my Lord, through Sister Water,
which is very useful and humble and precious and chaste.

Praised be You, my Lord, through Brother Fire,
through whom you light the night and he is beautiful
and playful and robust and strong.

Praised be You, my Lord, through Sister Mother Earth,
who sustains us and governs us and who produces
varied fruits with colored flowers and herbs.

All sheep and oxen,
  even the beasts of the field,
The birds of the air, the fish of the sea,
  and whatever swims the paths of the seas.
O LORD, our Lord,
  how awesome is your name through all the earth!

(Verses 4,8–10)

How do you answer the call to care for God's creation?

For Review

1. What does it mean that human beings are made in God's image?

2. How is Jesus a model of full humanity for us?

3. Describe the gifts of intellect and free will, and explain how God wants us to use them.

4. How did Jesus model love for us?

5. How does Jesus want us to love?

6. What does being a steward of creation mean?

7. In what ways does stewardship help to describe the relationship we should have with the earth?

Chapter 10

Jesus Reveals Our Inherent Dignity

Introduction

Jesus Christ, the Eternal Son of God, saved us by reconciling us with God when he fully assumed our human nature in the Incarnation. Jesus restored the original image of God in us, an image that sin had tarnished. Through the mystery of his Passion, death, Resurrection, and Ascension, Jesus redeemed us, offering us a share in the communion of the Blessed Trinity even while we live on earth and ensuring our ultimate destiny: eternal life in the glory of God's holy presence. Finally, Jesus, first in the Incarnation and later through the Paschal Mystery, revealed our inherent human dignity.

As we seek to honor this fundamental human dignity, we must remember that all people have been created in the image and likeness of God and redeemed by the saving work of Jesus Christ. We must also acknowledge women and men as equal partners, meant to serve the Creator side by side. Furthermore, we must uphold the sanctity of human life, at all its stages, from conception to natural death.

Article 45: Created, Redeemed, and Bound for Glory

At the core of human dignity lie three fundamental truths: (1) we are created as good, (2) we are in need of salvation, and (3) we are meant for eternal life in the glory of God's holy presence.

We Are Created as Good

The opening chapter of the Book of Genesis states that humanity has been created in the image and likeness of God: "Then God said: Let us make human beings in our image, after our likeness. . . . / God created mankind in his image; / in the image of God he created them; / male and female he created them" (1:26–27). As creatures who occupy this unique place in creation, we have a dignity that can never be taken away from us. The Incarnation— when God became flesh—further affirms the basic goodness of the world, particularly that of humanity. If our world were not good, God would not have come to live in it. Likewise, if humanity were not good, God would never have assumed human nature and lived among us as Jesus of Nazareth.

But what about free will? Are humans able to achieve goodness through our own freely chosen actions? In the fifth century, Saint Augustine, Bishop of Hippo in North Africa, and Pelagius, a monk from the British Isles, argued for years over this basic question. Can we achieve goodness through our own free will, or do we always need the help of God's grace to do good?

Pelagius believed that we are capable of choosing good through our own freely chosen actions, without the benefit of God's grace. He maintained that we can use our free will to pray, love others, engage in works of service and justice, and follow God's will. Pelagius thought it was possible not to sin at all if we just try hard enough.

In contrast, Saint Augustine believed that Original Sin left humanity permanently wounded. There-fore, according to Saint Augustine, we cannot create or experience goodness on our own. However, God's grace supports us in our weakness and enables us to choose the good. We may think we have made our own choice in favor of goodness, but Saint Augustine would say that God planted the initial desire for good in our hearts. Saint Augustine recognized that God's abundant and powerful grace always comes first.

After years of controversy, the Church acknowledged that Saint Augustine correctly understood human nature: We are created as good but are in constant need of redemptive grace. Consequently, Pelagius's views were judged to be heretical, or false.

In Need of Redemption

Although humanity was created by God as fundamentally good, we are still in need of redemption because of the Fall. As a direct consequence of the Fall from Grace, sin first entered our world and has been a part of our human experience ever since. This fallen nature,

Pray It!

Saint Augustine and Prayer

Saint Augustine believed that we should pray not for what we need or want, because God already knows what we need. Instead we need only ask that our desire for God be increased, so that we may be ready and able to receive his grace. In the following mediation, attributed to Saint Augustine, we pray to seek God continually:

O Lord my God, I believe in you, Father, Son and Holy Spirit. Insofar as I can, insofar as you have given me the power, I have sought you. I became weary and I labored. O Lord my God, my sole hope, help me to believe and never to cease seeking you. Grant that I may always and ardently seek out your countenance. Give me the strength to seek you, for you help me to find you and you have more and more given me the hope of finding you. Here I am before you with my firmness and my infirmity. Preserve the first and heal the second. Here I am before you with my strength and my ignorance. Where you have opened the door to me, welcome me at the entrance; where you have closed the door to me, open to my cry; enable me to remember you, to understand you, and to love you. Amen.

transmitted to every person born into the world, is called Original Sin. Although this first sin committed by Adam and Eve was a personal sin, all of human nature thereafter has been affected and shares a fallen state of existence. The doctrine of Original Sin does not mean we are born with personal faults. Rather, it means we enter the world as imperfect beings, with a strong tendency or predisposition to sin, and in need of redemption. Original Sin makes it hard for us to say no to temptation and inclines us to act for our own selfish pleasures rather than to do what is right.

Our redemption flows from God's initiative of love for us, because "he loved us and sent his Son as expiation for our sins" (1 John 4:10). Jesus freely offered himself for our salvation, and through his Passion, death, Resurrection, and Ascension, we are redeemed. Saint Paul explained that Jesus' fidelity to the will of his Divine Father essentially redeems all of the human race by redeeming the sin of Adam: "Therefore, just as through one person sin entered the world, and through sin, death, and thus death came to all . . . if by that one person's transgression the many died, how much more did the grace of God and the gracious gift of the one person Jesus Christ overflow for the many" (Romans 5:12,15). The Exultet is the Church's song of thanksgiving prayed at the Great Vigil of Easter. It further explains this connection between Adam and Christ: "O truly necessary sin of Adam, destroyed completely by the death of Christ! / O happy fault that earned so great, so glorious a Redeemer!" (*Roman Missal*). It is through the Sacrament of Baptism that we first gain access to the grace of our Redeemer, Jesus, who saves us from our own sins and brings us back to God.

Bound for Glory

The fact that we have been created as good and redeemed by Christ ensures our ultimate destiny: eternal life in the glory of God's holy presence. Jesus revealed this truth when he stated: "In my Father's house there are many

immortal
Living forever; not
subject to death.

dwelling places. If there were not, would I have told
you that I am going to prepare a place for you?" (John
14:2–3). Similarly, the First Letter of John states that "we
shall be like him, for we shall see him as he is" (3:2). The
scriptural witness is clear: we have a heavenly home with
God awaiting us. When we share in the sacramental life
of the Church, we are able to find our ultimate destiny
and we are strengthened on our journey toward it. The
Sacraments reinforce our fundamental identity: We are
people destined to share in the eternal glory of the One
who created us in perfect goodness and redeemed us in
perfect love.

Why is the Church concerned with human dignity?

Article 46: The Inherent Dignity of All People

We learn in the Book of Genesis that God is the Creator
of the universe, the earth, and all of its people. Therefore, all of creation—plants and trees, animals and birds,
sun and moon—comes from God, but only humans are
created in his divine image. Our sharing in this common
divine origin reveals a central truth about humanity: All
of us—women, men, and children of every race, language, age, and way of life—have a unique, inherent dignity given to us by God. *Inherent* means that this dignity
is so much a part of us that no one can ever take it away.

Body and Soul United

In creating us with inherent dignity, God has fashioned
humanity as truly unique among creation, for only
we have a spiritual, **immortal** soul. Though our parents
provide the genetic material that grows into our physical bodies, our souls are created directly by God. While
we live on earth, our bodies and souls dwell together, as
one unified being. Indeed it is due to our spiritual side,
or soul, that our bodies, which are made up of matter,
become living, human bodies. When we die, our souls

separate from our bodies. At the final resurrection, our souls will be reunited with our glorified, resurrected bodies.

Dignity of the Individual: Not Some*thing*, but Some*one*

The *Catechism of the Catholic Church (CCC)* states that "being in the image of God the human individual possesses the dignity of a person, who is not just something, but someone" (357). You may be wondering what the phrase "not just something, but someone" means exactly. It means we must not treat people as objects or things. People are individuals who should never be used simply to suit our own purposes. Such abuse of any individual

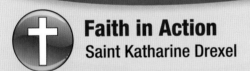

✝ Faith in Action
Saint Katharine Drexel

© Bettmann / CORBIS

Saint Katharine Drexel (1858–1955) was born in Philadelphia. The daughter of a successful banker, she used her enormous inheritance to establish schools for Native Americans and African Americans. At this time in history, nearly a century before the civil rights movement, black Americans were still overcoming a legacy of oppression and slavery. Both Native Americans and African Americans were often the victims of prejudice and often did not have access to the same education afforded to other Americans. Saint Katharine saw the inherent dignity of all people, especially those who were disenfranchised and disadvantaged. In 1891, she founded a new religious order, the Sisters of the Blessed Sacrament, specifically committed to educating Native Americans and African Americans. In 1894, Mother Drexel and her religious order opened the first mission school for Native Americans, in Santa Fe, New Mexico. At the time of her death, more than five hundred Sisters of the Blessed Sacrament were teaching in sixty-three schools and missions in twenty-one states. With her religious order, Saint Katherine Drexel had also established Xavier University in New Orleans, the first and only predominantly African American Catholic university.

Saint Katharine Drexel was canonized by Pope Saint John Paul II in 2000, making her only the second American-born saint. Her feast day is March 3.

or group of individuals is a grave violation of the dignity God has given to us all.

This is why, during his lifetime, Jesus treated every person he met—sinners, outcasts, the sick, and the poor—equally, with care and compassion. Jesus looked beyond the limits that so often stop us from seeing the dignity of others. For example, in the Gospel of John, Jesus engaged in a lengthy conversation with a Samaritan woman even though she was a member of a group the Jews despised and scorned (see John 4:4–42). Furthermore, Jesus healed the servant of a Roman official despite the fact that the Romans were hated as a foreign occupying power in Judea (see Matthew 8:5–13). Finally, Jesus cured the daughter of a Canaanite woman while his disciples were urging him to send her away (see Matthew 15:21–28). The Jews of the time, the people Jesus lived among and taught, commonly viewed Samaritans,

Live It!
Respecting Others

Is it challenging to always treat others with respect at your school? It can be difficult sometimes to recognize the inherent dignity of the people we encounter in our daily lives. That might be because people we see on a daily basis do not always treat us with respect. Or we may be too busy to think much about how we are treating other people. At the start your school day, ask yourself the following questions:

- Do I greet others with a friendly and welcoming spirit?
- Do I treat everyone fairly and avoid judging or disregarding people who seem different from me?
- Do I avoid prejudging people based on how they look, their perceived intelligence, or who their friends are?
- Do I look for the good in every person I encounter?
- Do I try to get to know and understand people I am unfamiliar with or people with whom I disagree?

When we make an effort to treat everyone in a way that respects their God-given, inherent dignity, we can discover the good that lies within each person.

Romans, and Canaanites with hatred and suspicion, but Jesus treated all people with kindness, respect, and concern.

The Church seeks to follow Jesus' example by protecting the dignity of every human person. Vatican II's *Pastoral Constitution on the Church in the Modern World (Gaudium et Spes*, 1965) states that "every form of social or cultural discrimination in fundamental personal rights on the grounds of sex, race, color, social conditions, language, or religion must be curbed and eradicated as incompatible with God's design[1]" (CCC, 1935). Therefore, the Church consistently speaks out against racism, sexism, abortion, human trafficking, and other oppressive, discriminatory practices.

> **Have you ever felt treated like a thing or an object and not with the dignity you deserve as a person? How did you maintain your own sense of dignity?**

Article 47: Jesus Restores Our Divine Image

As we saw have seen in the last chapter and earlier in this chapter, the Book of Genesis reveals that we have been created in God's image. Although sin has distorted that image, the saving work of Jesus Christ restores it.

The Human Being: God's "Noblest Fruit"

The first Creation account in Genesis tells of God's creative work through six days. Biblical scholars believe this beautiful, poetic story was originally a liturgical song. In the first chapter of Genesis, God created human beings on the sixth day, after preparing all the earth and heavens. Because only people are made in God's own image, we are God's crowning achievement, the summit of all his work. During his papacy, Saint John Paul II said this about the dignity and prominence of human beings in God's work of Creation: "On the previous days, marking as it were the rhythm of the birth of the cosmos, Yahweh had created the universe. Finally he created the human being, the noblest fruit of his design" ("Letter of His Holiness Pope John Paul II to Artists," 1). Throughout the narrative in the Book of Genesis, God describes each part of creation as "good." It is truly fitting that on this sixth day only, God looked at "everything he had made, and found it very good" (Genesis 1:31).

Jesus: Restoring What We Lost to Sin

The third chapter of the Book of Genesis recounts the Fall from Grace, in which the first man and woman chose to sin by disobeying God. Because of their sin, our likeness to God was disfigured or distorted. The image of God is no longer clear in us. Jesus, as both perfect God and perfect man, restores the image and likeness of God in us. Jesus, our Redeemer and Savior, gives us back what we once lost to sin: our original divine image full of the beauty and grace of God. Because Jesus is the "image of the invisible God" (Colossians 1:15), we are thus "inwardly renewed" (*The Church in the Modern World,* 22) when we become like him. In this way, Jesus is truly the firstborn of a multitude of brothers and sisters all united in him.

> **How would you describe the "image of the invisible God"?**

Article 48: Women and Men: Partners in God's Plan

From the beginning God willed the creation of humanity as male and female (see Genesis 1:27). In creating men and women as equal partners in his plan of salvation, God gave us the gift of sexuality and affirmed that we are not meant to be alone in the world.

Created for Each Other

Human beings were created by God to be in loving relationships with one another. In the Book of Genesis, when God fashioned the first person (in Hebrew, *adam*) from the clay of the ground, he declared: "It is not good for the man to be alone. I will make a helper suited to him" (2:18). After creating wild animals, birds, and cattle, God finally brought forth another person, whom Adam welcomed as "bone of my bones / and flesh of my flesh" (2:23). The Book of Genesis goes on to explain the communion made possible by this partnership between

Did You Know?

Models of Cooperation in Sacred Scripture and in Church History

© Scala / Art Resource, NY

Throughout the Bible and the history of the Church, we see numerous examples of men and women cooperating with one another and with God in the divine plan of salvation history.

In the Old Testament:

- Moses was helped by his brother, Aaron, and his sister, Miriam, in leading the Israelites to freedom.
- Joshua led the Israelites into the Promised Land with the assistance of a woman named Rahab, who hid the Israelite spies in her home, protecting them from danger.

In the New Testament:

- Mary and Joseph cooperated with God's plan for the Incarnation and as spouses in raising the child Jesus.
- Saint Paul traveled throughout the Mediterranean world to bring the Good News of salvation to countless people.

In Church History:

- Saint Francis and Saint Clare of Assisi both served the Church in the Late Middle Ages by founding religious orders: the Franciscans and the Poor Clares, respectively.
- Dorothy Day and Peter Maurin cofounded the Catholic Worker movement in 1933. Catholic Worker members commit themselves to taking care of the basic material needs of the poorest and most marginalized people, living simply and in community, and advocating for social change.

man and woman: "That is why a man leaves his father and mother and clings to his wife, and the two of them become one body" (2:24).

Created as Equals

Because God created men and women in his own divine image as equals, both women and men are born with a God-given dignity. As creatures made in God's image, we reflect his wisdom and goodness. Thus, even though men and women are physically different from each other, we are the same in the ways that matter most. We are equal in our dignity, in our rights, and in our capacity to be signs of God's presence in the world.

Historically, the dignity and rights of women have not been universally respected. Many ongoing social problems demonstrate the unfair and unjust treatment of women in society. For example, women and girls are often the victims of violence, especially sexual violence. Many girls in developing countries also lack access to education. The Second Vatican Council took note of this more than fifty years ago: "It is deeply to be deplored that these basic personal rights are not yet being respected everywhere, as is the case with women who are denied the chance freely to choose a husband, or a state of life, or to have access to the same educational and cultural benefits as are available to men" (*The Church in the Modern World*, 29). The Second Vatican Council urged our support of efforts to promote social justice, equity, and human dignity so that all God's people, both women and men, might flourish.

Created with the Gift of Sexuality

In creating us male and female, God has given us the wonderful gift of sexuality. Initially, our sexuality is rooted in our physical bodies, making us either male or female. Later, as we develop, we prepare for the possibility of marriage and family life. If God calls us to the Sacrament of Marriage, we will join our body with that of our future spouse. If God wills it, we will then bring

forth new life into the world by having children. However, sexuality is broader than just our physical capacity for **procreation**. "*Sexuality* affects all aspects of the
human person. . . . It especially concerns affectivity, the
capacity to love and to procreate, and in a more general
way the aptitude for forming bonds of communion with
others" (CCC, 2332). Our sexuality is a sign of our call
to love and to live in communion with God and one
another.

The gift of sexuality, however, also comes with the
responsibility to cultivate the virtue of **chastity**. To be
chaste means to live a life of sexual integrity. This is
easier to understand when we recognize that integrity
comes from the root word *integer,* meaning "whole." To
be chaste is to be whole. We must integrate our sexuality within our whole selves so that what we do with our
bodies is also fully united with the spiritual dimension of
our selves. A chaste person's thoughts, words, and actions

procreation
The act or process
of conceiving and
bearing children.

chastity
The virtue by
which people
are able to
successfully
and healthfully
integrate their
sexuality into
their total person;
recognized as one
of the fruits of the
Holy Spirit. Also
one of the vows of
religious life.

Primary Sources

Reflecting God's Goodness: "Letter of His Holiness Pope John Paul II to Artists"

In his letter to artists, issued on Easter Sunday of 1999, Pope Saint John
Paul II draws particular attention to how artists reflect and embody God's
creative love. He writes of the "vocation and mission" of poets, writers, sculptors, architects, musicians, actors, painters, playwrights, and filmmakers.
Perhaps Saint John Paul II had a special insight into the mission of artists
because as a young man he was an actor and playwright himself before
becoming a priest.

Addressing individual artists of all types directly, the Pope writes:

None can sense more deeply than you artists, ingenious creators of
beauty that you are, something of the pathos with which God at the dawn
of creation looked upon the work of his hands. A glimmer of that feeling
has shone so often in your eyes when—like the artists of every age—captivated by the hidden power of sounds and words, colours and shapes,
you have admired the work of your inspiration, sensing in it some echo of
the mystery of creation with which God, the sole creator of all things, has
wished in some way to associate you. (1)

genocide
The systematic and planned extermination of a national, racial, ethnic, or cultural group.

all reflect God's purpose for the gift of sexuality. All the baptized are called to develop the virtue of chastity in a way that is in keeping with their states of life.

> **How does the communion between Adam and Eve described in Genesis reflect the true communion we are all meant to share?**

Article 49: The Inherent Dignity of All Human Life

Throughout his ministry and life on earth, Jesus revealed that all people have an inherent dignity. Therefore we must respect human life in all its forms. Catholics call this reverence for, and protection of, human life the *consistent ethic of life*. This ethic applies to life in all its stages—at its very beginning, at its very end, and at every point in between.

The Sacred Gift of Life

Catholics understand life to be a sacred gift because we are created in the image and likeness of the one true and living God. Because God is the author and originator of all life, only he can decide the time for an individual human life to end. Any attempt to alter this course of events is a violation of the Fifth Commandment, "You shall not kill" (Exodus 20:13). Killing another person, at any stage of that person's life, is an offense against her or his own dignity and against the holiness of the Creator.

There are many facets to the Church's consistent ethic of life. Vatican II's *The Church in the Modern World* lists ways this ethic may be violated, including **genocide**, suicide, torture, human trafficking, and degrading working conditions (see 27). Central to the Church's teachings on issues of life are the ethics surrounding life's very beginnings and its very end.

The Beginning of Life

Human life begins at the moment of conception—when the egg and the sperm unite and a baby, a new human being with a unique genetic code, begins the long process of development in the womb. For this reason, the Church strongly opposes abortion—the intentional termination of a pregnancy—in all circumstances. Abortion ends the life of the most vulnerable individual in society, the developing child in its mother's womb.

Because a human **embryo** or **fetus** is a human being, created in God's image and likeness, it must be respected and protected from the moment of conception. From the first moment of existence, a human being has the rights of a full person, including the right to life. Medical science has advanced to such an extent that many diseases can be diagnosed, and some even treated, while the embryo or fetus remains in the womb. Doctors can even operate on an embryo or fetus. The Church accepts such procedures only if they respect the integrity and life of the embryo. The procedures must not involve "disproportionate risks" (CCC, 2275) to the developing child, and they must be "directed toward its healing, the improvement of its condition of health, or its individual survival" (2275).

embryo
The unborn child from the time it implants in the uterine wall through the eighth week of its development.

fetus
The unborn child from the end of the eighth week after conception to the moment of birth.

The End of Life

Euthanasia is a direct action, or deliberate and purposeful lack of action, that causes the death of a person who is disabled, sick, or dying. The most common justification given for euthanasia is that it relieves pain and suffering by hastening death.

We act on our respect for the sanctity of life by treating those who are at the end of life with dignity, care, and compassion.

The Church recognizes the reality of suffering for those at the end of life but definitely rejects the perspective that hastening death can ever be a truly moral choice. Instead of offering death as a solution to pain and suffering, we must guide dying people to see a great truth in their final days, that they are deeply united with the sufferings of the Crucified Christ. We must also strive to relieve the suffering of

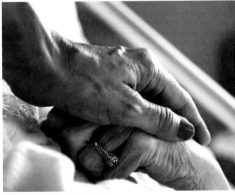

© Dennis Sabo / shutterstock.com

those at the end of life through the use of medicines as well as emotional and social support. As people of God, we must never try to determine the day or the hour when our earthly journey will be complete. The decision to end our earthly existence should be left entirely to God.

Why is it important to protect human life during all its stages?

For Review

1. What three basic truths are at the heart of human dignity?

2. If God created humans as essentially good, why do we need redemption?

3. What is most significant in the idea that a person is "not just something, but someone"?

4. Describe how Jesus respected the dignity of others during his earthly ministry.

5. How does Jesus restore what was lost through sin?

6. How can we participate in God's creative work?

7. Describe an example from the Bible of individuals cooperating with one another and with God in the divine plan of salvation.

8. Even though men and women are physically different, how are they created as equal?

9. What is the consistent ethic of life?

10. Define *abortion* and *euthanasia,* and explain why they are wrong.

We Are Children of God

Introduction

Through his saving work on earth, Jesus enables us to become adopted children of his Divine Father. Through the life-giving waters of the Sacrament of Baptism, we are transformed anew by the power of the Holy Spirit. Thus we are able to build our lives on the certain knowledge that God desires our happiness. While we live on earth, God listens attentively to our prayers, responding to us with abundant love, mercy, and compassion. God also gives us sanctifying grace so we can live in a way that reflects our inherent Christian dignity. At the end of our earthly lives, God offers us a new life in Heaven: perfect and unending joy in the holy presence of the Blessed Trinity. We are indeed fortunate and blessed to share in God's divine life both on earth and in Heaven, a life that overflows with bountiful, compassionate love for all creation.

Heaven
A state of eternal life and union with God, in which one experiences full happiness and the satisfaction of the deepest human longings.

Article 50: God Desires Our Happiness

The universal axiom *everyone wants to be happy* is easy to understand. However, we may wonder if God also wants us to be happy. The Church teaches us that God most definitely wants us to be happy; in fact, he created us to be truly and deeply happy, both during our time on earth and eternally with him in **Heaven**. We know that our desire for happiness comes from God. As the *Catechism of the Catholic Church* (*CCC*) explains, our desire for happiness is "of divine origin," for "God has placed it in the human heart" (1718). Because God is the source of our desire, only he can truly fulfill it. As Saint Augustine said in his *Confessions,* "You have made us for yourself, O Lord, and our hearts are restless until they rest in you."

Original Happiness: Lost by Sin, Restored by Christ

The Book of Genesis offers us a vision of the state of happiness that God originally intended for us. At first, humankind lived in harmony with God, with one another, and with nature in a state of holiness and justice. After the Fall from Grace, this original, blessed state of unity and peace was lost due to human sinfulness.

Because of the Fall, humanity is in need of redemption. We need God to restore our ability to live in right relationship with one another and to give us again the happiness that results from living as he desires. To ensure our redemption, God the Father sent Jesus Christ the Eternal Son to save us through the Paschal Mystery— Jesus' Passion, death, Resurrection, and Ascension. Like the suffering servant of whom the prophet Isaiah wrote, Jesus "surrendered himself to death, / was counted among the transgressors" and "bore the sins of many" (Isaiah 53:12). Or, as Saint Paul described it, Jesus "died for our sins in accordance with the scriptures" (1 Corinthians 15:3). Although Jesus was the Perfect and Eternal Son of God, he lived and died as a man. Jesus gave his life "as a ransom for many" (Matthew 20:28), dying for all people everywhere and throughout time. Truly, the saving work of the Paschal Mystery gives us cause for happiness, gratitude, and hope.

True Joy

When we believe in the saving, redemptive work of Jesus Christ, we are not guaranteed happiness every single day. Like all people, we too experience good days and bad days, happiness and sorrow, success and failure. Yet we can find comfort and reassurance in the promise Jesus offered his disciples shortly before his sacrificial death on the cross: "I have told you this so that my joy may be in you and your joy may be complete" (John 15:11). Indeed joy is one of the fruits of the Holy Spirit, one of the "perfections that the Holy Spirit forms in us as the first fruits of eternal glory" (CCC, 1832). True joy is the mark of the authentic Christian. In fact, Saint Paul urges us: "Rejoice in the Lord always. I shall say it again: rejoice!" (Philippians 4:4). Despite the inevitable ups and downs of daily

Primary Sources

Joy through Faith

The first encyclical by Pope Francis, *The Light of Faith (Lumen Fidei)*, is part of a series of encyclical letters on the Theological Virtues of faith, hope, and charity first begun by his predecessor, Pope Benedict XVI. *The Light of Faith* focuses on the many dimensions of faith, God's gift of salvation, and the role of Jesus in the Revelation of God. The following excerpt explores the joy that young people—and all of us—can experience through a life committed to Christ:

> We have all seen, during World Youth Days, the joy that young people show in their faith and their desire for an ever more solid and generous life of faith. Young people want to live life to the fullest. Encountering Christ, letting themselves be caught up in and guided by his love, enlarges the horizons of existence, gives it a firm hope which will not disappoint. Faith is no refuge for the fainthearted, but something which enhances our lives. It makes us aware of a magnificent calling, the vocation of love. It assures us that this love is trustworthy and worth embracing, for it is based on God's faithfulness which is stronger than our every weakness. (53)

sanctifying grace

The grace that heals our human nature wounded by sin and restores us to friendship with God by giving us a share in the divine life of the Trinity. It is a supernatural gift of God, infused into our souls by the Holy Spirit, that continues the work of making us holy.

life, faith in Jesus offers us a solid foundation on which to build a life that is full of deep and abiding joy.

The Beatitudes and Happiness

The Beatitudes present us with a specific vision of the happiness God desires for us. The Beatitudes are found in the Gospel of Matthew (see 5:3–11) and the Gospel of Luke (see 6:20–26). They are part of the Sermon on the Mount in Matthew and the Sermon on the Plain in Luke. In both Gospel accounts, we find some of the key teachings of Jesus distilled and clearly delineated. Interestingly, the word *beatitude* is derived from the Latin and means happy, fortunate, or blissful. In the Beatitudes, Jesus proclaims certain groups of people to be blessed, such as mourners, the meek, the poor in spirit, the merciful, the clean of heart, and the persecuted.

Characteristics like being poor, persecuted, or meek may seem like odd qualifications for happiness. Indeed the vision of the Kingdom that Jesus offers in the Beatitudes thwarts our common understanding of happiness. Like the prayer of Mary of Nazareth, which praises God as the One who fills the hungry and sends the rich away (see Luke 1:53), Jesus teaches us in the Beatitudes that real happiness does not lie in money, possessions, power, or prestige. As Christians, our sense of joy and gratitude is found when we show mercy, fight for righteousness, and make peace.

Why does God want us to be happy?

Article 51: Baptism: Becoming God's Adopted Children

Through the saving work of Jesus Christ on earth, we are able to become children of God. We become God's children through the Sacrament of Baptism, in which we receive **sanctifying grace** and come to share in the life of the Blessed Trinity.

God's Children and Heirs

Through the Sacrament of Baptism, we enter into a whole new relationship with God. When we are baptized, we become God's freely adopted children and heirs to his promises. The Sacrament of Baptism transforms the newly baptized person and makes him or her a Temple of the Holy Spirit, united with Christ and his divine nature. Saint Paul contrasts the new status of the baptized person—a freely adopted son or daughter of God—with his or her former state—a slave to sin. In his Letter to the Romans, Saint Paul writes:

> For those who are led by the Spirit of God are children of God. For you did not receive a spirit of slavery to fall back into fear, but you received a spirit of adoption, through which we cry "*Abba*, Father!" The Spirit itself bears witness with our spirit that we are children of God, and if children, then heirs, heirs of God and joint heirs with Christ, if only we suffer with him so that we may also be glorified with him. (8:14–17)

Saint Paul expressed a similar idea concerning our heirship to God's Kingdom in his letter to the Galatians: "So you are no longer a slave but a child, and if a child then also an heir, through God" (4:7).

Baptism also gives us a whole new relationship with other fellow believers in Christ. Because all baptized people have become God's adopted children, our differences, which may sometimes seem to define us, are not important in the Church. Baptism creates profound equality among believers, for through the Sacrament we are reborn as "the one People of God of the **New Covenant**, which transcends all the natural or human limits of nations, cultures, races, and sexes" (CCC, 1267). Saint Paul described the reality of this universal oneness in Christ in a biblical passage used in the baptismal liturgies of the early Church: "For through faith you are all children of God in Christ Jesus. For all of you who were baptized into Christ have clothed yourselves with Christ. There is neither Jew nor Greek, there is neither slave nor free person, there is not male and female; for you are all one in Christ Jesus" (Galatians 3:26–28).

New Covenant
The covenant or law established by God in Jesus Christ to fulfill and perfect the Old Covenant or Mosaic Law. It is a perfection here on earth of the divine law. The law of the New Covenant is called a law of love, grace, and freedom. The New Covenant will never end or diminish, and nothing new will be revealed until Christ comes again in glory.

The Role of Grace

The sanctifying grace of Baptism transforms both our relationship with God and our relationship with other believers. Because grace is a freely offered gift of God, it is not something that we have to earn, work for, or deserve. The grace we receive in Baptism enables us to share in the closeness of the Blessed Trinity and to respond wholeheartedly to our Christian vocation of living in a way that is worthy of God's adopted children.

Why do you think God freely offers us grace?

Did You Know?

Rite of Christian Initiation for Adults (RCIA)

When a baby is born into a Catholic family, the baby is usually baptized as an infant. For adults, the process of becoming baptized, known as Christian initiation, springs from the practice of the early Church. In the time of the early Church, people who wished to become Christians were invited to learn about Christianity before being admitted to the Church as children of God through the Sacrament of Baptism. The early converts to Christianity followed a series of steps that gradually formed them into disciples of Jesus.

Today this process is called the Rite of Christian Initiation of Adults (RCIA). During the course of about a year, adults in this program learn about Jesus, the Church, and what the Christian life is all about. At first, the initiates begin as inquirers, asking questions about the Catholic faith. Next they continue on as catechumens, or those preparing to be baptized. When the catechumens have been accepted for Baptism, usually in a ceremony at the cathedral of their diocese or archdiocese, they are called the elect. Catechumens are baptized and confirmed during the Easter Vigil, when they become children of God and part of the Body of Christ. At the Easter Vigil, the newly baptized receive the Eucharist for the first time. Now they are ready to live their faith in Christ for the rest of their lives!

Sometimes adults who have been baptized in another Christian Church or faith community wish to become Catholics. These individuals are not baptized again, but are received into full Communion with the Church through the Sacrament of Penance and Reconciliation, and, usually at the Easter Vigil, a Profession of Faith (the Creed), followed by the Sacraments of Confirmation and the Eucharist.

Article 52: Eternal Life: Our Ultimate Destiny

As God's beloved children, created in love and redeemed by grace, we are destined to live forever in the glory of his holy presence. Faith in God leads us to turn to him alone because it is God who first created us and it is God to whom we will return. We should neither prefer anything to God nor substitute anything for him, for nothing can take the place of God in our lives.

Sharing in Jesus' Resurrection

After Jesus had freely submitted himself to suffering and death, God the Father raised him up to a glorious new life. This event is called the Resurrection, and it is

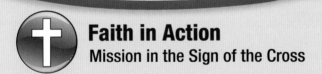

Faith in Action
Mission in the Sign of the Cross

When we are baptized, we are baptized in the Sign of the Cross: in the name of the Father, and of the Son, and of the Holy Spirit. The priests, brothers, sisters, and associates of the international Holy Cross family confront the mystery of the Cross—the life, death, Resurrection, and Ascension of Jesus—in the needs of the people they serve.

The Congregation of Holy Cross is a congregation of priests and brothers. Founded by Father Basil Moreau in Le Mans, France, in 1835, this congregation's mission grew out of service to a particular place and time: the village of Sainte-Croix (Holy Cross), on the outskirts of Le Mans. Today the Congregation of Holy Cross can be found across the United States and around the world. It sponsors and staffs institutes of Catholic higher education (including the University of Notre Dame in South Bend, Indiana), parishes, and ministries on five continents. The congregation also offers laypeople the opportunity to serve in mission lands through Overseas Lay Ministry.

A group of women religious also founded by Father Moreau form three distinct congregations today: the Sisters of the Holy Cross based in South Bend, Indiana; the Marianites of the Holy Cross based in Louisiana and in Le Mans, France; and the Sisters of Holy Cross, based in Canada. The Sisters of the Holy Cross in South Bend also sponsor an associate program that welcomes laypeople to share their spirituality and mission: to meet the unmet needs of people today, through compassion, faith, prayer, and community.

Purgatory
A state of final purification or cleansing, which one may need to enter following death and before entering Heaven.

the heart of the Paschal Mystery. You may be wondering, how exactly do we fit into the Resurrection of Jesus? Through the Sacrament of Baptism, we are baptized into Christ's death so that when we die, we may also share in his Resurrection. Saint Paul explains it this way:

> Or are you unaware that we who were baptized into Christ Jesus were baptized into his death? We were indeed buried with him through baptism into death, so that, just as Christ was raised from the dead by the glory of the Father, we too might live in newness of life.
>
> For if we have grown into union with him through a death like his, we shall also be united with him in the resurrection. (Romans 6:3–5)

To put it more simply, we who have been baptized into Christ's own body will, like him, be raised to immortality. We will live forever with God, sharing in the life of the Blessed Trinity.

Heaven

When we experience the presence and communion of the Blessed Trinity, we will know Heaven. In Heaven we will find complete happiness and spiritual perfection with all the blessed who are united in Christ. Through his death and Resurrection, Jesus made Heaven accessible to all people. Heaven is the final resting place for those who die in God's grace and friendship, who have been faithful to

Pray It!

The Act of Hope

Are you familiar with the prayer called the "Act of Hope"? Traditionally, an Act of Hope would be preceded by an Act of Faith and then followed by an Act of Charity, all important meditations in the Catholic prayer life. The Act of Hope affirms that Jesus is our Redeemer and expresses our hope for eternal life. Pray this prayer often. Consider making it a part of your daily prayers.

O my God, trusting in your infinite goodness and promises, I hope to obtain pardon of my sins, the help of your grace, and life everlasting, through the merits of Jesus Christ, my Lord and redeemer. Amen.

God's will, and who are perfectly purified. Some people are already perfectly purified when they die; others will experience a final cleansing in **Purgatory** before entering Heaven.

What is Heaven like? Heaven is a mystery that surpasses our human comprehension. Although words cannot fully express the joy of Heaven, we understand it as the perfect communion with God himself and with all those united in Christ. Sacred Scripture conveys the beauty and joy of Heaven through symbolic words and images, like light, peace, wedding feast, wine of the kingdom, the Father's house, the heavenly Jerusalem, and paradise. Although we may attempt to put the beauty and peace of Heaven into human terms, we always fall short: "What eye has not seen, and ear has not heard, / and what has not entered the human heart, / what God has prepared for those who love him" (1 Corinthians 2:9). No symbol or image, however, can fully capture the power and awe of seeing God face-to-face, "as he is" (1 John 3:2).

© 26kot / shutterstock.com

Live It!
Living the Beatitudes

In the Beatitudes, Jesus presents us with a set of instructions for how we are to live that are contrary to attitudes and values society often promotes. For example, Jesus says, "Blessed are the poor in spirit" (Matthew 5:3) and "Blessed are the meek" (Matthew 5:5), and tells us that these people will be rewarded. Society, on the other hand, often encourages us to seek power, control, and glory, and praises and values those who attain these attributes.

Read the Beatitudes in Matthew's Gospel (see 5:3–11). Select two beatitudes and reflect on how young people today can live them out. Then think of specific ways you can live them out in your own life today and every day. Repeat this exercise each day with another beatitude until you have reflected on each. Make a commitment to truly live by the Beatitudes every day.

Particular Judgment
The judgment that occurs immediately at time of our death, when our immortal souls will be judged as worthy or unworthy of Heaven.

When do we go to Heaven? Immediately upon our death, our immortal souls are judged to be either worthy or unworthy of their place in Heaven alongside the Blessed Trinity. This event is called the **Particular Judgment**. Furthermore, Jesus Christ will pass judgment on the entire human race at his Second Coming, at the time of the Last Judgment, also known as the Final Judgment. In the Gospel of Matthew, this event is depicted as the Judgment of the Nations (see 25:31–46).

Preparing for Eternal Life with God: The Catholic Funeral Liturgy

Although funerals are often sad occasions, the rituals and symbols of the Catholic funeral liturgy strengthen our belief that the baptized are destined to share in eternal life with God. In fact, many elements of the funeral liturgy explicitly connect with the liturgy of Baptism:

- **Holy water** Sprinkling the coffin or urn with holy water "reminds the assembly of the saving waters of Baptism" (*Order of Christian Funerals,* 36).

© Bill Wittman / www.wpwittman.com

- **Funeral pall** Covering the coffin with a white cloth, called a pall, is a sign of Christian dignity, which calls to mind the same white "baptismal garment of the deceased" (38).

- **Paschal candle** The lighting of the Paschal (Easter) candle "reminds the faithful of Christ's undying presence among them, of his victory over sin and death, and of their share in that victory by virtue of their initiation" (35).

- **Incense** Incensing the coffin or urn is "a sign of honor to the body of the deceased, which through Baptism became the temple of the Holy Spirit" (37).

Even as we grieve for the loss of a loved one, we can find comfort, and even joy, in our confident hope that he or she will share in the glorious life of the Blessed Trinity—a life we hope, one day, to experience ourselves.

What do people sometimes substitute for God?
How can you put God first in your life?

For Review

1. Where does the human desire for happiness come from?

2. What do the Beatitudes tell us about happiness?

3. What are the effects of the Sacrament of Baptism?

4. What is sanctifying grace?

5. In what way is the Resurrection of Jesus also about us?

6. What is Heaven?

7. Explain how the rituals and symbols of a Catholic funeral connect with the liturgy of Baptism.

Chapter 12

Jesus Reveals
Our Call to Holiness

Introduction

One of the best ways to learn about Jesus' teachings is to read the Gospels. Though all four Gospels, in their entirety, are worthy of our prayerful reflection, certain passages make our call to holiness especially clear. In passages like the Sermon on the Mount, Jesus' conversation with the rich man, the Great Commandment, and the parables, we clearly see what Jesus asks of his disciples. Through these biblical accounts, we glimpse the vision of the Reign of God, in which Jesus invites us to share. Furthermore, when we study the teachings of Jesus contained in the Gospels, we begin to understand how remaining faithful to the Word of God allows us to be participants in God's Reign on earth. By reading, studying, and living the teachings of Christ in Sacred Scripture, we receive strength for our journey toward our ultimate destiny—union with the life of the Blessed Trinity.

Article 53: The Sermon on the Mount

The Sermon on the Mount is a collection of Jesus' teachings on many important topics, which the Gospel of Matthew presents as a speech given by Jesus. In it Jesus speaks about love of enemies, anger, adultery, divorce, retaliation, judging others, and prayer, among other things. The following section considers several key points of this sermon.

The Beatitudes: Our Doorway to the Kingdom of Heaven

The Sermon on the Mount (see Matthew 5—7; called the Sermon on the Plain in Luke's Gospel [see 20–49]) begins with the Beatitudes (see Matthew 5:3-12, the series of teachings in which Jesus pronounces as "blessed" certain unlikely groups of people, such as the poor in spirit, the meek, and the persecuted). In this way, the Beatitudes identify the actions and attitudes that are most characteristic of the Christian life and show us our final goal as people of God: the state of beatitude. Beatitude—also known as the Kingdom or Reign of God, the vision of God, the joy of the Lord, or God's rest—is our ultimate vocation as disciples of Christ, for it allows us eternal blessedness with God in Heaven. Furthermore, beatitude enables us to share in the glory of Christ and in the joy of the Trinitarian life. This gift that God freely offers to us is love.

We know that our ultimate end is sharing in the life of the Blessed Trinity in Heaven. This fact invites us to conduct our lives in a way that is worthy of this destiny. The Beatitudes encourage us to put aside our desire for riches, fame, power, or prestige and to instead make mercy, peacemaking, and righteousness our priorities. In this way, we enter into the blessings of the Kingdom of Heaven, which we experience now in an incomplete way while looking forward to their fullness at the end of time.

Abba
A way of addressing God the Father used by Jesus to call attention to his—and our—intimate relationship with his Heavenly Father. *Abba* means "my Father" or "our Father" in Aramaic.

mammon
An Aramaic word meaning wealth or property.

God or Money: You Cannot Serve Both

Do you put most of your trust in yourself, other people, or what you have? What about putting all of your trust in God? In the Sermon on the Mount, Jesus stresses the importance of our dependence on God. He begins by stating: "Therefore I tell you, do not worry about your life, what you will eat [or drink], or about your body, what you will wear. Is not life more than food and the body more than clothing? Look at the birds in the sky; they do not sow or reap, they gather nothing into barns, yet your heavenly Father feeds them. Are not you more important than they?" (Matthew 6:25–26). Here Jesus challenges us to put our trust in God with our whole hearts. In talking about how people worry about what they will eat or drink, about what they will wear, and about their physical health and appearance, Jesus is addressing the same material concerns that preoccupy us today. Jesus invites us to let go of unproductive worries, "Can any of you by worrying add a single moment to your life-span?" (Matthew 6:27), and to make faith in the One he called **Abba** our first priority. God alone knows what we truly need, and God alone will provide for us.

Jesus also recognizes that when we are worried, we often place our trust where it does not belong: in money or in material possessions. Jesus cautions against this when he says: "No one can serve two masters. He will either hate one and love the other, or be devoted to one and despise the other. You cannot serve God and **mammon**" (Matthew 6:24). Jesus reminds us that "treasures on earth" can be destroyed or stolen, whereas "treasures in heaven" last eternally (6:19,20). He warns us that trusting in material things can distort our perspective regarding what is really important, and may lead us to value things more than people, status more than service, and money more than God. As we see in Matthew 6:24, Jesus confronts us with a clear choice: God or material riches. If we choose God, we will find true and lasting joy; if we choose worldly gain, we will find only a fleeting, temporary happiness.

Jesus' Teachings on Prayer, Fasting, and Almsgiving

In the Sermon on the Mount, Jesus explicitly teaches us about the value of almsgiving, prayer, and fasting, offering concrete and clear instruction. A portion of the Sermon on the Mount (see Matthew 6:1–6,16–18) is always read on Ash Wednesday, the beginning of the liturgical season of Lent. This passage teaches us about the traditional Lenten disciplines, or practices.

parables
Short stories that use everyday images to communicate religious messages. Jesus used parables frequently in his teaching as a way of presenting the Good News of salvation.

- **Prayer** Jesus urges us to pray sincerely, seeking God's presence with humility. We should not pray in a way that tries to draw the approval of others.

- **Fasting** Jesus invites us to fast as an act of genuine repentance, not as a ploy to impress other people.

- **Almsgiving** Jesus wants us to share generously with our sisters and brothers in need. We should act out of an authentic desire to lessen their suffering, and not to gain reward or recognition for ourselves.

Prayer, fasting, and almsgiving are interrelated practices. Prayer strengthens our resolve to fast and our generosity in giving alms. Fasting turns our hearts toward God, the Source of all we need, and cultivates compassion in us for those who will benefit from our almsgiving. Almsgiving ensures that our prayer and fasting give rise to a concrete response to the needs of the poor. Together these practices are hallmarks of Christian spirituality, both during the season of Lent and throughout the year.

Why is it important to pray, fast, and give alms without regard for reward or recognition?

© Bill Wittman / www.wpwittman.com

Article 54: The Parables of Jesus

Parables are stories that use everyday images and metaphors to convey religious truths. Parables are intended to bring about the self-knowledge and conversion of the listener by an implicit comparison of the listener to something in the parable. Jesus' parables are an important part of his proclamation of the Kingdom of God and of his invitation to all people to enter and take their places at the feast of the Kingdom. As a great teacher, Jesus knew the power of a vivid story to captivate the imagination and stir the hearts of his listeners. Although his parables are not long (the shortest is just one verse; the longest is twenty-one verses), they are memorable, powerful, and thought provoking. They often contain a narrative twist, or some element of surprise, that shocks us into thinking differently about ourselves, the world, or God. The parables of Jesus force us to confront ourselves, to examine our priorities, and to make difficult choices. Jesus used the parable as a kind of teaching tool, demonstrating through story the Good News of salvation.

The following section considers several of the more than thirty parables of Jesus contained in the Gospels.

The Treasure in the Field and the Pearl of Great Price (Matthew 13:44–46)

These parables are among Jesus' shortest—two stories in a mere three verses. In both parables, a man sells everything he has to buy only one thing. In the first parable, that one thing is a field in which the man has found a buried treasure; in the second parable, it is a fine, valuable pearl. Both stories invite us to commit ourselves fully to leading lives of discipleship, responding wholeheartedly to Jesus' proclamation of the Kingdom. This level of commitment often carries a great cost and involves sacrifice on our part. However, we should take note of the attitude of the man in the first parable. He sells all he has in a spirit of absolute happiness: "The kingdom of heaven is like a treasure buried in a field, which a person finds and hides again, and out of joy goes and sells all that he has and buys that field" (verse 44). When we are open to the presence and grace of the Holy Spirit, making a sacrifice for the sake of the Kingdom need not be burdensome; it should, in fact, be welcomed as a delight.

The Parable of the Great Feast
(Luke 14:16–24)

In Luke's Gospel, Jesus tells a parable about a man who hosts an elaborate dinner party. The invited guests all give reasons why they cannot attend the event. Although their excuses seem reasonable (for example, they have made major purchases and must tend to them, or have just been married), the host is angered. In his rage, the man decides to fill his home with the poor, the crippled, the blind, and the lame. When this is done and there is still room at the feast, the man has people pulled from the street in order to fill his home. The parable concludes with the host stating, "For, I tell you, none of those men who were invited will taste my dinner" (verse 24). Through this rather simple and straightforward parable, Jesus offers us a profound and stirring image of the Kingdom of Heaven—a great feast at which all people are welcome, especially those who may not be welcome anywhere else. The parable invites us to think about how our actions and decisions—especially our decisions to include or exclude others—should reflect this vision of the Kingdom.

Primary Sources

Jesus of Nazareth: From the Baptism in the Jordan to the Transfiguration, by Pope Benedict XVI

In his 2007 book *Jesus of Nazareth*, Pope Benedict XVI devotes a chapter to the message of the parables. He explores the nature and purpose of the parables and discusses the Parable of the Good Samaritan, the Parable of the Lost Son, and the Parable of the Rich Man and Lazarus. Below is an excerpt from the chapter "The Message of the Parables: The Nature and Purpose of the Parables":

> There is no doubt that the parables constitute the heart of Jesus' preaching. While civilizations have come and gone, these stories continue to touch us anew with their freshness and their humanity. Here we have a very immediate sense . . . of the closeness to Jesus as he lived and taught. At the same time, though, we find ourselves in the same situation as Jesus' contemporaries and even his disciples: We need to ask him again and again what he wants to say to us in each of the parables (cf. Mk 4:10).

The Parables of the Lost Sheep, the Lost Coin, and the Lost Son (Luke, Chapter 15)

Chapter 15 of Luke's Gospel contains three of the best known and most loved parables of Jesus, all of which express a common theme, that of great loss and joyous return. In the Parable of the Lost Sheep, a shepherd leaves his flock of ninety-nine sheep in the desert to search for one lost sheep. When he finds the lost one, he invites his friends and neighbors to rejoice with him. The Parable of the Lost Coin is similarly structured: a woman who has lost one of her ten silver coins diligently searches her home until she finds it. Like the shepherd, she also calls her friends to celebrate with her when she finds it.

The third and final parable in this sequence, the Parable of the Lost Son, commonly known as the Parable of the Prodigal Son, depicts the loss of a son in emotional and spiritual terms. When the son finally makes his way back home, his father runs to greet him, welcoming him with great rejoicing and celebration.

Read Luke 15:11–32. Whom in the parable can you identify with? When in your life have you felt lost, like the younger son? abandoned like the father? jealous like the older son?

These three parables tell us much about the Good News of salvation and the Kingdom of God that Jesus proclaimed. When we reflect on the symbolic meaning of the lost sheep, the lost coin, and the lost son, we can come to understand that no matter how long we have been lost in sin or how far we have strayed from God, it is never too late to turn our hearts back toward his saving grace. If we imagine God as the shepherd searching for his sheep, as the woman hunting for her coin, or as the father waiting for his son to return home, we see his infinite mercy and unending patience. God's love will never fail to find us, welcome us home, and rejoice at our return.

Do you think that the parable is a useful and effective teaching tool? Why do you think Jesus employed it so often in his Gospel teachings?

© North Carolina Museum of Art / CORBIS

Article 55: Jesus and the Rich Man (Mark 10:17–22)

Through the Gospels, Jesus teaches us what we must do to grow in holiness and in goodness. Although he invites us, by his example, to lead lives committed to the service of our fellow sisters and brothers, we may find that other priorities can stand in our way, interfering with our wholehearted commitment to Christian discipleship. We may find that a love of money or attachments to material things limit our ability to fully engage in the Gospel message and Jesus' call to discipleship. As we see in chapter 10 of Mark's Gospel, Jesus' words to the rich man challenge us to radically rethink our priorities and our lives: "Go, sell what you have, and give to [the] poor and you will have treasure in heaven; then come, follow me" (verse 21). Although there are parallel passages in the other **synoptic Gospels**, here we will focus on the one-on-one conversation Jesus has with a rich man in Mark's Gospel.

synoptic Gospels
From the Greek for "seeing the whole together," the name given to the Gospels of Matthew, Mark, and Luke, because they are similar in style and content.

"Good Teacher, What Must I Do?"

After the Gospel account of the blessing of the children (see Mark 10:13–16), Jesus is approached by the rich

Pray It!

When Jesus Calls

In the following prayer, we ask Jesus to grant us the ability to transcend the material and unimportant things of this world. With Jesus' help, we hope to achieve a new openness to the needs of others.

Dear Jesus, help us not to be afraid of your call, whether in small or big things. Sometimes we can get comfortable and think we are doing enough in response. Sometimes we get too concerned about what others will think about us. When these things happen, help us to be fearless and to strive to do more.

Jesus, help us to be open in our prayer to hear your call. Open our ears to your Word so we can better live its meaning in our daily lives. Give us the grace we need to become more like you. Amen.

man: "As he was setting out on a journey, a man ran up, knelt down before him, and asked him, 'Good teacher, what must I do to inherit eternal life?'" (10:17). Jesus answers the man by quoting a shortened version of the Ten Commandments, laws that would have been very familiar to a faithful Jew in the time of Christ. When the man indicates that he has observed these laws since the days of his youth, Jesus looks at him with love, saying: "You are lacking in one thing. Go, sell what you have, and give to [the] poor and you will have treasure in heaven; then come, follow me" (10:21). You may wonder, why does Jesus love this man? He does not seem to have done anything extraordinary or heroic, yet Jesus recognizes in the man a sincere desire to follow him. The rich man has sought out Jesus, making an effort to ask his question

Faith in Action
Dorothy Day and the Catholic Worker

© Bettmann / CORBIS

Dorothy Day was born in 1897 in Brooklyn, New York, and made her career as a journalist. Baptized Episcopalian, she did not practice her faith until after she became pregnant out of wedlock and decided to have her daughter baptized as a Catholic. She herself soon followed suit, becoming Catholic in 1927. When she met the activist Peter Maurin several years later, the two started an organization called the Catholic Worker. Together they published a newspaper that advocated for the rights of workers and opened a "house of hospitality" to provide food, shelter, and other assistance to the many people of New York City struggling during the Great Depression.

The Catholic Worker soon grew into a nationwide, and then worldwide, movement. Today houses of hospitality continue the work Day and Maurin began by serving the poor in the name of Christ and by advocating for just social policies.

Dorothy Day died on November 29, 1980. She had truly lived out the words of Jesus to the rich man: "Go, sell what you have, and give to [the] poor" (Mark 10:21). Her example challenges each of us to examine our own willingness to make service of the poor and the transformation of unjust social structures priorities in our lives.

and to listen to Jesus' response. Although the man since childhood has been living in a way that is pleasing to God, he desires to do more.

"Go, Sell What You Have"

Jesus recognizes that the rich man's possessions and wealth are obstacles to his further growth in holiness. Jesus tells the man to sell what he has and to give to the poor, and then the rich man will have his "treasure in heaven." Jesus invites the man to a life that is focused not on acquiring more possessions but on caring for all those in need. Jesus asks the man to live in a way that witnesses to the power and presence of the Kingdom of Heaven on earth.

The man has no further response to Jesus' instructions. Mark's Gospel simply states that "his face fell, and he went away sad, for he had many possessions" (10:22). The rich man's story ends here. We don't know if the man accepted Jesus' invitation to discipleship and eternal life or not. Was he able to overcome his sadness and take up Christ's call to follow? Or was he too afraid to let go of his many possessions, too frightened to radically alter the priorities in his life? We can only speculate about the possible outcome of the story of the rich man. However, we can ask some difficult questions of ourselves: How important are the material possessions in our lives? Are we willing to live with less in order to help our fellow sisters and brothers? Are we willing to serve Christ, who was materially poor during his earthly life, by serving the poor in our world today?

> **What sometimes stands in the way of your own commitment to Christ?**

Article 56: The Greatest Commandment (Matthew 22:34–40)

In Matthew's Gospel, a Pharisee asks Jesus which commandment in the Jewish Law is the greatest, or most important. Jesus responds by invoking passages from the Old Testament. First, Jesus quotes from the Book of Deuteronomy: "Therefore, you shall love the LORD, your God, with your whole heart, and with your whole being, and with your whole strength" (6:5). Next he quotes from the Book of Leviticus: "You shall love your neighbor as yourself" (19:18).

Amazingly, in just two short sentences, Jesus managed to summarize the entirety of Jewish tradition of the "law and the prophets" (Matthew 22:40), as well as the essential message of the Gospel—love. Yet we are still left with important questions: How exactly should we love God? How should we love our neighbor? The Ten Commandments (see Exodus 20:1–17) provide us with insight into the specifics of how we are to live out this Great Commandment of love.

How Do We Love God?

Of the Ten Commandments, the first three focus on how we are to love God:

- **I am the Lord your God; you shall not have strange gods before me.** The First Commandment invites us to faithfully believe and hope in God, loving him above all else. We live this Commandment when we worship God and pray faithfully, resisting the temptation to make other things—like power, pleasure, or possessions—the gods we serve in our lives.

- **You shall not take the name of the Lord your God in vain.** The Second Commandment echoes the words of Psalm 8: "O LORD, our Lord, / how awesome is your name through all the earth!" (verse 2). We are to speak God's name only in reverence, love, and respect, never using it in a way that expresses hatred, dishonesty, or violence.

- **Remember to keep holy the Lord's Day.** The Third Commandment reminds us that Sunday, as the day on which our Lord Jesus rose from the dead, is the holiest day of the Christian week. God asks us to respect the sacredness of this day by participating in the celebration of the Eucharist, resting from our usual business of work or school, and enjoying the company of family and friends.

How Do We Love Our Neighbor?

Commandments four through ten focus on how we are to love our neighbor:

- **Honor your father and mother.** In the Fourth Commandment, God wills that we honor our parents with respect and gratitude for the life they have given us. Parents, likewise, are to love their children by providing them with a safe, nurturing home and by educating them in the Christian faith.

- **You shall not kill.** The Fifth Commandment declares that all human life, at every stage of its development, is sacred based on the fact that we have all been created with love in the image and likeness of God. For this reason, we must never participate in the intentional taking of an innocent human life, whether through abortion, euthanasia, suicide, or war. However, we may defend ourselves and others against harm and aggression by rendering the aggressor unable to harm us.

- **You shall not commit adultery.** In the Sixth Commandment, God asks that we respect the gift of our sexuality, accepting our identity and dignity as male or female willingly. This commandment also instructs us to reserve intimate sexual activity for marriage.

- **You shall not steal.** The Seventh Commandment reinforces what our parents and other adults have been teaching us from a very young age: respect the property of others and do not take what does not belong to you. However, we also must recognize the demands of charity and justice: to share our goods and property generously with others. Failure to do so is a form of theft from those who are hungry or poor.

- **You shall not bear false witness against your neighbor.** The Eighth Commandment calls us to always speak and act truthfully, and to never deceive others or ruin reputations by spreading lies, rumors, or gossip.
- **You shall not covet your neighbor's wife.** We are invited by God in the Ninth Commandment to be pure in our hearts, bodies, and minds, recognizing that the human body—both our own and that of others, is itself a holy temple, radiating the beauty and goodness of God.
- **You shall not covet your neighbor's goods.** We are asked by God in the Tenth Commandment to resist greed, envy, and the desire for wealth and material possessions. Instead we must cultivate goodwill toward our neighbors, a spirit of humility, and a sense of trust that God will never fail to provide all we need.

In your own words, how would you express the Greatest Commandment?

Live It!
Corporal Works of Mercy

How can you live the Corporal Works of Mercy in your own life? You may think, "I don't have much money, power, or experience, so what can I really do to make a difference?" In fact, there is a lot you can do. You can volunteer at a soup kitchen, shelter, food pantry, or similar place of community outreach. You can give time to the sick and elderly in hospitals and nursing homes, or get involved in clothing and food drives. You can help with fundraisers to benefit people in need, from the homeless to the imprisoned. You can donate the money you would have normally spent on going to the movies or downloading music to a charity that helps the poor. With a little creativity, you can find countless ways to live the Corporal Works of Mercy. You can also invite your friends and family to participate with you. What will you do today to live out Christ's call to love through works of mercy?

Article 57: The Judgment of the Nations (Matthew 25:31–46)

Jesus always makes the poor a priority in his teaching, healing, and proclamation of the Kingdom of God. From the very beginning of his public ministry, when he announces that he has been sent to "bring glad tidings to the poor" (Luke 4:18), to his declaration that the Kingdom itself belongs to the poor (see 6:20), Jesus invites us to experience a new awareness of, and response to, the plight of the oppressed and the poor. Sometimes known as the Judgment of the Nations, Jesus' teaching about the Last Judgment (see Matthew 25:31–46) clearly demonstrates that we must actively love the poor if we hope to enter the Kingdom of Heaven.

Parousia
The Second Coming of Christ as judge of all the living and the dead, at the end of time, when the Kingdom of God will be fulfilled.

The Parable of the Sheep and the Goats

Jesus' teaching about the Last Judgment is centered on a parable about a shepherd separating his sheep from his goats: "When the Son of Man comes in his glory, and all the angels with him, he will sit upon his glorious throne, and all the nations will be assembled before him. And he will separate them one from another, as a shepherd separates the sheep from the goats" (Matthew 25:31–32). The deeper meaning of the story quickly becomes clear: it describes the **Parousia**, and it reveals the criteria by which all people will one day be judged. In this judgment, the *sheep* are invited into the Kingdom of the Divine Father because they have consistently responded to the needs of the suffering by offering food, drink, clothing, hospitality, care, and companionship. In contrast to the compassion and empathy of the *sheep,* the *goats,* because they have failed to respond to the hungry, the poor, the sick, and the imprisoned, are considered accursed and sent "into the eternal fire prepared for the devil and his angels" (Matthew 25:41). The narrative twist or surprise of this story lies in the presence of Jesus: he is hidden within the "least ones" (25:45), much to the shock of both the compassionate and the accursed. Jesus seems to have been so well concealed that the *sheep* did not realize that in serving the least amongst them, they served Christ, and the *goats* did not realize that in ignoring the hungry, the thirsty, the ill and imprisoned, they ignored the Son of Man.

The Challenge of True Discipleship

The Parable of the Sheep and the Goats makes clear that the standard for genuine discipleship is not what we say but what we do. If we merely say we want to serve the poor or alleviate the suffering of the hungry and do not

Did You Know?

The Works of Mercy

The Parable of the Sheep and the Goats has given rise to the Church's teaching about the Corporal and Spiritual Works of Mercy.

Practicing the Corporal Works of Mercy means offering care for a person's basic needs:

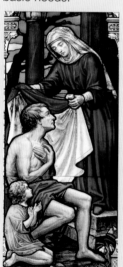

© Bill Wittman / www.wpwittman.com

- Feed the hungry.
- Give drink to the thirsty.
- Shelter the homeless.
- Clothe the naked.
- Care for the sick.
- Help the imprisoned.
- Bury the dead.

The Spiritual Works of Mercy care for a person's emotional, intellectual, or spiritual needs:

- Share knowledge.
- Give advice to those who need it.
- Comfort those who suffer.
- Forgive those who hurt you.
- Correct those who need it.
- Pray for the living and the dead.

Both the Corporal and Spiritual Works of Mercy invite us to share with others the bountiful mercy and goodness God shares with us. When we share mercy with others, we stand in **solidarity** with them, knowing that we are united in our common need for God's healing love and grace.

follow through with concrete actions, Jesus himself will confront us with our hypocrisy.

It is significant that Jesus teaches with this parable just shortly before his Passion begins. As the last parable in the Gospel of Matthew, the story of sheep and the goats is among Jesus' parting words to his disciples. As he is about to undertake the saving work of the Paschal Mystery, Jesus teaches the disciples that their lives of generous service must also embody the same spirit of willing sacrifice that lies at the heart of his Passion and death.

> **Why do you think Jesus included the Parable of the Sheep and the Goats among his parting words?**

solidarity
Union of one's heart and mind with all people. Solidarity leads to the just distribution of material goods, creates bonds between opposing groups and nations, and leads to the spread of spiritual goods such as friendship and prayer.

For Review

1. What are the Beatitudes and what do they teach us?

2. Identify and explain three traditional Lenten practices.

3. What is a parable?

4. What do the Parables of the Lost Sheep, the Lost Coin, and the Lost Son tell us about the Kingdom of God?

5. What does Jesus tell the rich man he must do in order to inherit eternal life? Why?

6. What is the Greatest Commandment?

7. What do the first three Commandments tell us about loving God?

8. At the Last Judgment, what is the standard by which all people will be judged?

9. What is the significance of Jesus' teaching the Parable of the Sheep and the Goats shortly before his Passion?

10. What are the Works of Mercy?

Unit 5

Faith and Our Response to Jesus

Faith, one of the Theological Virtues, is a gift from God and our response to his Revelation. As we study what constitutes faith, we examine the intricacies of the relationship between faith and religion. When we look to Sacred Scripture and the history of the Church, we find numerous examples of individuals—such as the saints and martyrs—who lived their faith, very often dramatically and impressively.

Prayer is essential to the virtue of faith. Prayer is a communication tool we employ to help nurture our relationship with God. There are many kinds of prayer, but all prayer seeks God in loving relationship. In Sacred Scripture, Jesus himself gave us the most well-known of all prayers—the Lord's Prayer, or the Our Father—and the Church offers us the Sacraments as cornerstones of prayer.

Beyond responding to God through prayer, we act on our faith through living a life of discipleship. Mary the Mother of God is our prime example of a life of faith and discipleship. As disciples of Christ today, we must overcome the temptation of evil and seek forgiveness for our sins. Furthermore, a life of Christian discipleship includes living the principles of Catholic social teaching and the call to evangelization.

If we truly seek to follow Christ through a life of faith, prayer, and discipleship, we will share in all that Christ promised us: eternal life with the Blessed Trinity and with the Communion of Saints in heavenly glory.

The enduring understandings and essential questions represent core concepts and questions that are explored throughout this unit. By studying the content of each chapter, you will gain a more complete understanding of the following:

Enduring Understandings

1. Faith is expressed and supported by the people and the religious practices of the faith community.

2. We nurture our relationship and connection with God through prayer.

3. Through discipleship we dedicate our lives to following Jesus and the example he set for us.

4. Our earthly lives shape the final destiny of our lives in Heaven.

Essential Questions

1. What is the relationship between faith and the practice of religion?

2. What is prayer, and why do we pray?

3. How can discipleship help us to grow in faith by being more like Jesus?

4. What does eternal life mean for Christians?

What Is Faith?

Introduction

What exactly is faith? Faith is not something physical, to be touched or held, nor is it something we can directly see or hear. The presence of faith in an individual person cannot be detected by science, nor can we verify which people from history, even religious history, have acted on genuine faith and which have not. If faith is so difficult to determine or measure, how are we to define it?

The term *faith* comes from the Latin word *fides,* meaning trust or belief, and is both God's gift to us and our free response to that gift. Through the Theological Virtue of faith, God prepares all of us to respond to his revealed truth with our whole hearts and minds. When our response is genuine and deeply rooted, truly a part of our lives, it transforms us. Thus we seek to understand it more fully and are moved to express it through our words and actions. We want to share our faith with others, hoping they too will find the same peace and joy we have found in freely surrendering our whole selves to the truth God has revealed to us.

Article 58: Faith and Religion

Faith always begins with God. God gives every person the **Theological Virtue** of faith to enable us to accept God's revealed truth and to be in union with him in our minds and hearts. Through faith we are able "to submit freely to the word that has been heard, because its truth is guaranteed by God, who is Truth itself" (*Catechism of the Catholic Church [CCC]*, 144).

Faith and Religion Are Inseparable

How are religious practices connected to faith? You can think of faith and religion as two sides of the same coin. In faith we accept God's Revelation, and we express that faith in our religious beliefs and practices. Faith is the surrendering of our whole selves—minds, hearts, and spirits—to God's saving love. On the other hand, religion is the practice of prayer, worship, and service, combined with the shared beliefs that result from surrendering ourselves to God's love.

Faith and religion are so closely connected that we cannot truly have one without the other. If we try to sustain our faith without expressing it through religion, it will eventually fade away. True faith is always expressed in religious worship and outreach. However, if we engage in religious practices that are not expressions of an authentic faith, we are not involved in real worship. Consequently, our religion becomes an empty ritual, a meaningless collection of words, gestures, and actions.

Religion: Worship and Adoration

When Jesus was confronted and tempted by the Devil in the desert, he quoted the Book of Deuteronomy: "You shall worship the Lord, your God, / and him alone shall you serve" (Luke 4:8). Worship of God is a key component of religion; without it we cannot say we are truly practicing our faith. Because God is the Source of all that we are, worship of God is our duty, and it is through worship that we give back to God all that we as his creation owe him.

Theological Virtues
The name for the God-given virtues of faith, hope, and love. These virtues enable us to know God as God and lead us to union with him in mind and heart.

lament

A prayer, petition, or ritual of grief that honors the death of a loved one. Many of the psalms are laments.

When we truly adore God, we acknowledge him as our Savior and as the Creator of all that we know and will ever know. Through adoration we lift our minds toward God and celebrate his endless mercy and love. In prayerful adoration we praise the One whose goodness and mercy holds us in life, recalling that every blessing we enjoy is a gracious gift from our kind and gentle God.

Religion: Service and Sacrifice

The religious practices through which we express our faith include not only worship and adoration of God but also service and sacrifice offered on behalf of our neighbor. In other words, our religion is not just something we practice in the confines of a church or in solitary prayer; rather, we practice our religion each time we share generously with those who are poor, offer assistance to our

Did You Know?

The Book of Psalms: Prayers of Praise

© Sybille Yates / shutterstock.com

The Book of Psalms is a beautiful resource we can use in our worship and adoration of God. It has been called the prayer book of ancient Israel, for the prayers it contains were frequently used in Temple worship. As a faithful Jew, Jesus would have prayed the Psalms regularly. Today the Psalms are commonly used in both Jewish and Christian prayer. In Catholic liturgy every celebration of the Eucharist includes a psalm as part of the Liturgy of the Word. The Church's official daily prayer, the Liturgy of the Hours, is entirely built upon praying all 150 Psalms within a four-week cycle.

The Psalms are an incredibly diverse collection of prayers. The various prayers express thanksgiving, petition, **lament**, and countless other human emotions and attitudes. However, praise of God's great and constant goodness is the consistent backdrop for all the psalms. Interestingly, even the psalms that express sadness, fear, doubt, frustration, confusion, and anger ultimately acclaim God's saving works—God's fidelity to his people in every time and place.

neighbors, and help our parents and other family members. In sacrificing our time, money, or other resources for the good of others, we unite ourselves more fully with the sacrifice Christ offered on the cross, and make our whole lives a sacrifice to God.

> **In your words, why is faith inseparable from religion?**

Article 59: Faith: A Gift from God

Faith is a supernatural gift that God freely offers to us. Through faith we come to accept the truth God has revealed to us. None of us can maintain faith on our own; rather, it is divine grace and the help of the Holy Spirit that make our faith possible.

God's Revelation: Belief and Faith

In Matthew's Gospel, Jesus confronts his disciples with the question "But who do you say that I am?" (16:15). Peter responds with a perfect confession of faith in Jesus: "You are the Messiah, the Son of the living God" (verse 16). Jesus goes on to say that "flesh and blood has not revealed this to you, but my heavenly Father" (verse 17). Here Jesus indicates that Peter has come to believe in something that God the Father has revealed to him—something Peter could not have known any other way. Through the grace of God the Father and the help of the Holy Spirit, Peter exercises the gift of faith.

We act on our own gift of faith when we willingly accept God's invitation to believe in Revelation, even when the truths of Revelation do not make perfect sense to us. The *Catechism* acknowledges that "revealed truths can seem obscure to human reason and experience" (157); yet we trust their authenticity because we wholeheartedly trust in the One who has revealed them to us.

Although believing the truths of Revelation is possible only with the Holy Spirit's help, doing so does not contradict our human freedom or reason. In fact, *to believe* is a fundamentally human act. On a daily basis, we believe what others—like friends, family members, or classmates— tell us. Shouldn't we also believe what God tells us? As a truly human act, our belief in God must come from our own free choice. Jesus invited—but never forced—all people to be his friends and followers during his earthly life. In the same way, Jesus invites us to believe in and follow him today. As with any invitation, we must freely choose to accept or reject it.

This painting depicts Genesis 18:2–15, where Abraham and Sarah are visited by God's messengers. Whom has God sent into your life to call you to deeper faith?

The Obedience of Faith

© Erich Lessing / Art Resource, NY

In his Letter to the Romans, Saint Paul writes about the "obedience of faith" (1:5). The word *obedience* comes from a Latin root meaning "to hear, listen, or pay attention to." When we are obedient to God in matters of faith, we listen carefully to his Word and then freely surrender our whole selves—intellect, personal will, heart, and mind—to it because only God offers eternal truth, for he is Divine Truth. In obedience to our faith in God, we pay attention to Revelation, even when it seems mysterious or incomprehensible. Through our faith, we humbly seek God's will for our lives, eager to trust in all God has communicated to us.

Faith Needs Nourishment

It is possible to lose the gift of faith if we do not attend to it, nourish it, and help it to grow. What can we do to strengthen and nourish our faith? One way to grow in faith is to read Sacred Scripture regularly and prayerfully. Additionally, we can engage in acts of charity and works of justice. We can seek the support of other believers to help us bolster our own gift of faith. In our prayers, we can also join the Apostles in asking the Lord to "increase our faith" (Luke 17:5). God, who first granted us the gift of faith, will surely hear our prayers of longing for that gift to grow and flourish.

> **Why do think faith needs to be attended to and nourished?**

Article 60: Biblical Figures, Saints, and Martyrs: Examples of Faith

Have you ever felt tired and discouraged when trying to succeed and excel at something difficult? Have you noticed that it helps to have others with you engaged in the same struggle and helping you to go on? When we struggle we are often inspired by the people around us

Faith in Action
Abraham: Our Ancestor in Faith

© Renata Sedmakova / iStockphoto.com

Abraham is our earliest ancestor in faith. Throughout his life he repeatedly trusted in the promises of God, even when those promises seemed mysterious or even impossible to fulfill.

First, Abraham answered God's call to leave his homeland and to go to a new land God showed him. In return, God promised to make of Abraham "a great nation" (Genesis 12:2). Even though Abraham and Sarah were elderly and childless, they firmly believed God's promise that they would have descendants. In time, Abraham and Sarah miraculously conceived Isaac, even though Sarah was long past her childbearing years. Later, when God commanded Abraham to offer Isaac as a sacrifice, Abraham set about to do as God instructed. When God saw Abraham's great faith and devotion, he stopped him, and promised him "descendants as countless as the stars of the sky" (Genesis 22:17).

Several New Testament books, including the Letter to the Romans and the Letter to the Hebrews, praise the faith of Abraham. Abraham has much to teach us about trusting completely in God's Revelation. Through the example of Abraham's faith, we can learn to place our trust in God and obediently follow wherever he leads.

to continue forward and give our best effort. In a similar way, others, through their lives and deeds, can inspire and encourage us to be faithful.

When our own faith is weak or struggling, the generations of faithful men and women who have gone before us can offer us help and encouragement. These models of faith include people from both Testaments of the Bible as well as the saints and martyrs.

Biblical Figures: The Old Testament

The Old Testament is filled with examples of people whose careful and committed response to God's

Pray It!

A Psalm Prayer

The Psalms offer us words to call out to God in a variety of circumstances and to express a variety of sentiments and desires. Psalm 27 expresses trust in God in difficult circumstances. As you pray this psalm, allow yourself to rest in God's presence and to feel the comfort and safety his loving protection.

The LORD is my light and salvation;
　　whom should I fear?
The LORD is my life's refuge;
　　of whom should I be afraid?

　. . . . .

Though an army encamp against me,
　　my heart does not fear;
Though war be waged against me,
　　even then do I trust.

One thing I ask of the LORD;
　　this I seek:
To dwell in the LORD's house
　　all the days of my life,
To gaze on the LORD's beauty,
　　to visit his temple.
　　　　　　　　(Verses 1,3–4)

Revelation, especially in difficult circumstances, can inspire our own faith.

- Ruth's abundant faith led her to care for her mother-in-law, Naomi, after both women had become widows. Ruth promised Naomi:

  > Wherever you go I will go,
  >
  > . . . .
  >
  > Your people shall be my people and your God, my God.
  >
  > (Ruth 1:16)

  They lived together in Naomi's hometown, Bethlehem, until Ruth remarried. Ruth later became the great-grandmother of King David and an ancestor of Jesus.

- Hannah showed great faith in her quest to have a child. In prayer she promised that if God gave her a son, she would "give him to the LORD all the days of his life" (1 Samuel 1:11). When she became pregnant, she made good on her promise, and her son grew up to become the great prophet Samuel.

- Jeremiah was terrified when God asked him to become a prophet. He told God he was too young to speak for him and wouldn't know what to say. But, in faith, he willingly trusted in God's will and did what was asked of him, becoming one of the greatest of the prophets.

Biblical Figures: The New Testament

Like the Old Testament, the New Testament also abounds with examples of holy men and women who freely surrendered to God's Revelation, even when that surrender required great sacrifice on their part.

- "The Virgin Mary most perfectly embodies the obedience of faith" (*CCC*, 148). From her freely offered "yes" in response to her role in God's plan of salvation as the Mother of Jesus, to her willingness to watch her son suffer and die on the cross, to her presence among the other disciples after Jesus' Resurrection, she is truly "the purest realization of faith" (149).

- Mary Magdalene was among the women from Galilee who accompanied Jesus and the Apostles in their traveling and preaching and provided financial support for them. In all four Gospels, she is among the first of the faithful witnesses of the Resurrected Lord Jesus, who entrusts her with the mission of proclaiming that Good News to the other disciples.

- Despite Peter's famous denials during Jesus' Passion, he was nonetheless an Apostle of great faith who had earlier confessed Jesus as "the Messiah, the Son of the living God" (Matthew 16:16). In John's Gospel, Peter professes his love for the Risen Lord three times, repenting of his three earlier denials. Peter shows us that even when our faith seriously falters, God's gracious mercy heals us, enabling us to trust in Revelation once again.

Saints and Martyrs: Lives of Faith

The lives of the saints, some of whom were also martyrs, are a rich resource of inspiration for us as we try to live our faith authentically. The Church's saints and martyrs show us through their example how to maintain and grow our faith, especially during our most trying times.

- Saint Ignatius of Loyola, who was a soldier, put all his trust in God's Revelation while resting from an injury he had sustained on the battlefield. After his full recovery, he gathered a group of companions around him. These people became the first members of a new religious order, the Society of Jesus, or Jesuits.

- Saint Catherine of Siena's faith gave her the courage to confront Pope Gregory XI, the last of the Avignon Popes. She urged him to return to the holy city of Rome. Perhaps to her great surprise, he listened to her.

- Saint Thomas More's fidelity to Revelation cost him his life. King Henry VIII of England ordered his execution when More would not support the king in rejecting the authority of the Pope.

The example of these and countless other holy women and men who have gone before us show us how to live a life of faith. They teach us how to surrender our whole selves—minds, hearts, and spirits—to the truth God has revealed to us.

Whom do you look to when you feel discouraged in faith?

© Brooklyn Museum / Corbis

Article 61: Faith: Our Response to Revelation

Faith is the dedication of our whole selves to God who has revealed himself to us through both words and deeds. Faith involves the consent of our human intellect and free will. In other words, God initiates a relationship with us through Revelation; we respond to God through faith.

Mary Magdalene was one of the women that supported Jesus' ministry. Who are women you see in the world today who actively support the mission of Jesus?

We Respond through Discipleship

When we have faith in Jesus Christ, we become his disciples, or followers. First, this means we seek to imitate the words and actions of Jesus. Through faith we try to make Jesus' values, attitudes, and priorities our own. Furthermore, we seek to treat people as Jesus treated everyone during his earthly life—with dignity, compassion, and love. Second, when we become disciples of Christ, we fully recognize and accept Jesus as the Second Person of the Blessed Trinity, the Eternal Son of God, who took on human flesh, died to liberate us from sin, and opened a path to new life for us through his glorious Resurrection and Ascension. As disciples we accept with grateful hearts the gift of grace that, through the power of the Holy Spirit, makes us adopted children of God the Father and therefore brothers and sisters of Jesus and of one another.

We Respond through Evangelization

All disciples of Jesus have a common vocation, rooted in our Baptism: "a vocation to holiness and to the mission of evangelizing the world" (CCC, 1533). To evangelize means to proclaim our faith in Jesus Christ and the Good News of his life, death, and Resurrection through words and deeds. There are many ways to witness to our faith through both our words and deeds. For example, we can actively participate in the liturgical and sacramental life of the Church and invite others to do the same. We can use our talents to proclaim and to share with others what God has revealed for our salvation. We can actively engage in acts of charity and works of justice. We can try to live "in a way worthy of the gospel of Christ" (Philippians 1:27) so others may be drawn to faith through our example.

Live It!
How Can You Evangelize?

How can you witness to the Kingdom of God in your life? Every one of us can help to spread the Good News of Jesus Christ through both our words and our actions. Below are some actions you can take to help make evangelization an active part of your life:

- Invite a friend to attend Mass with you on Sunday.
- Volunteer with a local food bank.
- Help out with your parish's elementary religious education program or vacation Bible school.
- Ask your friends to say grace before lunch at school.

These are only a few ideas; there are countless other ways you can evangelize. We all have gifts and talents we can use to help spread the Good News of Jesus Christ. What are two things you can do this week to evangelize?

How is your faith a response to God's Revelation?

Article 62: The Theological Virtues: Faith, Hope, and Love

A virtue is a good habit, a continual and firm disposition to do good. The three Theological Virtues—faith; hope; and charity, or love—enable us to respond to God's Revelation and live in relationship with the Blessed Trinity. They are God-given principles that allow us to directly commune with the Divine Trinity.

- **Faith** enables us to believe what God has revealed, and allows us to respond to Revelation by uniting ourselves to Christ as living members of his Body, the Church. As disciples we must profess our faith with confidence, bearing witness to it in the words and actions of our daily lives.

- **Hope** invites us to trust in the love of God the Father, the promises of Christ, and the grace of the Holy

Primary Sources

Faith, Hope, and Love: Stars in Our Spiritual Lives

The Theological Virtues—faith, hope, and love—are essential to our lives as disciples of Christ. As pope, Saint John Paul II expressed their importance in this way:

> Faith, hope and love are like three stars that rise in the sky of our spiritual life to guide us to God. They are the theological virtues *par excellence:* they put us in communion with God and lead us to him. They form a triptych, whose apex is found in love, the *agape* excellently praised by Paul in a hymn of the First Letter to the Corinthians. It is sealed by the following declaration: "So faith, hope, love abide, these three; but the greatest of these is love" (13:13).
>
> To the extent that they enliven the disciples of Christ, the three theological virtues spur them on towards unity, in accordance with Paul's words . . . : "One body . . . , one hope . . .; one Lord, one faith . . . , one God and Father" (Eph 4:4–6). ("John Paul II, General Audience, November 22, 2000, 1")

Spirit, especially when we feel discouraged, abandoned, or disheartened. Through the virtue of hope, we trust that our destiny is to share in the life of the Blessed Trinity and the joys of Heaven.

- **Charity** asks that we follow the Greatest Commandment , loving God above all else and loving our neighbors as ourselves, out of our love for God.

How are the virtues of faith, hope, and charity part of your everyday life?

For Review

1. Why are faith and religion inseparable?

2. What are some of the religious practices through which we can express our faith?

3. Explain why it is true that faith is both a gift from God and also rooted in human freedom.

4. What can we do to nourish our faith?

5. How can the generations of faithful men and women who have gone before us help us in our own faith?

6. What does it mean to be a disciple of Jesus?

7. What is evangelization?

We Respond to God through Prayer

Introduction

Think about a good friend, one you are especially close to. How did you first get to know and connect with this person? Furthermore, think about exactly how your relationship has grown into the close friendship you now enjoy.

Any lasting friendship takes time to develop. We must spend extended periods of time with a person to really get to know his or her personality, interests, and values. In forming friendships, we must develop a sense of trust before we begin to share our hopes, dreams, and fears with each other.

Like a good, solid friendship, our relationship with God has the same qualities and demands. As with all the important relationships in our lives, the one we have with God does not develop overnight, and it does not grow without time, effort, and commitment on our part. Prayer is the time we spend with God seeking to nurture our mutual relationship. Although Christian prayer can take many forms, it is always rooted in the example and teachings of Jesus as found in the Gospels and in the sacramental life of the Church.

Article 63: What Is Prayer?

Prayer is fundamentally a relationship—a personal, vital, and intimate connection with the living God. Throughout the whole history of salvation, prayer unfolds as a reciprocal call between God and his people, an unceasing invitation to each and every person to encounter him in prayer. In a sense, prayer is a back-and-forth dialogue between God the Father and his children: God calls to us, and we respond; God calls again, and we respond more deeply and completely.

Saint John Damascene offers a classic definition of *prayer*: "Prayer is the raising of one's mind and heart to God or the requesting of good things from God." We will now consider these two aspects of prayer.

Raising the Mind and Heart to God

Raising our minds and hearts to God means that we are always conscious of God's presence within us. Our faith teaches us that God is always with us, for we dwell constantly with the One who loved us into being and redeemed us in grace. However, we sometimes temporarily lose sight of God's presence due to the distractions and stresses of daily life. During prayer, our minds, hearts, and spirits are focused on God's loving presence, as we seek to be drawn into greater union with the Blessed Trinity. Prayer enables us to open ourselves more fully to the goodness and mercy of God's gracious will for our lives.

We support and strengthen one another through communal prayer. What opportunities do you have for praying with others? Use one of those opportunities this week.

© Bill Wittman / www.wpwittman.com

In addition to the consciousness of God's presence, raising our hearts and minds to God also means we worship God as our Creator, never forgetting that we, as his creatures, are wholly and completely dependent on him. This recognition—that only God is truly God—is called humility. A well-developed sense of humility is essential to prayer. Humility does not mean self-loathing or being overly self-critical; rather, it means seeing ourselves as we really are: beloved children of God who are in constant need of divine grace as we journey toward the ultimate perfection of God's Reign.

One way you can increase your continual awareness of God's presence is through a prayer known as an **aspiration**. An aspiration is a short prayer that one memorizes and simply repeats throughout the day, perhaps even while doing other things. Examples include "My Lord and my God" or "Lord, have mercy." Aspirations can become a habitual and natural part of our everyday life; in fact, aspiration comes from the Latin word meaning "to breathe upon". Thus our prayer lives, following the rhythm and regularity of our own bodies, can always be turned toward God.

Requesting Good Things from God

Many of our prayers ask God for something. This type of prayer is called a **prayer of petition**. In a prayer of petition, we may ask God for forgiveness of our sins. We may ask, as in the Lord's Prayer, for the coming of God's Reign and for the courage and strength to do God's will. When we share in God's love and promise of salvation, we see that all of our needs can be addressed with prayers of petition.

When we ask God for good things on behalf of other people, we engage in **intercessory prayer**—interceding with God for the needs of others. We may pray for those who are sick or suffering, for those who are poor, or for those who are mourning the loss of a loved one. When we pray intercessory prayers, we must be generous in our prayer, praying not only for our own friends or family members but also for the many people throughout the world who are in great need, especially those who have no one else to pray for them.

aspiration
A short prayer meant to be memorized and repeated throughout the day. The word comes from the Latin *aspirare*, "to breathe upon." In this way, we can heed Saint Paul's injunction to pray without ceasing and continually turn our thoughts toward God.

prayer of petition
A prayer form in which we ask God for something we need.

intercessory prayer
A prayer form in which we ask God's help for other people's needs; also called intercession.

© Bill Wittman / www.wpwittman.com

Saint Ignatius encouraged his followers to do a daily examen as part of their prayer life. For the next several days, set aside time each night to pray and do an examen, following the steps to the right.

The Practice of Prayer

Even though we know God is active in our lives, in order to be consciously and continually aware of his presence, we must commit ourselves to frequent prayer, asking the Holy Spirit to teach and guide us. In order to meet such needs, Saint Ignatius of Loyola recommended that his followers conduct an *examen* at the end of each day. This prayer exercise would serve as a way of increasing their awareness of God's presence. An *examen* can take many forms, but the basic steps are as follows:

- quieting ourselves, asking God to enlighten and guide our minds and hearts

- reviewing the experiences of our day, noticing how we responded to and interacted with people (When did we act with love? When did we act with selfishness?)

- asking for God's forgiveness for the times in the day when we sinned

- offering gratitude for the blessings of the day

- seeking strength for all we will face the next day

When we engage regularly in the practice of the *examen* or a similar form of daily prayer, we will grow spiritually and begin to see more with eyes of faith. Frequent, daily prayer allows us to notice God's grace, love, and wisdom offered to us in the midst of a conversation, a class, a game, or a quiet moment. When we harness the profound power of prayer, we realize, with the great Jesuit poet Gerard Manley Hopkins, that "the world is charged with the grandeur of God."

Tips for Prayer

We often have the desire to further develop our relationship with God through prayer, but we are unsure how to get started. Here are some pointers on how to build a fulfilling and strong prayer life:

- **Who?** You can pray with anyone or with no one. When you pray with family members or friends, they support your spiritual life. But praying alone can also be very fulfilling.
- **Where?** Many people find it helpful to dedicate a specific place, like a table or a corner of a bedroom, to prayer. Keep a Bible there, along with a cross or holy image, and a candle to make the prayer space appealing and beautiful.
- **When?** Prayer becomes a good habit when we set aside time for it. Think about when you could carve out some time in your day for prayer—perhaps in the morning on the way to school, during your lunch break, or before going to sleep.
- **How?** There are countless ways to pray. You can pray through Sacred Scripture, the Rosary, or meditation; through prayer that is vocal or silent; through prayer that praises God or asks for what you need. But remember that the *how* of prayer is not the most important part of prayer—actually praying is what matters.

© Brand X / Corbis

Pray It!

Teach Us to Pray!

In the following prayer, we ask Jesus to be our teacher and to guide us in our life of prayer.

Lord, teach us to pray. Give us the heart and the humility to speak in our own words with you about our hopes and fears, joys and sorrows, weaknesses and strengths. Help us to be honest with ourselves and sincere before you. Teach us to listen. Guide us to see more clearly the gifts you have given us and the good ways we can use them.

Lord, fill us with great desires to speak with you. Stir within us a holy ambition to spread your word to others and to work to share your message with the world. Give us the strength to be constant in our prayer so that we may rely on you as our great friend throughout our lives. Amen.

In your own words, how would you define prayer?

Article 64: The Lord's Prayer

In Luke's Gospel, we see the disciples ask Jesus to teach them to pray: "He was praying in a certain place, and when he had finished, one of his disciples said to him, 'Lord, teach us to pray just as John taught his disciples'" (11:1). Jesus responded with what has become the best-known and best-loved of all Christian prayers—the Lord's Prayer, also known as the Our Father. In this prayer, Jesus neatly summarizes the key elements of the Gospel message: praise of God the Father's holy name, desire for the Kingdom, prayer that our needs will be met, and a plea for forgiveness.

The Lord's Prayer Teaches Us about God

Christian prayer is always Trinitarian: prayers are addressed *to* the Father, the First Divine Person of the Trinity; prayers are said *in the name of* Jesus, the Second Divine Person of the Trinity; and prayers are requested *through the power of* the Holy Spirit, the Third Divine Person of the Trinity. Because the Lord's Prayer is clearly addressed to the First Person of the Blessed Trinity, it speaks of our belief in a Triune God.

The Lord's Prayer also teaches us that Jesus, the Eternal Son of God, who assumed human nature, has revealed God the Father to us. In his earthly life, Jesus called his Divine Father *Abba,* a term of respect that means "Father." In teaching us to pray in the words of the Lord's Prayer, Jesus invites us to share in a filial relation-ship of intimacy and love as adopted sons and daugh-ters through Baptism. Indeed praying the Lord's Prayer brings us into closer communion with the Blessed Trin-ity, enabling us to experience the mystery, wonder, and joy of the divine life of Father, Son, and Holy Spirit.

The Lord's Prayer Teaches Us about Ourselves

Have you ever noticed that the Lord's Prayer is such an important prayer in the life of the Church? We pray it at every liturgical and sacramental celebration, including the Liturgy of the Hours, Baptism, Confirmation, and the Eucharist. This is not only because The Lord's Prayer contains the words that Jesus himself taught us but also because it reflects our fundamental identity as Christians. Through the Sacrament of Baptism, we are incorporated into Christ's own Body, the Church, and adopted as children of God the Father. Praying the Lord's Prayer reminds us that as God's own adopted children, we must speak and act in a way that is worthy of this dignity. In addition, praying to God our Father should develop in us the will to be like him and foster in us humility and trust, the same trust as that of a child who relies totally on a loving parent for all of her or his needs.

> **Why do you think the Lord's Prayer, or the Our Father, is such a popular prayer?**

Article 65: Jesus Teaches Us about Prayer

In the Gospels, Jesus teaches us about prayer through the example of his actions and through his words.

Learning from Jesus' Example

During his earthly life, Jesus often took time alone to pray. For example, the Gospel of Mark recounts the actions of Jesus after a very busy day of teaching and healing in the town of Capernaum: "Rising very early before dawn, he left and went off to a deserted place, where he prayed" (1:35). In Mark's Gospel, in the account of the Feeding of the Five Thousand (see Mark 6:34–44), Jesus asks the Apostles to come away with him "to a deserted place and rest a while" (verse 31). However, crowds of people follow them, and Jesus, moved with compassion, teaches them and feeds them. When the people at last disperse, Jesus goes off by himself "to the mountain to pray" (verse 46). Luke's Gospel also tells us that despite the great crowds that assembled to listen to Jesus and be healed by him, Jesus would make the effort to "withdraw to deserted places to pray" (5:16).

These Gospel accounts make clear that Jesus needed prayer to sustain him in his ministry. Jesus consciously made time for prayer, often by getting up very early and finding a place where he could be alone. We lead busy lives, full of activities, work, school, and people who

Faith in Action
"Our Daily Bread": Catholic Relief Services

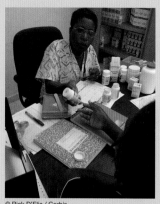

© Rick D'Elia / Corbis

"**G**ive us this day our daily bread." Do you sometimes just glide by that phrase of the Lord's Prayer without really considering its meaning? When we pray these words, we should not simply ask God to meet our own needs. Rather, we must think of our sisters and brothers who suffer from a lack of "daily bread."

One organization that works to ensure that all people have access to "daily bread" is Catholic Relief Services (CRS), the official international humanitarian agency of the United States Catholic community. CRS sponsors efforts in more than a hundred countries around the world where people suffer from hunger and lack adequate nutrition, shelter, and health care. Further, CRS always responds quickly to natural disasters like earthquakes, floods, and famines. CRS also initiates long-term projects to help local people become more self-sufficient. For example, CRS teaches people to grow their own vegetables, to practice proper sanitation, to start small businesses, and to send their children to school. By serving the word's poor and disadvantaged, CRS lives out the words of the Lord's Prayer, creating conditions for providing daily bread that will endure for generations to come.

The next time you pray the Lord's Prayer, pause after "our daily bread." Remember all those whose basic needs are not met. Ask God to show you how you can help to ease poverty and hunger, both in your own community and around the world.

demand our time and attention. Therefore, it can be challenging to find a time and a place to pray. But Jesus' example teaches us that prayer is not a luxury—it is a necessity. The *Catechism* states that "prayer and *Christian life* are *inseparable*" (2745). This means that prayer is the strong foundation on which all the other aspects of our lives can rest—studies, work, activities, and relationships. Without prayer our daily lives can become overburdened or meaningless. With prayer our every thought, word, and deed can be transformed and directed toward loving service of God and neighbor.

A Parable about Prayer

In the Parable of the Pharisee and the Tax Collector, Jesus teaches us how to approach God in prayer. Like many of Jesus' parables, this one contains a narrative twist or surprise. The parable concerns two men who go to the temple area to pray—one a Pharisee, a strictly observant Jew; the other a tax collector, a hated agent of Rome. Jesus' listeners would have assumed that the person worthy of holiness and respect would be the Pharisee. But Jesus overturns their expectations. It is the tax collector who, with eyes cast down and beating his breast, prays: "O God, be merciful to me a sinner" (Luke 18:13). Jesus concludes with the statement: "I tell you, the latter went home justified, not the former; for everyone who exalts himself will be humbled, and the one who humbles himself will be exalted" (verse 14).

It is interesting to note the specific audience to whom Jesus addressed this parable: "those who were convinced of their own righteousness and despised everyone else" (Luke 18:9). Could we be like the Pharisee, overly convinced of our own honesty and righteousness? Like the Pharisee, are we overly confident in our own superiority, certain that our thoughts and actions are pleasing to God? If so, we have fallen into

Jesus not only taught the importance of praying but also modeled faithful prayer. How can you make prayer a more important part of your life?

© The Gallery Collection / Corbis

the same trap as the Pharisee in the parable, who prays, "O God, I thank you that I am not like the rest of humanity—greedy, dishonest, adulterous—or even like this tax collector" (verse 11). The reality is that all human beings sin. We all need the infinite mercy of God to flood our hearts and heal our souls. The tax collector, who stands at a distance and prays with humility, knows this. Do we?

Why do you think Jesus used a tax collector to illustrate the power of humble prayer?

Article 66: Sacred Scripture on the Need for Prayer

As God's beloved children, we know we can confidently approach God with our needs, desires, and concerns through prayer. But sometimes we find that prayer is difficult; we may wonder whether God is listening to us or whether our prayers will be answered. During these times of doubt, passages from Sacred Scripture can help us to stick it out and allow us to persevere in our prayers despite our doubts. We will now explore what exactly some of these passages can teach us about prayer.

How do you pray when you need to bring your cares and concerns to God?

The Friend at Midnight (Luke 11:5–8)

© Bill Wittman / www.wpwittman.com

This parable, a story that uses metaphor to teach, is about a man who has an unexpected guest arrive at midnight. Completely unprepared, the man asks a friend to loan him three loaves of bread so he might extend hospitality to his guest and offer him a meal. Although the friend may be annoyed at being disturbed in the middle of the night and refuse to get up, "if he does not get up to give him the loaves because of their friendship, he will get up to give him whatever he needs because of his persistence" (verse 8).

Jesus uses this story to teach us that our prayers should always be persistent and courageous. Like the man who boldly knocks on a friend's door at midnight, asking for food, we can be forthright with God and share our needs, concerns, and problems with him anytime. And like the friend who responds to the man in need of bread, we know that God will likewise always respond to our needs with merciful love.

Ask, Seek, Knock: The Answer to Prayers (Matthew 7:7–11)

In this passage, Jesus continues to teach us about prayer by assuring us that if we ask, we will receive; if we seek, we will find; and if we knock, the door will open. Jesus compares the love and fidelity of his Divine Father to the love of a human father for his children. If a human father knows how to provide for his children, then "how much more will your heavenly Father give good things to those who ask him" (verse 11)?

The Parable of the Persistent Widow (Luke 18:1–8)

In order to understand this parable's teaching on prayer, we must reflect on the vulnerable position of widows during the time of Jesus. During this time, a widow had to rely on the goodwill of her own family or her deceased husband's family to ensure her survival. The families' failure to provide for the widow could mean the difference between life and death. The widow in the parable may have been in a situation like this, for she actively seeks a "just decision" against her adversary (verse 5).

The judge before whom she places her case "neither feared God nor respected any human being" (verse 2). Yet because the widow persistently makes her request, never giving up and never backing down, she succeeds and the judge renders a verdict in her favor.

The Parable of the Persistent Widow teaches us that to pray always "without becoming weary" (verse 1) is a necessity. As Jesus tells us, if the corrupt and unjust judge can be persuaded to do the right thing: "Will not God then secure the rights of his chosen ones who call out to him day and night? Will he be slow to answer them? I tell you, he will see to it that justice is done for them speedily." (verses 7–8).

When Prayers Seem to Go Unanswered

All these Scripture passages teach us to be faithful and persistent in our prayer, to never lose heart and become weary. What about the times when our prayers seem to go unanswered? Is God not listening? Is he just being slow in responding? Or is something else going on?

The *Catechism* states that God is not "an instrument to be used" (2735). In other words, our prayer requests are not specific demands made on God. He is indeed faithful to our prayers and petitions, but sometimes this fidelity does not take the form we expect or desire. For example, what we ask of God may not be in our best interest. God may have a plan for us that differs from what we ask for or want—a plan that gradually unfolds and becomes clear. Or God may answer our prayers in an unexpected way, different from what we had hoped for, a way we cannot yet understand. If we follow the advice of Saint Paul and "pray without ceasing" (1 Thessalonians 5:17), we will grow in our ability to trust in God's goodness and grace. Even when our prayers seem to go unanswered, we will come to believe that God never fails to embrace us in our time of need, offering us gentle mercy and abundant compassion.

When we pray it is important to focus not on our will but on God's will. God hears all our prayers; he often answers them in ways we do not see.

© Annie Griffiths Belt / CORBIS

Why is it important to be persistent in prayer?

Article 67: The Sacraments: Cornerstones of Prayer

Participation in the sacramental life of the Church is an essential aspect of the prayer life of a Catholic. In particular, the Sacrament of the Eucharist and the Sacrament of Penance and Reconciliation, which we celebrate repeatedly throughout our lives, can be continual sources of grace for us. Through these Sacraments we experience the ministry of Christ through the power of the Holy Spirit and are drawn closer to God the Father. The Church offers us the Sacraments as the cornerstones of our life of prayer.

The Eucharist

Saint Thomas Aquinas called the Eucharist the "Sacrament of sacraments." The Second Vatican Council's *Constitution on the Sacred Liturgy (Sacrosanctum Concilium, 1963)* elaborates on the idea of the Eucharist as chief Sacrament by describing the Eucharist as "the summit toward which the activity of the Church is directed; it is also the source from which all of its power flows" (10). Why is celebration of the Eucharist so crucial for Catholics?

- The Eucharist unites us more fully with Christ. Just as physical food nourishes and strengthens our bodies, the food of the Eucharist sustains our spiritual lives of Christian discipleship. It "preserves, increases, and renews the life of grace received at Baptism" (CCC, 1392).

- The Eucharist unites us with our fellow Christians. Through Holy Communion, we deepen and renew our baptismal unity with one another as brothers and sisters in Christ Jesus. Saint Paul saw this reality when he wrote, in one of the earliest texts on the Eucharist in the New Testament: "The bread that we break, is it not a participation in the body of Christ? Because the loaf of bread is one, we, though many, are one body, for we all partake of the one loaf" (1 Corinthians 10:16–17).

- The Eucharist commits us to the poor. "To receive in truth the Body and Blood of Christ given up for us, we must recognize Christ in the poorest" (CCC, 1397). As we are nourished at the table of the Eucharistic feast with the Body and Blood of Christ, we must also commit ourselves to nourishing those members of Christ's own Body who suffer from poverty and deprivation. The Christ whom we receive in the Eucharist is the same Christ who is present in the "least ones" (Matthew 25:45): the hungry, the thirsty, the sick, the naked, the foreign, and the imprisoned.

Did You Know?

Celebrating the Sacrament of Penance and Reconciliation

© Bill Wittman / www.wpwittman.com

Has it been awhile since you celebrated the Sacrament of Penance and Reconciliation? If so, here is a quick review of the rite:

- **Greeting and welcome** The priest welcomes you, makes the Sign of the Cross with you, and reminds you of God's infinite mercy.
- **Confession of sin** You tell the priest your sins. He may offer you spiritual advice.
- **Penance** The priest gives you a penance, which will help to repair the harm your sin has caused and help you to grow as a Christian disciple. A penance could be a prayer, a good work, or some other type of offering.
- **Act of Contrition** During this prayer you express sorrow for your sins. There are many versions of this prayer. You can also make up your own, praying with the words of your own heart.
- **Absolution** The priest speaks the words of Absolution. He offers you God's pardon and peace through the ministry of the Church.
- **Conclusion** The priest blesses you and tells you to go in peace.

Penance and Reconciliation

The Sacrament of Penance and Reconciliation must also be a regular part of the prayer life of a Catholic. Though the Church asks, minimally, that we confess serious sin once a year, celebrating the Sacrament of Penance and Reconciliation more often gives us the chance to experience the consolation and healing of God's grace and mercy. When we confess our sins to a priest, we admit that we have harmed other people and damaged our bond with the Body of Christ, the Church. And when we receive the words of Absolution from the priest, we are forgiven, healed, and welcomed back to our rightful place in loving relationship with God.

© Bill Wittman / www.wpwittman.com

In the Sacrament of Penance and Reconciliation, the priest continues the ministry of forgiveness entrusted by Christ to the Apostles.

> **How is the Sacrament of Penance and Reconciliation related to prayer?**

Article 68: Mary: Our Model of Discipleship and Faith

The belief that Catholics worship Mary and the saints is a common misunderstanding among non-Catholics. In fact, Catholics worship only the Blessed Trinity, for only our Triune God is worthy of adoration. In addition, Catholics believe that only God can answer prayers, so we never ask Mary or any other saint to answer our prayers because only God is able to do so. We do, however, ask Mary to intercede for us, and we honor her as the Mother of God.

Mary, Our Intercessor

When Catholics offer prayers directed to Mary, such as the Hail Mary, we are asking for Mary's intercessory help. Just as we ask our faith-filled friends on earth to pray for us, we can also ask our friends in Heaven to pray for us, and Mary is surely one of those friends.

New Eve
A reference to Mary, "mother of all the living," emphasizing her role in the new creation brought about by Christ. It is because Mary is the New Eve that in statues she is often portrayed standing on a snake, which represents the devil in the Book of Genesis.

A prayer to Mary is really a prayer asking that she offer that same prayer to God on our behalf. Because Mary is already in Heaven with God, she knows better than us how best to offer prayer to God.

In her earthly life, Mary cooperated completely with God's plan for our salvation. She is a model of true discipleship for us. Our prayers to Mary acknowledge that in her heavenly life, she can continue to do good with us and for us as she did during her earthly life with Jesus.

Honoring Mary

Although Catholics worship God alone, we venerate Mary and the saints. To venerate means to show honor, respect, and devotion. Catholics venerate Mary with various titles, the foremost of which is Mother of God. We celebrate various feasts and solemnities in her honor. These include the Feast of the Immaculate Conception, on December 8, which honors Mary's having been free of Original Sin from the moment of her conception; the Annunciation, on March 25, which celebrates Mary's yes to God's invitation to be the Mother of his Son; and her Assumption, on August 15, which commemorates

Primary Sources

Saint Justin Martyr on the Virgin Mary as the New Eve

Many Church Fathers and Doctors have regarded Mary as "the **New Eve**." The second-century apologist, Saint Justin Martyr, was one of the earliest Church Fathers to do so. He wrote:

For Eve, who was a virgin and undefiled, having conceived the word of the serpent, brought forth disobedience and death. But the Virgin Mary received faith and joy, when the angel Gabriel announced the good tidings to her that the Spirit of the Lord would come upon her, and the power of the Highest would overshadow her: wherefore also the Holy Thing begotten of her is the Son of God; and she replied, "Be it unto me according to your word" (Luke 1:38). And by her has He been born, to whom we have proved so many Scriptures refer, and by whom God destroys both the serpent and those angels and men who are like him; but works deliverance from death to those who repent of their wickedness and believe upon Him.

Mary's having been taken body and soul into Heaven at the time of her death. We also have many traditions of prayer and devotion associated with Mary, such as **litanies**, **novenas**, the wearing of medals, and the Rosary. Our veneration of Mary through these and other practices honors the unique role she played in God's plan of salvation and brings us closer to her Son.

litanies
Prayers consisting of a series of invocations and responses.

novenas
From the Latin word for "nine," public or private devotions that extend for a period of nine days.

The *Magnificat*

One way we can truly pray *with* Mary is to pray in her own words. The Gospel of Luke gives us Mary's prayer, the *Magnificat,* also called the Canticle of Mary (see 1:46–55).

After learning that she will be the Mother of Jesus, Mary visits her cousin Elizabeth, who is also with child. The two women—one old, one young, and both pregnant through a miracle of God's grace—rejoice together. In this context Mary offers her *Magnificat.* In this prayer, she praises the "Mighty One" (Luke 1:49) who has done great things for her and whose gracious mercy has changed the world. The God she "magnifies" is the One who fills the

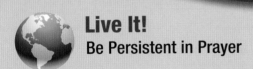

Live It!
Be Persistent in Prayer

Did you ever think that nagging could get you somewhere with God? Nagging is certainly not valued in our friendships or family relationships. But in different passages of Scripture, such as the example of the Friend at Midnight (see Luke 11: 5–8), Jesus advises us to essentially nag God for the things we really need—that is, to be persistent in our prayers. In his teaching about prayer, Jesus tells us:

> And I tell you, ask and you will receive; seek and you will find; knock and the door will be opened to you. For everyone who asks, receives; and the one who seeks, finds; and to the one who knocks, the door will be opened. (Luke 11:9–10)

Don't ever give up asking God for what you need for yourself and others. Be persistent in prayer, and, of course, always be open to God's response.

© Brooklyn Museum / Corbis

hungry but sends the rich away and who lifts up the lowly but throws down the powerful.

At the time when Mary prayed the *Magnificat,* her people, suffering under Roman oppression, were longing for justice. When we pray in her words, we not only honor Mary, we also stand in solidarity with all those suffering people today who live in the hope that God will, one day, do "great things" (Luke 1:49) for them.

What about the Virgin Mary makes her the ideal model of discipleship and faith?

For Review

1. What is prayer?

2. What is a prayer of petition? What is an intercessory prayer? What is an aspiration?

3. What is the purpose of a daily *examen*? How is it accomplished?

4. What does the Lord's Prayer teach us about God?

5. What does the Lord's Prayer teach us about ourselves?

6. What do Jesus' actions teach us about prayer?

7. Why are the Eucharist and the Sacrament of Penance and Reconciliation a crucial part of our prayer lives?

8. If only God can answer prayers, why do we pray to Mary and other saints?

We Respond through a Life of Discipleship

Chapter 15

Introduction

The word *disciple* comes from the Latin word meaning *student* or *pupil*. The disciples whom Jesus called to accompany him in his earthly life learned from all his words and actions. Jesus' whole life was a model for living a holy life. In fact, some Gospel texts refer to Jesus as *rabbi*, which is Hebrew for *teacher*.

Today being a disciple of Jesus means dedicating our whole lives to him and basing our decisions on his words and actions. We follow Christ's example of total self-giving by serving God and others. We seek forgiveness when we sin, and we extend forgiveness to those who harm us, just as Jesus forgave those who persecuted and crucified him. We act as true disciples of Jesus when we share the Good News of the Gospel with all those we meet, trusting that God is always at work in our efforts to witness to our faith.

Article 69: Mary: First Disciple of Jesus and Model of Faith

As we seek to respond to Jesus with a life of authentic Christian discipleship, the lives of the many holy women and men who have gone before us can be models for us. Foremost among these models is Mary, Jesus' mother and his first disciple.

The First Disciple of Jesus

As Jesus' own mother, Mary was among the first people to believe in him and to follow him as a disciple. We see evidence of this in New Testament texts. For example, in the account of the wedding at Cana (see John 2:1–11), Mary instructed the servers to "Do whatever he tells you" (verse 5). She clearly believed Jesus could and would reveal his glory through a miracle, or "sign." In fact, he did, by turning water into wine: "Jesus did this as the beginning of his signs in Cana in Galilee and so revealed his glory, and his disciples began to believe in him" (verse 11).

After Jesus' death, Resurrection, and Ascension, Mary gathered with the community of believers in Jerusalem who eventually became the Church: "All these devoted themselves with one accord to prayer, together with some women, and Mary the mother of Jesus, and his brothers" (Acts 1:14). Because this is before Pentecost, Mary is "imploring the gift of the Spirit" (*Dogmatic Constitution on the Church* [*Lumen Gentium*, 1964], 59) to be poured out upon them. In fact, we can safely say that Mary "aided the beginnings of the church by her prayers" (69). For this reason, she is herself not only the first disciple but also the Mother of all other disciples. Thus Mary is the Mother of the Church.

Model of Faith

The *Catechism of the Catholic Church* (CCC) states that "by her complete adherence to the Father's will, to his Son's redemptive work, and to every prompting of the Holy Spirit, the Virgin Mary is the Church's model of faith and charity" (967). We must remember that Mary was not a passive pawn in the hands of God. She was not a puppet whose every word and action God controlled; rather, it was Mary's faith that led her to the active, free choice to cooperate with God's plan for our salvation.

When the angel Gabriel appeared to Mary in the **Annunciation**, she questioned him, seeking to understand how it could be possible for a virgin to have a child. Ultimately she said yes, even though it is likely she did not fully understand all she was taking on. As the years went by, she watched her Son grow up and fulfill his mission of salvation. When that mission reached its completion, she courageously stayed by Jesus' side as he suffered the shameful, violent, and torturous death of a condemned criminal. At every turn, her trust in God's goodness and her surrender to his will make her a model of faith for us.

Mary's role in salvation history places her in a long line of courageous and holy women from Sacred Scripture who, in their own way and their own time, cooperated with God's plan for their people. Biblical women such as Deborah, the judge; Ruth, the Moabite daughter-in-law of Naomi; Hannah, the mother of Samuel; Judith, the widow and warrior; and Esther, the Persian queen are Mary's foremothers in faith. Like her, they confidently hoped for God's deliverance. Among this company of women, Mary stands out as unique, for "after a long period of waiting for the promise, the times are fulfilled" (Church, 55). In Mary, God's divine plan reaches its definitive moment as the Eternal Son of God takes on

Annunciation
The biblical event in which the Archangel Gabriel visits the Virgin Mary to announce that she is to be the Mother of the Savior.

This mosaic is from a chapel in the Church of the Assumption in Jerusalem. Which of these six women from the Old Testament can you identify from their images?

human flesh in her very body. Because of this she is also truly the Mother of God.

In what way is Mary uniquely suited for her role as a model of faith?

Article 70: Discipleship: Resisting Evil, Seeking Forgiveness

In our lives of Christian discipleship, we must open ourselves to God's grace so we can resist sin and evil as best we can. When we do give in to the temptations of sin, God's divine grace helps us to seek forgiveness for our failings.

Resisting Evil

As humans we enjoy the gift of freedom, or free will, that God has given us. Having free will means that God never forces us to choose the good. Instead we must freely decide for ourselves. However, the grace of Jesus' death and Resurrection has made us adopted children of God the Father and has given us a new life in the Holy Spirit.

Pray It!

A Prayer of Penance

The Sacrament of Penance and Reconciliation frees us from our sins and challenges us to have compassion for those who sin against us. Through this holy Sacrament, we are liberated to become forgivers. In the following prayer from the Rite of Penance, the priest prays on our behalf, asking God for his healing mercy and his help in living a life filled with grace. Reflect on the words of this prayer and ask God for his grace:

May the Passion of Our Lord Jesus Christ,
the intercession of the Blessed Virgin Mary and of all the saints,
whatever good you do and suffering you endure,
heal your sins,
help you grow in holiness,
and reward you with eternal life.
Go in peace.

(Rite of Penance, 93)

Our new life in Christ delivers us from the power of sin, making it easier for us to choose the good and resist evil. When we believe in Jesus and in the saving power of his death and Resurrection, we are strengthened to follow the example of his words and deeds. In "acting rightly and doing good" (CCC, 1709), we become holy: "The disciple attains the perfection of charity which is holiness. Having matured in grace, the moral life blossoms into eternal life in the glory of heaven" (1709).

Seeking Forgiveness

As imperfect creatures, none of us will ever resist sin and evil every single time we are confronted with them. Sinful behavior can seem attractive to us when our minds and hearts are misguided, divided, or disordered. When we give in to temptation, Jesus teaches us to repent, to turn ourselves back toward him, seeking forgiveness and a new start.

In order to experience the mercy and forgiveness of God, we must first freely admit our sin. The First Letter of John puts it this way: "If we say, 'We are without sin,' we deceive ourselves, and the truth is not in us. If we acknowledge our sins, he is faithful and just and will forgive our sins and cleanse us from every wrongdoing" (1:8–9). The *Catechism* uses the image of a doctor treating a patient to describe the way grace can heal our sin, once we have confessed it: "To do its work grace must uncover sin so as to convert our hearts. . . . Like a physician who probes the wound before treating it, God, by his Word and by his Spirit, casts a living light on sin" (1848).

When we have admitted and confessed our sin— brought it out of the darkness and into the marvelous light of God's mercy—God can truly heal us, forgive us, and put us back on the path of Christian discipleship. Though we can confess our sins to God and ask for forgiveness at any time, a true and heartfelt confession made within the context of the Sacrament of Penance and Reconciliation reminds us that we are part of a community of faith, a community harmed by the sin of any one of its members. This Sacrament grants us the gift of God's pardon and peace and strengthens us in our life of faith.

When we sin, what Sacrament brings us back to right relationship with God?

Article 71: Discipleship: Concern for the Common Good

Although our life of Christian discipleship must be rooted in prayer and in a close relationship with Jesus Christ, it cannot end there. When we are truly in communion with Jesus, we are attuned to his presence in the "least ones" (Matthew 25:45) and moved to serve them in his name. Indeed active involvement in the world is a key element of our baptismal call.

Catholic Social Teaching

In working for the common good, we participate in Christ's ministry of love and healing. As a disciple of Christ, how do you work for the common good?

The Church teachings that guide our efforts to create a more just and peaceful world are called Catholic social teaching (CST). The *Catechism* describes CST as "a body of doctrine, which is articulated as the Church interprets events in the course of history, with the assistance of the Holy Spirit, in the light of the whole of what has been revealed by Jesus Christ[1]" (2422). Though the tenets of CST are rooted in the Gospel message, Catholics credit Pope Leo XIII as the first Church leader to address the issue directly. His encyclical *On the Condition of Labor (Rerum Novarum)* was issued in 1891. Since that time seven key principles have emerged as crucial elements of Catholic social teaching:

© Con Tanasiuk / Design Pics / Corbis

- **Life and dignity of the human person** All human life is sacred and must be respected and protected at all times.

- **Call to family, community, and participation** We must be concerned about not only our own success and well-being but also the common good of all people, especially those most in need.

- **Rights and responsibilities** We all have the right to life and to life's basic needs, like food, shelter, and health care. We also have the duty to ensure that these rights are always protected. All persons have a right to participate in the cultural, economic, and political life of society.

- **Option for the poor and vulnerable** The needs of the poor must have first priority in how we spend our time, money, and other resources.

- **The dignity of work and the rights of workers** Workers have a right to a fair wage and to decent working conditions. Further, workers have the right

Primary Sources

"Sharing Catholic Social Teaching: Challenges and Directions"

The United States bishops' document "Sharing Catholic Social Teaching: Challenges and Directions" explains the main themes of Catholic social teaching (CST). You can find a full-text version of the publication on the website of the United States Conference of Catholic Bishops (*www.usccb.org*).

In the following passage, the Church urgently declares the need to proclaim the Gospel of life and call to justice, hallmarks of the Catholic faith:

The Church's social teaching is a rich treasure of wisdom about building a just society and living lives of holiness amidst the challenges of modern society. It offers moral principles and coherent values that are badly needed in our time. In this time of widespread violence and diminished respect for human life and dignity in our country and around the world, the Gospel of life and the biblical call to justice need to be proclaimed and shared with new clarity, urgency, and energy. ("Sharing Catholic Social Teaching: Challenges and Directions")

evangelization
The proclamation of the Gospel of Jesus Christ through word and witness.

to organize and join unions and to go on strike when their basic rights are not being respected.

- **Solidarity** We must support and care for one another as brothers and sisters in one global human family. Governments must protect human life and human rights, promote human dignity, and build the common good.

- **Care for God's creation** We must protect the resources of our planet, preserving them for future generations.

> **Which of the seven principles of Catholic social teaching do you think most needs to be promoted in your world?**

Article 72: Discipleship: The Call to Evangelization

When we see a good movie or hear a great song, we want to share it with others; we want others to experience the same joy we feel. It is natural to want to share something exciting and wonderful. This is exactly what we are called to do when we hear the message of the Gospel.

As baptized Christians we have been given the mission of sharing the Good News of Jesus Christ with all those we meet. Proclaiming the beauty and truth of Christ through our words and our actions is called **evangelization**. *Evangelization* comes from the Greek word *evangelion*, which means "good news." Because the life, death, and Resurrection of Jesus is truly Good News for all humanity, we want to share it with others.

Jesus and the Mission of the Disciples

We can see the roots of our call to evangelize in the mission Jesus gives to the disciples. For example, in the Gospel of Luke (see 10:1–20), Jesus sends out seventy-two disciples in pairs. He directs them to various cities and towns, asking them to teach and heal in his name. When his disciples return from their mission, they rejoice at all they have been able to accomplish. In the same way, in the Gospel of Matthew, the Risen Christ commissions the eleven Apostles with these famous words: "Go, therefore, and make disciples of all nations, baptizing them in the name of the Father, and of the Son, and of the holy Spirit, teaching them to observe all that I have commanded you. And behold, I am with you always, until the end of the age" (28:19–20). In carrying out their mission, the Apostles appoint successors as their own deaths draw

Did You Know?

Saint John Baptist de La Salle: Education for All

© Saint Mary's Press / Vicki Shuck

Saint John Baptist de La Salle was born into a wealthy family in Reims, France, in 1651. As a young man, he studied theology and was ordained a priest in 1678.

In seventeenth-century France, there were many poor people, and only the rich could afford to provide schooling for their children. De La Salle was moved by the plight of the poor he saw every day. He became determined to provide them with access to education. He believed that despite the poverty of their circumstances, they had a basic human right to better their lives. Eventually his passion for education became his only priority, and he renounced his family wealth to devote himself to it fully. He lived in community with the companions he had recruited to teach with him. Together they offered education to all children, regardless of families' ability to pay. These companions eventually became the members of a new religious order, the Brothers of the Christian Schools, also known as the Christian Brothers. Before De La Salle died in 1719, the Christian Brothers had created a network of schools all across France.

Today more than 900,000 students are taught in Lasallian schools, sponsored by the Christian Brothers in more than eighty countries around the globe. The mission of each of these schools is in keeping with De La Salle's original vision: to give a human and Christian education to the young, especially the poor.

De La Salle's feast day is April 7.

missionaries
People who devote themselves to spreading the Gospel—in word and service—to those who have not heard it or to those who have rejected it. Missionaries often serve in foreign countries.

near. Thus the work of evangelization can continue "until the end of the age" (28:20).

Jesus and Our Mission

Jesus has entrusted us with the same mission of evangelization as the original disciples. We are able to bear authentic witness to our faith in Jesus right here today in our own world. We hope that this witness may, in time, lead others to faith in him. For example, we can pray regularly; share generously, especially with the poor; and speak freely and without embarrassment of our Christian faith. In our efforts to encourage faith in Christ, God will surely give us courage and wisdom so that, in our words and actions, "the power of the Gospel may shine out" (*Dogmatic Constitution on the Church [Lumen Gentium, 1964]*, 35).

✝ Faith in Action
Maryknoll: Evangelizing in Mission

© Horace Bristol / CORBIS

Maryknoll is a Catholic organization, based in the United States, which sends sisters, brothers, priests, and lay **missionaries** throughout the world to engage in works of service, justice, and evangelization. Since its founding in 1911, members of Maryknoll have witnessed to the Gospel of Jesus Christ by working with refugees in war zones; ministering to the sick, elderly, and orphans; and building communities of faith. Most missionaries serve in a particular location in Africa, Asia, or Latin America for three or four years. Other members decide to dedicate their whole lives to this ministry.

Maryknoll missionaries use their words and their deeds "to announce and to give witness to the Good News of the Reign of God." However, their proclamation of the Gospel message takes into account the needs of the whole person—both body and soul. The missionaries of Maryknoll also deeply respect human freedom, which, as part of our inherent dignity, is God's gracious gift. Regardless of whether a particular person chooses to embrace the Good News of Jesus Christ, Maryknoll trusts that its missionaries have planted seeds of faith that, one day, may bear fruit.

Evangelizing, Not Proselytizing

In some Christian denominations, the mission to evangelize has become distorted by proselytism, the active, even aggressive, seeking of converts to one's own religious faith, often away from another religion. Usually with the best of intentions (the salvation of souls), proselytizers will sometimes relentlessly pursue people, even individuals who have never shown interest in their message.

The Catholic approach to evangelization is different, guided by an understanding that God calls each person to an authentic relationship with him. We know that we must be "on the lookout for occasions to proclaim Christ by word, either to unbelievers . . . or to the faithful" (*Decree on the Apostolate of Lay People [Apostolicam Actuositatem],* 6); however, we also recognize that we must respect people's basic freedom to accept or reject the Gospel message. The witness of our own faithful lives and our proclamation of the Good News may not have

Live It!
Go and Make Disciples: Renewed Evangelization

In 1990, the United States Conference of Catholic Bishops unveiled *Go and Make Disciples*, a plan for a renewed effort of evangelization. This document presented three goals:

- **Goal 1:** To bring about in all Catholics such an enthusiasm for their faith that, in living their faith in Jesus, they freely share it with others. (46)
- **Goal 2:** To invite all people in the United States, whatever their social or cultural background, to hear the message of salvation in Jesus Christ so they may come to join us in the fullness of the Catholic faith. (53)
- **Goal 3:** To foster Gospel values in our society, promoting the dignity of the human person, the importance of the family, and the common good of our society, so that our nation may continue to be transformed by the saving power of Jesus Christ. (56)

Reflect on these goals and seek ways to live them out in your life.

any immediate effect on another person. However, we trust that God is always at work, in ways we cannot fully understand, and that slowly, even without being noticed, the Gospel is spreading throughout the world.

What is your experience with evangelization?

For Review

1. Why is Mary considered to be the first disciple of Jesus?

2. How is Mary a model of faith for us?

3. How does the grace of Jesus' death and Resurrection empower us to resist sin and evil?

4. Why is the Sacrament of Penance and Reconciliation important?

5. What is Catholic social teaching?

6. Describe three principles of Catholic social teaching.

7. How is the Catholic approach to evangelization different from that of proselytization?

Our Response to Jesus

Chapter 16

Introduction

Have you ever wondered if believing in Jesus makes any real difference? Have you ever thought, in the end does it really matter what we believe or in whom we believe?

If you have, be assured that the answer to both questions is a definitive yes, it matters a lot! Our response to Jesus during our lives on earth shapes the ultimate destiny of our eternal lives in Heaven. If we seek to follow him through faithful lives of prayer and discipleship in the company of the Church, we will share in all that Jesus has promised us: new and resurrected life, union with the Blessed Trinity, and a vision of our Triune God in heavenly glory.

Jesus wants us to directly experience the Beatific Vision after our earthly lives end. Yet, at all times we remain utterly free people. We are free to accept or reject the grace and blessings Jesus offers to us. If, however, we exercise our freedom wisely, we can make choices that bring us closer to the ultimate destiny Jesus desires for all of us: eternal life and happiness with him in Heaven.

Article 73: Our Destiny: Union with God

We are created and destined to be fully united with God forever in Heaven. God wants this so much that he sent his Son to redeem us so we can share a life of love with him eternally. Even in our earthly lives, we experience a degree of union with God through our participation in the Sacraments and through our efforts to follow a path of holiness by engaging in discipleship and prayer. If our earthly lives are faithful, we will attain our final destiny: complete union with the Blessed Trinity.

Faith and Our Destiny

"Believing in Jesus Christ and in the One who sent him for our salvation is necessary for obtaining that salvation[1]" (*Catechism of the Catholic Church [CCC]*, 161). In other words, without faith, we cannot have salvation. Faith in Jesus is our path to eternal life, assuring us that we will one day enjoy the company of the Blessed Trinity and all the angels and saints. Faith is an act of the entire Church, for the faith of the Church as a whole is an important part of the faith of every member of the Body of Christ. The faith of the Church calls forth our own individual faith and nurtures and supports our belief in God. Saint Thomas Aquinas described faith as "a foretaste of the knowledge that will make us blessed in the life to come[2]" (184). The blessedness of the afterlife to which Saint Thomas referred is called the Beatific Vision.

The Beatific Vision

The Beatific Vision is the encounter with and sight of God in the glory of Heaven after we die. Whether we acknowledge it or not, the desire to see God, to know God, is built into us. Thus the Beatific Vision is the ultimate goal of our lives. When the journey of our earthly lives is complete, God opens the divine mystery to us, giving us the capacity to contemplate, understand, and appreciate his heavenly glory.

Although no one has come back to earth from Heaven to tell us what the Beatific Vision is like, several New Testament passages refer to it. In the Beatitudes, Jesus proclaims: "Blessed are the clean of heart, / for they will see God" (Matthew 5:8). Similarly, Saint Paul writes in his First Letter to the Corinthians: "At present we see indistinctly, as in a mirror, but then face to face. At present I know partially; then I shall know fully, as I am fully known" (13:12). Finally, the First Letter of John says that "we shall be like him, for we shall see him as he is" (3:2).

Some of the early Church Fathers also wrote about the Beatific Vision. For example, Saint Augustine described it in this way: "God himself will be the goal of our desires; we shall contemplate him without end, love him without surfeit, praise him without weariness. This gift, this state, this act, like eternal life itself, will assuredly be common to all." As we live our earthly lives, these reflections on the Beatific Vision help us to keep in mind the ultimate goal of our heavenly life.

What are some examples of earthly union with God from your life?

Article 74: The Church: Visible and Spiritual

Our baptismal call to live lives of faithful discipleship does not happen in isolation. We are members of the Church, the Body of Christ, and we are brothers and sisters to one another. There is a visible reality of the Church that is clear to all, but there is also an invisible, spiritual reality that is known only through the eyes of faith. This invisible reality is often described as the Mystical Body of Christ and as the Communion of Saints.

The Mystical Body of Christ

When we are baptized into Christ and become members of his Body, the Church, we become part of both a visible, human society and an invisible, divine reality. The

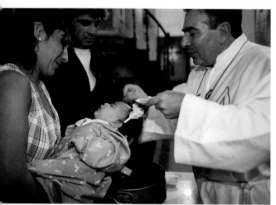

© Pablo Corral V / CORBIS

What invisible spiritual reality is signified by the visible sign of being immersed in the waters of Baptism?

visible aspect of the Church is easy for us to see. For example, we can study history to see the Church's presence and involvement in many human achievements and affairs. Additionally, we can look to the present day and the many ministries of the Church in parishes, schools, hospitals, and social service agencies. We can also simply look around us to see one another. The visible organization of the Church includes hierarchical leaders, ordained ministers, members of religious orders, and the laity.

The invisible reality of the Church is more difficult to perceive: in fact, it can be seen from only a perspective of faith. This spiritual component of the Church is called the Mystical Body of Christ, which the *Catechism* describes as a "supernatural unity . . . a single mystical person[3]" (1474). This means that all members of the Church are truly and spiritually united as one Body in the divine life of the Blessed Trinity. The members include those living on earth, those being purified in Purgatory, and those living in Heaven. Think about that: Nothing can separate us from the Mystical Body of which we are a part, not even death.

The Communion of Saints

Although we often think of saints as only those people who have been officially canonized, or recognized, as such by the Church, a saint is really anyone who is trying to live a holy and Christian life, through the grace of Christ. This includes people living on earth, individuals who have died and are in Purgatory, and the people who are, even now, dwelling in the glory of God's holy presence in Heaven. This union of all God's holy ones—on earth, in Purgatory, and in Heaven—is called the Communion of Saints.

As part of the Communion of Saints, we are united "in holy things" and "among holy persons" (CCC, 948). The "holy things" in which we are united are the Sacraments, especially the Eucharist, and other spiritual gifts. The "holy persons" with whom we are joined as one are all those members of Christ's own Body, the great "cloud of witnesses" (Hebrews 12:1) who have faithfully kept their "eyes fixed on Jesus, the leader and perfecter of faith" (12:2).

Why do you think we have both an invisible and a visible reality of the Church?

Article 75: The Christian Understanding of Death

Just as our response to Jesus affects every aspect of our daily living, it also affects our approach to death and dying.

Live It!
Start with the End in Mind

Have you ever heard the phrase "start with the end in mind"? This means that before you begin something, you decide what end result you would like. Whether you are writing an essay, planning a mission trip, or going sight-seeing, you can have a better experience if you have the end result in mind.

Being conscious of the end can help us to cope with death. The truth is that we have a limited time on earth, and eventually our earthly life will end. We are called, though, to a greater end—eternal life with God in Heaven. How would your life be different if you made your decisions with the goal of Heaven in mind? Start each day by asking yourself the following questions:

- What can I do today to grow closer to God?
- What can I do today to help others recognize God's loving presence in their lives?
- What can I do today to share the Gospel message with others?

The Resurrection of the Body

God created human beings with both bodies and souls. After the physical body dies, the soul separates from the body and goes to meet God. At the Final Judgment, when Christ comes again in glory, the soul will be reunited with the body in a new and glorified state. Our bodily resurrection has been a central truth of Christian faith from the beginning, being consistently proclaimed in every book of the New Testament and even in some

Faith in Action
Cardinal Joseph Bernardin of Chicago

© Ralf-Finn Hestoft / CORBIS

Cardinal Joseph Bernardin had been archbishop of Chicago for thirteen years when he was diagnosed with pancreatic cancer in June 1995. After undergoing surgery, chemotherapy, and radiation, his cancer was in remission and he began a new phase of his ministry as a priest and bishop: outreach to cancer patients. He visited hundreds of suffering people in hospitals, in hospices, and in their homes, and he corresponded with many more. He encouraged them to view "death as a friend, as the transition from earthly life to life eternal" (*New York Times*, August 31, 1996). Cardinal Bernardin was willing to take up the cross of cancer and journey with others through the final days of their earthly pilgrimage.

At the end of August 1996, Cardinal Bernardin announced that his cancer had returned and that he had less than a year to live. Since he was no longer able to keep up his busy schedule of public appearances and sacramental ministry, Cardinal Bernardin turned to writing. He completed his spiritual autobiography *The Gift of Peace* (Chicago: Loyola Press, 1997) just days before his death on November 14, 1996.

For many people Cardinal Bernardin was a model of how to die—with grace, dignity, and faith. When asked what he expected in the afterlife, he replied: "I don't have a crystal ball, but I know the Lord's promises—to be with him and to be happy with him. In faith I know the Lord will be waiting for me and his promises will be fulfilled" (*New York Times*, August 31, 1996).

books of the Old Testament. For example, in the Second Book of Maccabees, a mother speaks to her seven sons who are facing martyrdom because of their fidelity to Jewish Law:

> I do not know how you came to be in my womb; it was not I who gave you breath and life, nor was it I who arranged the elements you are made of. Therefore, since it is the Creator of the universe who shaped the beginning of humankind and brought about the origin of everything, he, in his mercy, will give you back both breath and life, because you now disregard yourselves for the sake of his law. (7:22–23)

This courageous woman recognizes that God, the Author of all life, will surely bring her sons to a new and eternal life that is both physical and spiritual.

"By Your Cross and Resurrection, You Have Set Us Free"

We proclaim these words in the Memorial Acclamation at a Eucharistic liturgy. We mean that Jesus' death has forever changed death into something positive. If you have been to a Catholic funeral Mass, you may recall hearing this prayer: "Lord, for your faithful people life is changed, not ended. When the body of our earthly dwelling lies in death we gain an everlasting dwelling place in heaven" (Eucharistic Prayer, *Rite of Christian Burial*). Because Christians enter into the death of Christ in Baptism, our physical death allows us to share in the glory of his Resurrection.

"Pray for us now and at the hour of our death." These words remind us that our destiny lies not in this world but in eternal happiness with God in Heaven.

Preparing for Death

Have you ever prayed the words of the Hail Mary—"pray for us sinners / now and at the hour of our death"? If so, then you have, in a small way, prepared for your own death. For a young person with many years ahead of you, this may sound odd or morbid. But it is in fact something the Church encourages for people of all ages. We need to remember our mortality, the fact that we will not live on this earth forever. It helps us to know that mortal time is limited and that we do not have forever to fulfill our earthly lives.

© Nikola Bilic / shutterstock.com

Considering our own mortality is also a way of growing in faith, of surrendering to God's divine will and trusting that our lives are truly in God's hands, from the moment of our conception to the moment of our last breath.

> **What do you think is meant by the phrase "life is changed, not ended"?**

Article 76: Heaven, Hell, and Purgatory

After death, all people will face divine judgment twice, in the Last Judgment and in each person's Particular Judgment. The Last Judgment will occur for everyone

Did You Know?

Dante's *Divine Comedy*

© Bettmann / CORBIS

Heaven, Hell, and Purgatory have always been popular subjects for artists. Perhaps because no one living has ever experienced these realities, painters, sculptors, filmmakers, and writers can allow their imagination free rein to show them creatively and vividly.

One of the most famous portrayals of Heaven, Hell, and Purgatory is in Dante's *Divine Comedy*. It is an epic poem composed by this devoutly Catholic writer in the early fourteenth century. The narrator is meant to be Dante himself. He recounts an imaginary journey he takes from the depths of Hell, through Purgatory, and finally to the paradise of Heaven. Along the way he meets people from history, literature, and his own native Florence, in Italy. He learns how these individuals' virtues and vices, strengths and weaknesses, and good and evil choices determined their final fate.

The three volumes of the *Divine Comedy*—*Inferno*, *Purgatorio*, and *Paradiso*—are considered classics of Western literature. They give us not only an artist's creative insight into the realities of the afterlife but also a renewed appreciation for the power of fiction and poetry to stir us to faith and conversion.

when Jesus comes again in glory, and no one but God the Father knows when that will be. At the moment of our death, we will face Christ, the judge of the living and the dead, in the Particular Judgment, which has three possible outcomes: Heaven, Hell, or Purgatory.

Heaven

Those who die in God's grace and friendship and are perfectly purified go immediately to Heaven. There they live in the company of the Blessed Trinity forever. The *Catechism* defines Heaven in various ways: as "communion of life and love with the Trinity, with the Virgin Mary, the angels, and all the blessed" (1024); as "the ultimate end and fulfillment of the deepest human longings, the state of supreme, definitive happiness" (1024); and as "the blessed community of all who are perfectly incorporated into Christ" (1026).

Though these definitions give us some glimpse into the reality of Heaven's glory, we cannot really know what Heaven is like until we are there. In fact, the idea of Heaven stretches the limits of human imagination

Primary Sources

Dante's *Paradiso*

In the following excerpt from the *Paradiso*, the third and final part of the *Divine Comedy*, Dante encounters his beloved Beatrice, his guide through Heaven, and beholds the sun as no mortal can:

> I saw Beatrice turn round
> and left, that she might see the sun; no eagle
> has ever stared so steadily at it. . . .
> [M]y action drew, and on the sun I set
> my sight more than we usually do.
> More is permitted to our powers there
> than is permitted here, by virtue of
> that place, made for mankind as its true home.
> I did not bear it long, but not so briefly
> as not to see it sparkling round about,
> like molten iron emerging from the fire.

and language. For this reason, Sacred Scripture uses metaphors in an effort to give us some sense of it. These metaphors include "life, light, peace, wedding feast, wine of the kingdom, the Father's house, the heavenly Jerusalem, paradise" (CCC, 1027).

Hell

Because God gave us the gift of free will, he never forces us to be good or to do the right thing. We must freely choose to do so for ourselves, for the only way to be in communion with God is to freely choose to love him. When we choose evil, we reject the love, grace, and redemption God offers to us, and instead choose Hell, the "state of definitive self-exclusion from communion with God and the blessed" (CCC, 1033). Those in Hell are eternally separated from God; this is Hell's chief punishment.

Pray It!

Prayer for the Dead

As Catholics we have the tradition of praying for our deceased brothers and sisters. This is a way of continuing our relationship with them and assisting them on their journey to Heaven. We pray for those who have died at every Mass. All Souls' Day, on November 2, is a special time set aside to pray for the dead.

This prayer for All Souls' Day helps us to remember those who have died:

O God who will that your Only Begotten Son,
having conquered death,
should pass over into the realm of heaven,
grant, we pray, to your departed servants
that, with the mortality of this life overcome,
they may gaze eternally on you,
their Creator and Redeemer.
Through our Lord Jesus Christ, your Son,
who lives and reigns with you
in the Unity of the Holy Spirit,
one God, for ever and ever.

(Roman Missal)

God does not send anyone to Hell. Rather, through our own choices, we can send ourselves there. By rejecting God's grace, we can condemn ourselves to separation from God for all eternity.

Purgatory

Purgatory is for souls ultimately destined for Heaven but who are not yet pure enough to enter it. Purgatory is a state of final purification or cleansing that allows these individual souls to achieve the holiness needed to experience eternal joy in Heaven. When we pray for the dead, we are interceding for those in Purgatory. We are asking that they may soon enjoy the everlasting glory, peace, and comfort of God's holy presence.

> **Why do you think there are two times of judgment for humankind?**

For Review

1. Explain why faith in Jesus is our path to eternal life.

2. Define the Beatific Vision.

3. What is the Mystical Body of Christ?

4. What is the Communion of Saints?

5. How did the death and Resurrection of Jesus change death for all of us?

6. Why is it important to remember that death is inevitable?

7. What are some ideas and images that help us to understand Heaven?

8. What is the relationship between Hell and God's gift of free will?

9. What is the purpose of Purgatory?

Glossary

A

Abba A way of addressing God the Father used by Jesus to call attention to his—and our—intimate relationship with his Heavenly Father. *Abba* means "my Father" or "our Father" in Aramaic. *(article 53)*

Annunciation The biblical event in which the Archangel Gabriel visits the Virgin Mary to announce that she is to be the Mother of the Savior. *(article 69)*

Apostolic Succession The uninterrupted passing on of apostolic preaching and authority from the Apostles directly to all bishops. It is accomplished through the laying on of hands when a bishop is ordained in the Sacrament of Holy Orders as instituted by Christ. The office of bishop is permanent, because at ordination a bishop is marked with an indelible, sacred character. *(article 19)*

aspiration A short prayer meant to be memorized and repeated throughout the day. The word comes from the Latin *aspirare,* "to breathe upon." In this way, we can heed Saint Paul's injunction to pray without ceasing and continually turn our thoughts toward God. *(article 63)*

B

Beatific Vision Directly encountering and seeing God in the glory of Heaven. *(article 28)*

beatitude The state of eternal happiness with God in Heaven. *(article 3)*

Beatitudes The teachings of Jesus that begin the Sermon on the Mount and that summarize the New Law of Christ. The Beatitudes describe the actions and attitudes by which one can discover genuine happiness, and they teach us the final end to which God calls us: full communion with him in the Kingdom of Heaven. *(article 31)*

C

canonized A deceased Catholic's having been publicly and officially proclaimed a saint. *(article 22)*

canon of Scripture The books of the Bible officially recognized by the Church as the inspired Word of God. *(article 17)*

chastity The virtue by which people are able to successfully and healthfully integrate their sexuality into their total person; recognized as one of the fruits of the Holy Spirit. Also one of the vows of religious life. *(article 48)*

Christ From the Greek translation of the Hebrew *Messiah,* meaning "anointed." It became the name proper to Jesus because he accomplished perfectly the divine mission of priest, prophet, and king, signified by his anointing as Messiah. *(article 4)*

Christological Having to do with the branch of theology called Christology. Christology is the study of the divinity of Jesus Christ, the Son of God and the Second Divine Person of the Trinity, and his earthly ministry and eternal mission. *(article 7)*

circumcision   The act, required by Jewish Law, of removing the foreskin of the penis. Since the time of Abraham, it has been a sign of God's covenant relationship with the Jewish people. *(article 30)*

collects Prayers offered by the person leading an assembly in communal prayer. *(article 28)*

conscience The "inner voice," guided by human reason and Divine Law, that enables us to judge what is good and what is evil. To make good judgments, one needs to have a well-formed conscience. *(article 42)*

consecrate To declare or set apart as sacred or to solemnly dedicate to God's service; to make holy. *(article 37)*

covenant   A personal, solemn promise of faithful love that involves mutual commitments and creates a sacred relationship. *(article 1)*

D

divine economy Also known as the economy of salvation, this refers to God's eternal plan and his actions for the salvation of humanity. *(article 2)*

doctrine An official, authoritative teaching of the Church based on the Revelation of God. *(article 1)*

domestic church A name for the first and most fundamental community of faith: the family. *(article 21)*

E

Ecumenical Council A gathering of the Church's bishops from around the world convened by the Pope or approved by him to address pressing issues in the Church. *(article 6)*

ecumenism The movement to restore unity among all Christians, the unity to which the Church is called by the Holy Spirit. *(article 19)*

embryo The unborn child from the time it implants in the uterine wall through the eighth week of its development. *(article 49)*

Eucharist, the Also called the Mass or Lord's Supper, and based on a word for "thanksgiving," it is the central Christian liturgical celebration, established by Jesus at the Last Supper. In the Eucharist, the sacrificial death and Resurrection of Jesus are both remembered and renewed. The term sometimes refers specifically to the consecrated bread and wine that have become the Body and Blood of Christ. *(article 9)*

Eucharistic species The gifts of bread and wine after they have become Christ's Body and Blood. *(article 37)*

evangelical counsels The call to go beyond the minimum rules of life required by God (such as the Ten Commandments and the Precepts of the Church) and strive for spiritual perfection through a life marked by a commitment to chastity, poverty, and obedience. *(article 40)*

Evangelists From a Greek word meaning "messenger of good news," the title given to the authors of the Gospels of Matthew, Mark, Luke, and John. *(article 17)*

evangelization The proclamation of the Gospel of Jesus Christ through word and witness. *(article 72)*

ex cathedra A Latin term literally meaning "from the chair," referring to pronouncements concerning faith or morals made by the Pope, acting with full Apostolic authority, as pastor and teacher of all Christians. *(article 19)*

F

Fall, the Also called the Fall from Grace, the biblical Revelation about the origins of sin and evil in the world, expressed figuratively in the account of Adam and Eve in Genesis. *(article 13)*

Fathers of the Church (Church Fathers) During the early centuries of the Church, those teachers whose writings extended the Tradition of the Apostles and who continue to be important for the Church's teachings. *(article 6)*

fetus The unborn child from the end of the eighth week after conception to the moment of birth. *(article 49)*

filial Having to do with the relationship of a child to his or her parent. *(article 3)*

free will The gift from God that allows human beings to choose from among various actions, for which we are held accountable. It is the basis for moral responsibility. *(article 15)*

G

genocide The systematic and planned extermination of a national, racial, ethnic, or cultural group. *(article 49)*

Gentile Someone who is not Jewish. *(article 16)*

grace The free and undeserved gift that God gives us to empower us to respond to his call and to live as his adopted sons and daughters. Grace restores our loving communion with the Holy Trinity, lost through sin. *(article 36)*

H

Heaven A state of eternal life and union with God, in which one experiences full happiness and the satisfaction of the deepest human longings. *(article 50)*

heresy The conscious and deliberate rejection by a baptized person of a truth of faith that must be believed. *(article 7)*

holy day of obligation Feast day in the Liturgical Year on which, in addition to Sundays, Catholics are obliged to participate in the Eucharist. *(article 26)*

hypostatic union The union of Jesus Christ's divine and human natures in one Divine Person. *(article 32)*

I

incarnate, Incarnation From the Latin, meaning "to become flesh," referring to the mystery of Jesus Christ, the Divine Son of God, becoming man. In the Incarnation, Jesus Christ became truly man while remaining truly God. *(article 2)*

infallibility The gift given by the Holy Spirit to the Church whereby the pastors of the Church, the Pope and the bishops in union with him, can definitively proclaim a doctrine of faith and morals without error. *(article 19)*

immortal Living forever; not subject to death. *(article 46)*

inspired Written by human beings with the guidance of the Holy Spirit to teach faithfully and without error the saving truth that God willed to give us. *(article 16)*

intercessory prayer A prayer form in which we ask God's help for other people's needs; also called intercession. *(article 63)*

interreligious dialogue The efforts to build cooperative and constructive interaction with other world religions. *(article 19)*

L

laity All members of the Church with the exception of those who are ordained as bishops, priests, or deacons. The laity share in Christ's role as priest, prophet, and king, witnessing to God's love and power in the world. *(article 40)*

lament A prayer, petition, or ritual of grief that honors the death of a loved one. Many of the psalms are laments. *(article 58)*

Last Judgment The judgment of the human race by Jesus Christ at his Second Coming. It is also called the Final Judgment. *(article 9)*

litanies Prayers consisting of a series of invocations and responses. *(article 68)*

liturgy The Church's official, public, communal prayer. It is God's work, in which the People of God participate. The Church's most important liturgy is the Eucharist, or the Mass. *(article 38)*

M

Magisterium The Church's living teaching office, which consists of all bishops, in communion with the Pope, the bishop of Rome. *(article 18)*

mammon An Aramaic word meaning wealth or property. *(article 53)*

martyrdom Witness to the saving message of Christ through the sacrifice of one's life. *(article 14)*

Messiah Hebrew word for "anointed one." The equivalent Greek term is *christos.* Jesus is the Christ and the Messiah because he is the Anointed One. *(article 4)*

missionaries People who devote themselves to spreading the Gospel—in word and service—to those who have not heard it or to those who have rejected it. Missionaries often serve in foreign countries. *(article 72)*

monotheism The belief in and worship of only one God. *(article 1)*

N

New Covenant The covenant or law established by God in Jesus Christ to fulfill and perfect the Old Covenant or Mosaic Law. It is a perfection here on earth of the Divine Law. The law of the New Covenant is called a law of love, grace, and freedom. The New Covenant will never end or diminish, and nothing new will be revealed until Christ comes again in glory. *(article 51)*

New Eve A reference to Mary, "mother of all the living," emphasizing her role in the new creation brought about by Christ. It is because Mary is the New Eve that in statues she is often portrayed standing on a snake, which represents the devil in the Book of Genesis. *(article 68)*

Nicene Creed The formal statement or profession of Christian belief originally formulated at the Council of Nicaea in 325 and amplified at the Council of Constantinople in 381. *(article 1)*

novenas From the Latin word for "nine," public or private devotions that extend for a period of nine days. *(article 68)*

O

Original Sin The sin by which the first humans disobeyed God and thereby lost their original holiness and became subject to death. Original Sin is transmitted to every person born into the world, except Jesus and Mary. *(article 26)*

P

parables Short stories that use everyday images to communicate religious messages. Jesus used parables frequently in his teaching as a way of presenting the Good News of salvation *(article 54)*

Paraclete A term meaning "advocate" or "helper," used in the Gospel of John to describe the Holy Spirit, the Third Divine Person of the Trinity, whom Jesus promised to the disciples as an advocate and counselor. *(article 5)*

Parousia The Second Coming of Christ as judge of all the living and the dead, at the end of time, when the Kingdom of God will be fulfilled. *(article 57)*

Particular Judgment The judgment that occurs immediately at time of our death, when our immortal soul will be judged as worthy or unworthy of Heaven. *(article 52)*

Paschal Mystery The work of salvation accomplished by Jesus Christ mainly through his Passion, death, Resurrection, and Ascension. *(article 15)*

patriarchs The ancient fathers of the Jewish People, whose stories are recounted in the Book of Genesis. *(article 12)*

Pentecost The fiftieth day following Easter, which commemorates the descent of the Holy Spirit on the early Apostles and disciples. *(article 5)*

personal sin Any deliberate offense, in thought, word, or deed, against the will of God. *(article 26)*

Pharisees A Jewish sect at the time of Jesus known for its strict adherence to the Law. *(article 30)*

philosophy In Greek this word literally means "love of wisdom." It refers to the study of human existence using logical reasoning. *(article 6)*

pluralistic Characterized by the presence of many different ethnic, religious, or cultural groups. *(article 31)*

prayer of petition A prayer form in which we ask God for something we need. *(article 63)*

procreation The act or process of conceiving and bearing children. *(article 48)*

Purgatory A state of final purification or cleansing, which one may need to enter following death and before entering Heaven. *(article 52)*

R

Reign of God The reign or rule of God over the hearts of people and, as a consequence of that, the development of a new social order based on unconditional love. The fullness of God's Reign will not be realized until the end of time. Also called the Kingdom of God. *(article 4)*

religious vows The promises made by members of religious communities to follow the evangelical counsels of poverty, chastity, and obedience. *(article 4)*

S

Sacrament An efficacious and visible sign of God's grace, instituted by Christ and entrusted to the Church, by which divine life is dispensed to us. The Seven Sacraments are Baptism, the Eucharist, Confirmation, Penance and Reconciliation, Anointing of the Sick, Matrimony, and Holy Orders. *(article 37)*

sacred The quality of being holy, worthy of respect and reverence; set apart for God. *(article 6)*

Sacred Tradition The process of passing on the Gospel message. Sacred Tradition, which began with the oral communication of the Gospel by the Apostles, was written down in Sacred Scripture, is handed down and lived out in the life of the Church, and is interpreted by the Magisterium under the guidance of the Holy Spirit. *(article 18)*

Sadducees A Jewish sect at the time of Jesus known for its strong commitment to the Temple in Jerusalem. *(article 30)*

salvation history The pattern of specific events in human history in which God clearly reveals his presence and saving actions. Salvation was accomplished once and for all through Jesus Christ, a truth foreshadowed and revealed throughout the Old Testament. *(article 11)*

Samaritan An inhabitant of Samaria, in the central hill country of Palestine. The Samaritans rejected the Jerusalem Temple and worshiped instead at Mount Gerizim. The New Testament mentions the Jewish rejection of Samaritans in both the Parable of the Good Samaritan (see Luke 10:29–37) and the account of Jesus' speaking with the Samaritan woman at the well (see John 4:1–42). *(article 41)*

sanctify To make holy; sanctification is the process of responding to God's grace and becoming closer to God. *(article 29)*

sanctifying grace The grace that heals our human nature wounded by sin and restores us to friendship with God by giving us a share in the divine life of the Trinity. It is a supernatural gift of God, infused into our souls by the Holy Spirit, that continues the work of making us holy. *(article 51)*

scribes Jewish legal scholars or teachers of Jewish Law. In the New Testament they are associated with the Pharisees and the High Priests as opponents of Jesus. *(article 30)*

solemnities Important holy days in the Catholic liturgical calendar, such as Christmas, Easter, Pentecost, and All Saints' Day. *(article 9)*

solidarity Union of one's heart and mind with all people. Solidarity leads to the just distribution of material goods, creates bonds between opposing groups and nations, and leads to the spread of spiritual goods such as friendship and prayer. *(article 57)*

Son of Man A messianic title from the Book of Daniel, used to describe a figure who receives authority over other nations from God; the only messianic title in the Gospels used by Jesus to describe himself. *(article 41)*

stewards People who are put in charge of managing, caring for, and protecting something, such as money or personal property. *(article 44)*

stewardship The careful and responsible management of someone or something that has been entrusted to a person's care. This includes responsibly using and caring for the gifts of creation that God has given us. *(article 44)*

synoptic Gospels From the Greek for "seeing the whole together," the name given to the Gospels of Matthew, Mark, and Luke, because they are similar in style and content. *(article 55)*

T

theodicy From the Greek words for "God" and "justice," referring to the study of evil and suffering in the world, which seems contrary to the existence of a presumably good God. *(article 15)*

Theological Virtues The name for the God-given virtues of faith, hope, and love. These virtues enable us to know God as God and lead us to union with him in mind and heart. *(article 58)*

theology Literally, "the study of God"; the academic discipline and effort to understand, interpret, and order our experience of God and Christian faith. *(article 23)*

Theotokos A Greek title for Mary meaning "God bearer." *(article 7)*

Trinity From the Latin *trinus*, meaning "threefold," referring to the central mystery of the Christian faith that God exists as a communion of three distinct and interrelated Divine Persons: Father, Son, and Holy Spirit. The doctrine of the Trinity is a mystery that is inaccessible to human reason alone and is known through Divine Revelation only. *(article 1)*

V

vocation A call from God to all members of the Church to embrace a life of holiness. Specifically, it refers to a call to live the holy life as an ordained minister, as a vowed religious (sister or brother), or in a Christian marriage. Single life that involves a personal consecration or commitment to a permanent, celibate gift of self to God and one's neighbor is also a vocational state. *(article 12)*

Index

Acknowledgments

The scriptural quotations in this book are from the *New American Bible, revised edition* © 2010, 1991, 1986, and 1970 Confraternity of Christian Doctrine Inc., Washington, D.C. All Rights Reserved. No part of this work may be reproduced or transmitted in any form or by any means, electronic or mechanical, including photocopying, recording, or by any information storage and retrieval system, without permission in writing from the copyright owner.

The excerpts marked *Catechism* and *CCC* are from the English translation of the *Catechism of the Catholic Church* for use in the United States of America, second edition. Copyright © 1994 by the United States Catholic Conference, Inc.—Libreria Editrice Vaticana (LEV). English translation of the *Catechism of the Catholic Church: Modifications from the Editio Typica* copyright © 1997 by the United States Catholic Conference, Inc.—LEV.

The excerpts on pages 14, 72–73, and 73 are from *Declaration on the Relation of the Church to Non-Christian Religions* (*Nostra Aetate*, 1965), numbers 4 and 2, respectively, in *Vatican Council II: Constitutions, Decrees, Declarations*, Austin Flannery, general editor (Northport, NY: Costello Publishing Company, 1996). Copyright © 1996 by Reverend Austin Flannery, OP.

The excerpt on page 16 is from "The Athanasian Creed," by James Sullivan, in *The Catholic Encyclopedia*, volume 2 (New York: Robert Appleton Company, 1907), at *www.newadvent.org/cathen/02033b.htm*.

The prayer on page 21 is from "Catholic Prayer: Novena Honoring the Body and Blood of Christ," at *www.catholicculture.org/culture/liturgicalyear/prayers /view.cfm?id=1194*.

The quotation from the Trinitarians on page 25 is from the Trinitarian website, at *www.trinitarians.org*.

The words of Pope Saint John Paul II on page 25 are from "Letter of Pope John Paul II to the Minister General of the Order of the Most Holy Trinity," number 4, at *www.vatican.va/holy_father/john_paul_ii/speeches/1998/june /documents/hf_jp-ii_spe_19980607_trinitarios_en.html*. Copyright © 1998 LEV.

The quotation on page 36 is from *General Instruction of the Roman Missal*, number 67, at *www.usccb.org/prayer-and-worship/the-mass/general-instruction -of-the-roman-missal/girm-chapter-2.cfm*. Copyright © 2003 by the United States Catholic Conference, Washington, D.C. All rights reserved.

The words of Saint Irenaeus on page 32 are from Against Heresies, book 1, chapter 10, translated by Alexander Roberts and William Rambaut, in *Ante-Nicene Fathers*, volume 1, edited by Alexander Roberts, James Donaldson, and A. Cleveland Cox (Buffalo, NY: Christian Literature Publishing Company, 1885), at *www.newadvent.org/fathers/0103110.htm*.

The words of Saint Augustine on page 48 are from *Confessions*, by Saint Augustine, translated with an introduction by R. S. Pine-Coffin (London: Penguin Classics, 1961), page 22. Copyright © 1961 by R. S. Pine-Coffin.

The excerpts on pages 45 and 49 are from *Dogmatic Constitution on Divine Revelation* (*Dei Verbum*, 1965), numbers 3 and 4, at *www.vatican.va /archive/hist_councils/ii_vaticancouncil/documents/vat-ii_const_19651118 _dei-verbum_en.html*.